1876 – 2001

THE ORIENTAL HOTEL
COOKBOOK

General Manager: **Kurt Wachtveitl**
Hotel Manager: **Jonas A. Schuermann**
PA to General Manager: **Duangrudee Siriwann**
Guest Relations Consultant: **Ankana Kalantananda**
Public Relations Manager: **Janice Nopvichai**
Food and Beverage Manager: **Michael Sorgenfrey**
Assistant Food and Beverage Manager: **Anthony Tyler**
Baan Rim Naam Manager: **Somnuk Nuntachaibuncha**
The Oriental Spa Manager: **Orawan Choeysawat**
Secretary to Executive Chef: **Nawarat Toonsakvorasan**

Editors: **Melisa Teo and Jonathan Cobb**
Designer: **Tan Seok Lui**
Food Stylist: **Susie Donald**

Published by Archipelago Press, an imprint of **Editions Didier Millet**.
64 Peck Seah Street. Singapore 079325
Tel: (65) 324 9260 Fax: (65) 324 9261 E-mail: edm@pacific.net.sg Website: www.edmbooks.com

Printed in Singapore © 2000 Editions Didier Millet
© Text William Warren © Photography Luca Invernizzi Tettoni
All rights reserved. No portion of the book may be reproduced in any form, or by any means, without the express written consent of the publisher.

The publishers would like to thank The Most Famous Hotels In The World's archives for the use of some historical images reproduced from *The Oriental Bangkok* by Andreas Augustin and Andrew Williamson in 'The Making Of A Legend'.

ISBN: 981-4068-08-X

THE ORIENTAL HOTEL
COOKBOOK

Text by

WILLIAM WARREN

Photography by

LUCA INVERNIZZI TETTONI

Recipes by

NORBERT KOSTNER
and the chefs of THE ORIENTAL, BANGKOK
ANDRE BUSER, *Executive Sous Chef*
PETER J. WEBBER, *Executive Pastry Chef*
VICHIT MUKURA, *Executive Thai Chef*
STEFAN MOERTH, *Chef – Le Normandie*
LEONG SIEW FYE, *Chef – The China House*
DOMINIQUE BUGNAND, *Sous Chef*

ARCHIPELAGO PRESS

CONTENTS

8 **THAI HOSPITALITY**

20 **CUISINES ACROSS CULTURES**
22 Sala Rim Naam
46 Lord Jim's
58 Ciao and The Verandah
82 The China House
94 Le Normandie
112 The Oriental Spa
120 More Tastes of The Oriental

140 **THE MAKING OF A LEGEND**

168 **ANNEXES**
169 Conversion Tables
170 Glossary
174 Culinary Index

Opposite: A spectacular ice sculpture in the Royal Ballroom for one of The Oriental's many social functions
Pg 2: Executive Chef Norbert Kostner (centre) with the Royal Project's Foundation Chairman HSH Prince Bhisatej Rajani (right)
Pg 6 to 7: The Oriental's Royal Ballroom is a regular host to the most lavish banquets in Bangkok

[THAI HOSPITALITY]

Countless visitors, past and present, have received their cultural introduction to Thailand during a stay at The Oriental Hotel in Bangkok.

Some of these discoveries are small but significant, like the graceful *wai* with which each arriving guest is greeted at the entrance. This prayer-like gesture is the traditional Thai way of showing respect. However, it is not quite as simple as it may appear since *wais* can vary considerably depending on the status of greeter and greeted (it may also be used to pay homage to a religious shrine), but it is always infinitely beguiling to a newcomer, especially when accompanied by a dazzling Thai smile, as it invariably is at The Oriental.

Other Thai touches also accompany this initial welcoming contact. The staff member assigned to the task, for instance, is usually attired in Thai dress – a richly brocaded silk skirt called a *phasin* for women, worn with a fitted blouse, or, for men, a voluminous length of shimmering silk called a *phanung*, pulled up between the legs and tucked in behind. These are adaptations of ancient court costumes, still worn by many Thais on special occasions.

Moreover, the welcome *wai* is followed by the presentation of a small jewel-like floral wreath, the customary Thai offering to honoured guests. Called a *malai*, this is a complex creation in which assorted blossoms are painstakingly strung together in a variety of fragrant patterns. The *malai* is used in countless aspects of Thai life and is often encountered at The Oriental.

Strolling across the lobby, more Thai features may be fleetingly noticed – a spectacular arrangement of flowers in season always including enough locally grown orchids to fill a florist shop; enormous temple bells that serve as chandeliers; a pair of wooden elephants, each regally caparisoned with a delicate blanket made from woven flowers; handsome expanses of carved teakwood; and, through the lofty windows along one side, a glimpse of the broad

Left: The malai, a signature of Thai hospitality
Opposite: Chandeliers in the form of huge temple bells and a dramatic floral arrangement adorn the lobby

Above: Malais, made from tightly-woven wreaths of flowers, are widely used as religious offerings
Right: Traditional floral arrangements form part of the setting for a Thai feast at The Oriental

river that dominated Bangkok life when The Oriental first opened its doors.

By the time a guest enters the elevator, Thailand has already made a memorable impression, one that will be expanded in numerous ways over the following days.

Spirits have always played a role in Thai life, influencing not only such natural phemenona as sufficient rainfall and bountiful crops but also the vagaries of individual fortune. Buddhism did not replace such beliefs but came to co-exist comfortably with them, often to the confusion of outsiders. Nearly every compound in Thailand, for instance, has a guardian spirit, who must be provided with a suitable residence. This may be a simple replica of a traditional Thai house or something much more elaborate in brightly-coloured cement resembling a temple structure. In either case, it is always neatly tended, and supplied with daily offerings of incense sticks, fresh flowers and fruit, and miniature figures representing attendants. Other supernatural forces are of Indian origin, absorbed with equal ease and also honoured with public shrines. These aspects of Thai culture are reflected in two structures standing beside the hotel's driveway.

Nestled amid the twisting roots of the Bodhi tree – a famous emblem of Buddhism, being the tree under which the Buddha attained enlightenment – is a little Thai-style structure,

surrounded by an eclectic assortment of gifts. The trunk of the tree itself is wrapped with lengths of brightly coloured cloth to signify its importance as a symbol of the faith followed by the majority of the Thai population.

The larger of the two edifices placed near the street shelters a multi-armed image of Brahma, the creator in the Hindu trinity of Gods. His traditional mount is the three-headed elephant Erawan, and for this reason, offerings to the shrine by both the hotel's staff and outsiders include carved wooden elephants in considerable quantities.

Floral offerings at shrines often include the sort of creations regularly displayed throughout The Oriental. Around three hundred of these can be seen at the hotel everyday, representing forty different types. Some employ heliconias, gingers, orchids, roses and numerous other specimens to form dramatic arrangements of striking originality. Others, though, display the Thai genius for transforming flowers into highly perishable works of living art.

This skill originated with the women of the royal palace, where it was one of the marks of ultimate refinement (skill at preparing certain kinds of food was another). The object was not to reproduce nature but rather to create something entirely different, closer perhaps to embroidery or jewellery design than anything a Westerner might consider in the category of flower-arranging.

At The Oriental, perhaps the most common of these ephemeral creations are the *malais*, which range from fairly simple ones like those presented to arriving guests to much more elaborate wreaths requiring hours to make.

Another type frequently seen is bowl arrangements known as *jad paan* or *poom*, in

Left: An introductory Thai experience awaits in the lobby of The Oriental with the presentation of jasmine garlands to arriving guests

which a core of moistened earth or sawdust is covered entirely with flowers to form a seamless display of intricate designs. Bachelor's Buttons, which fit tightly together and last for weeks, are generally employed (and sometimes dyed to obtain a wider range of colours), though for grander occasions like those when members of the Thai royal family are in attendance, blossoms such as the fragrant jasmine or other short-lived varieties are used instead.

Once a year, banana leaves and flowers are weaved into little lotus-shaped vessels for the Loy Krathong festival, in honour of the all-important water spirits. The Oriental is a popular gathering place to view the thousands of *krathongs* set adrift on the moonlit river, each adorned with a lit candle and burning incense sticks.

From the Authors' Wing, the oldest part of The Oriental, just beyond a cool arcaded terrace leading into a lush garden, stands a curious little monument that recalls another ancient custom. Atop the marble base is a bright-red replica of the Giant Swing, once the focus of one of Bangkok's most unusual festivals.

The original, consisting of two immense teak pillars with a crossbar at the top from which a swing was hung, towers some 90 feet above a

Above: The garden of The Oriental, leading to the river, is planted with a wide range of tropical specimens
Right: A special offering of food and traditional floral arrangements at the spirit house near the entrance to the hotel; in the background, lengths of cloth are tied around a sacred Bodhi tree

square outside Wat Suthat and was used in an annual Brahmin ritual honouring the God, Siva.

Annually, teams of young men swung to dizzying heights in an effort to snatch sacks of money with their teeth, the highest sack being suspended from a 76-foot pole and requiring an arc of nearly 180 degrees to reach.

The last Giant Swing Ceremony was held in 1935, and the swing itself seemed in danger of slow deterioration in the years that followed. Then Louis T. Leonowens and Company, founded by a former owner of the hotel, replaced the teak pillars and so saved the landmark.

The replica of the Giant Swing in The Oriental's garden marks the location of a time capsule installed in 1980. This will be opened in 5 June 2055, revealing an assortment of items from what by then will no doubt seem a distant era – some of them collected at the hotel itself.

The surrounding garden provides strolling guests with an introduction to the luxuriance of tropical horticulture. Stately coconut palms – used for so many purposes in Thailand, culinary and otherwise – spread feathery fronds over a smooth lawn; orchids bloom flamboyantly here and there; and huge bird's nest ferns mingle with creepers to create an exotic jungle atmosphere. Water jars are planted with the sacred lotus, its pink and white flowers rising above the large leaves, while such shrubs as jasmine and mock-orange fill the area with fragrance after dark.

Just beyond, flows the broad Chao Phraya. Murals in the hotel's Royal Ballroom pay tribute to the old days of this majestic river, described as "Bangkok's principal highway" by one late 19th-century visitor. As a short time spent on the terrace will attest, this is an endlessly fascinating artery of communication with its long processions of hump-backed barges, crowded public ferries, the hotel's shuttle and slender *hang-yao*, or long-tail motorboats, flashing in the sunlight.

Guests can also become part of this busy scene by taking a cruise on the hotel's sleek Oriental Queen. This vessel follows the winding course of the Chao Phraya upstream, passing such city landmarks as Wat Arun, the Temple of Dawn; Pak Klong Talad, Bangkok's wholesale market for fresh flowers, fruit, and vegetables; the Grand Palace, all multi-tiered roofs and golden spires, an amazing mile-square enclosure that comprises the world's greatest display of classic Thai art and architecture; and handsome old riverside houses and palaces where most of the city's elite once lived.

Outside the metropolitan area, the river enters the vast, flat central plains, whose rice fields and orchards have sustained Thailand's people for centuries. The final destination of most cruises is Bang Pa-In, a picturesque island used by rulers of both Ayudhaya and Bangkok as a retreat from the summer heat.

The buildings scattered around the island today date mostly from the 19th-century reign of King Chulalongkorn, and display a remarkable diversity of styles – a Buddhist chapel built in the form of a gothic church with stained glass windows; a gaudy, red-and-gold Chinese throne hall presented to the King by the Chinese community; a neo-classic palace from the Victorian era; and perhaps most memorably, a little Thai pavilion rising like a dream from a serene lake.

Many of The Oriental's most effective lessons in the country's culture can be found concentrated in a cluster of buildings on the west bank of the river. The most striking of these is the Sala Rim Naam, with its northern-style,

Above: A selection of Thai snacks; artful display is important in the preparation of a Thai meal

carved temple facade, where guests can enjoy a sumptuous feast of Thai delicacies and, in the evenings, watch performances of Thai classical dance and martial arts. The oldest building of the group is a colonial-style bungalow that once belonged to a nobleman. In 1986, this traditional structure with louvred shutters, breezy verandahs and Victorian fretwork set in a shady garden, became a perfect home for the Thai Cooking School, one of the hotel's most popular features.

Thai cuisine by that time had become an international phenomenon. Through Thai restaurants as far flung as London and New York, not to mention those in Thailand itself such as the Sala Rim Naam, countless people had come to appreciate its distinctive blend of flavours and healthy ingredients. With increasing numbers of visitors also interested in learning how to prepare some of these classic dishes, The Oriental came up with the concept of an in-house school.

Behind the cooking school and designed to blend architecturally with the old building, another unique Thai experience awaits at The Oriental Spa.

One of the first such facilities to be opened in Thailand, the Spa offers over thirty different treatments to soothe and beautify in luxurious surroundings ranging from a 30-minute Oriental foot massage to ease pain and 'release blocked energy'; to full-day programmes that include treatments such as hydrotherapy, papaya body polish, herbal wraps and facials.

For those who really want to pamper themselves, there is a selection of packages that could span over three days and cover everything from airport transfers by the hotel limousine to spa-cuisine meals and treatments, a class at the Thai Cooking School and a programme devoted to Thai culture.

The Oriental's Thai Culture Programme undoubtedly forms the most comprehensive introduction to the country and its ways for any visitor. Created fifteen years ago, this consists of afternoon sessions taught by renowned professors and scholars from leading universities and has attracted many heads of state, diplomats, journalists and other travellers.

An introductory course called 'Thai Ways' explores such matters as history, society, behaviour, customs and traditions, culminating by boat through the *klongs* of Thonburi to observe traditional lifestyles only superficially changed over the years.

Another course, 'Thai Beliefs', covers Buddhism, Brahminism and Animism, along with a visit to Wat Pho, the Temple of the

Right and opposite: The 'Khon', or classical dance, is one of the glories of Thai culture. Performances are presented nightly as part of a cultural show at the Sala Rim Naam

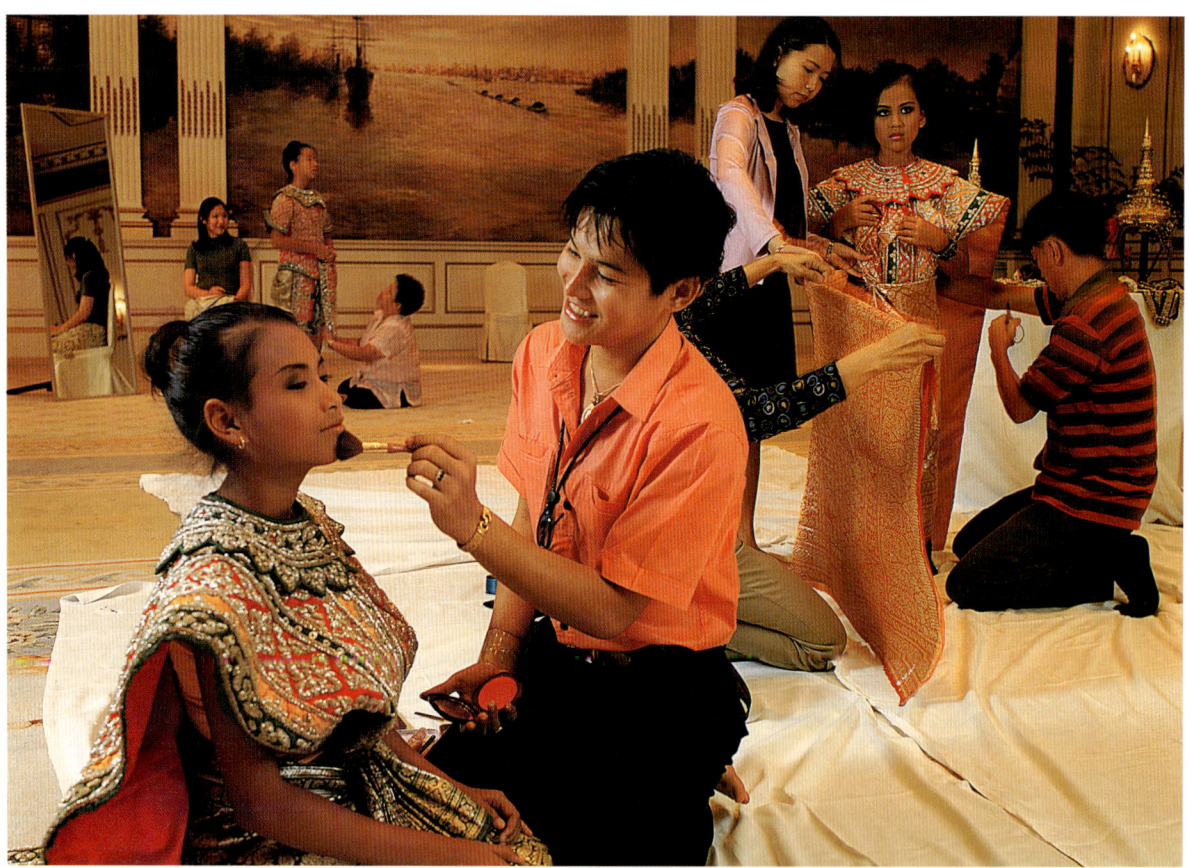

Left and opposite: The art of carving fruit and vegetables into exquisite shapes originated in the royal palace. Examples adorn many of the dishes served at The Oriental
Page 18–19: A sumptuous spread of Thai specialities

Reclining Buddha, or a meditation class in the serene surroundings of The Oriental Spa. Another explains classical Thai dance and music with performances by members of the Fine Arts Department; while one on 'Contemporary Thai Culture' examines such institutions as the monarchy, government, politics and society, as well as business etiquette. 'Thai Arts and Architecture' deals with both classical and folk art and includes a visit to the National Museum.

From The Oriental's rooms, guests can look out on the various aspects of Thailand's capital city, from the low, wooden buildings and timeless river traffic of its past, to the proud skyscrapers and teeming highways of its present. As an institution itself and an established part of Bangkok's history and social life, it is only natural that the hotel should also provide an inner guide to the delights and mysteries of Thai culture.

[CUISINES ACROSS CULTURES]

SALA RIM NAAM

The 'Pavilion on the River' combines classic Thai architecture with equally traditional dishes, highlighting the individuality of regional Thai cuisines.

LORD JIM'S

The Oriental pays tribute to Joseph Conrad's seafaring hero with a collection of succulent recipes dedicated to seafood, complemented with a tempting variety of meat and vegetarian dishes.

CIAO

Bangkok's only *al fresco* Italian restaurant is known not only for its unencumbered view of the Chao Phraya, but also its delicious Mediterranean menu.

THE VERANDAH

An outlet for all-day dining, The Verandah features dishes that blend the familiar with the exotic in the most innovative ways.

THE CHINA HOUSE

Explore the versatility of classical Cantonese cuisine with The China House's exquisite creations, ranging from casual dim sum to dishes designed for an elaborate Chinese banquet.

LE NORMANDIE

The height of French gastronomy finds its place within the four elegant walls of Le Normandie – the restaurant which offers a dazzling view of the city of Bangkok and the winding Chao Phraya.

THE ORIENTAL SPA

Health-conscious cuisine, enhanced with good looks and great taste, and a delicious menu of invigorating health drinks, complement the luxurious treatments at The Oriental Spa.

MORE TASTES OF THE ORIENTAL

A compilation of culinary favourites from the Authors' Lounge, the Bamboo Bar, the Bakery and Salon de l'Oriental.

Left: Place setting for a Thai meal; the napkin is decorated with a malai
Opposite: Assorted canapés; a highlight of cocktail parties at The Oriental

SALA RIM NAAM

Sala Rim Naam – 'Pavilion on the River' – was opened in 1983 on the west bank of the Chao Phraya, a site formerly occupied by tall rice silos. The elegant building is in classic Thai style, with a roof of layered green tiles and a carved wooden facade that recalls those seen on temples of the far north. The food is equally classic, a selection drawn from different parts of the country and prepared in traditional ways by skilled chefs.

The spiciness of Thai cuisine is probably its most celebrated feature. However, as diners at the Sala Rim Naam will discover, chilli is by no means the only ingredient. It is not even the predominant one. "There must always be harmony in a dish," says Chef Vichit Mukura, a veteran of fourteen years at The Oriental who is in charge of the Sala Rim Naam. "In a curry dish, for instance, the sharpness from the chilli and spices is toned down by the sweetness of coconut milk, which also enhances the flavour of fish sauce and the remaining ingredients." As such, a well-balanced and skilfully prepared Thai meal always offers a wide range of tastes and textures.

Guests at the Sala Rim Naam have a choice of venues in which to embark on their culinary explorations. Outside, on the Terrace Rim Naam, they can order *à la carte* while taking in the ever-changing river scene; alternatively, they can enjoy a lavish buffet in the restaurant. Dinner comes with entertainment in the form of classical masked Thai dance drama and a demonstration of ancient martial arts.

A meal might start with a few appetisers such as *Yaam Pla Grob Gub Piw Som-Sa* (spicy crisp fish served wih sparkling lime rind) or *Jaeng Ron* (fish dumplings with cucumber-chilli dip) to accompany drinks. It could then proceed to a salad (possibly *Yaam Grapao Pla Gub Med Mamuang*, a fried fish maw and cashewnut salad), a soup (*Gaeng Liang Ghoong*, concocted with fresh herbs, vegetables and shrimps, is a popular favourite), a curry or two (such as *Gaeng Moo Ta Po*, a pork and water spinach curry), and a couple of other dishes such as *Tom Gathi Sai Bou Gub Goong* (herbed blue river prawns and lotus stems in coconut milk) and *Pla Gao Thod Gub Prik Sam Ros* (fried red coral reef garoupa with sweet-salty chilli sauce). For dessert, there's always a selection of traditional Thai treats and seasonal fruit to choose from.

Sala Rim Naam offers diners a sumptuous range of Thai dishes, as well as good views across the Chao Phraya River to The Oriental Hotel

THAI COOKING SCHOOL

Besides the service of drinks and snacks before the meal and sweets at the end, there are no fixed courses in Thai dining. The dishes are served simultaneously and arranged around a big bowl of steamed rice on the table. An average family usually tucks into only two or three dishes in one meal, but if guests are expected, the spread improves to include a soup, a curry, one or two steamed or stir-fried dishes, and a spiced salad, served with assorted condiments and dips. Seasonal fruit or perhaps, a special Thai dessert, completes the experience.

Led by Culinary Instructor Sansern Gajaseni and The Oriental's chefs, students who sign up for a course with the Thai Cooking School will stand to gain greater insight into the intricacies of Thai cuisine within four fun-filled days.

Not only will they be introduced to the various herbs, spices and ingredients responsible for the popularity of Thai cooking around the world, the students can also look forward to participating in interactive cooking demonstrations. These are designed to equip them with the culinary know-how to prepare and present a sumptuous home-cooked meal.

Since an authentic Thai dish is never without an exquisite piece of fruit or vegetable carving, participants will be given the opportunity to dabble in this art form, which can transform a humble radish, papaya or spring onion into a decorative blossom; a slice of pineapple into a sunburst; and a watermelon into a basket of flowers.

1. Long dried chillies
2. Green chillies
3. Yellow chillies
4. Bird's eye chillies
5. Small dried chillies
6. Star anise
7. Kaffir lime
8. Green peppercorns
9. Szechuan peppercorns
10. Allspice
11. Bay leaves
12. Mace
13. Coriander seeds
14. White peppercorn
15. Nutmeg
16. Shallots
17. Black peppercorns
18. White cloves
19. Matore ginger
20. Fresh turmeric
21. Ground turmeric
22. Cumin seeds
23. White cardamom pods
24. Young turmeric
25. Lesser galangal
26. Cardamom pods
27. Green cardamom pods
28. Lemongrass
29. Kaffir lime leaves

GRILLED GREEN EGGPLANT SALAD
Yaam Makhuea Yow (opposite, back)

Serves 4–5

Eggplant Salad

3	Firm and long green eggplants
30 g	Ground roasted dried shrimps
10	Cooked shrimps, peeled, de-veined and cut in half lengthwise
8	Shallots, peeled and finely sliced into rings
1–2	Red chillies, finely sliced
A few sprigs of coriander leaves	
2	Eggs, hard boiled, peeled and cut into 8 wedges

Salad Dressing

1	Garlic clove, very finely minced
1 tbsp	Small pumpkin cubes, boiled until tender but firm
2 tbsp	Fish sauce (*nam pla*)
1 tsp	Crystal sugar
2 tbsp	Lime juice

PREPARATION
Preheat oven at 170–180°C.
Scorch the eggplants over an open flame until the skin becomes black and blistered all over (this gives the eggplant salad its unique smoky flavour).
Line the eggplants on a roasting tray and bake them for about 20 minutes until they are soft, but not mushy.
Remove from the oven, peel off the skin and trim off the stems.

PRESENTATION
Cut each eggplant into 4 or 5 pieces and arrange on a serving dish. Sprinkle the dried shrimps over, then top with the cooked shrimps and shallots.
Combine the dressing ingredients in a small bowl, mix well and pour over the grilled eggplant salad. Garnish with the sliced chillies, coriander leaves and egg wedges and serve immediately.

FRIED FISH MAW AND CASHEWNUT SALAD
Yaam Grapao Pla Gub Med Mamuang (opposite, front)

Serves 4–5

1.5 litres	Vegetable oil for frying
170–200 g	Small dried fish maw
40–50 g	White onion, peeled and cut into small crescents
4	Spring onion, including the green leaves, cut into 3–4 cm pieces
70–80 g	Fried cashewnuts
12–15	Small dried red chillies, fried until crispy
3–4	Small fresh red chillies, crushed
3	Garlic cloves, peeled and finely chopped
30–40 g	Shallots, peeled and finely sliced
20–30 g	Ginger, peeled and shredded
3–4 tbsp	Fish sauce (*nam pla*)
1 tsp	Granulated sugar
2–3 tbsp	Freshly squeezed lime juice
1 tsp	Roasted chilli jam
Salt and pepper to taste	
A few sprigs of fresh coriander leaves	

PREPARATION
Heat the vegetable oil in a deep saucepan and fry the fish maw until it becomes light brown in colour. Remove from oil with a slotted spoon and drain on paper towels. Leave aside to rest for 10 minutes.
Combine all remaining ingredients (except coriander leaves) with the fried fish maw in a medium-sized bowl and mix well. This should be done quickly so that everything remains crisp and crunchy.
Season with salt and pepper to taste if necessary and transfer mixture to a serving plate.
Garnish with fresh coriander leaves and serve immediately.

SARDINE SALAD IN LETTUCE CUPS
Yaam Pla Too (above)

Serves 4

8	Fresh sardines (approx. 80 g each)
6	Small red chillies, finely sliced
80 g	Fresh coconut flesh, chopped
45 g	Spring onion (green part only), sliced
75 g	Ginger, finely sliced into threads
30 g	Coriander leaves, finely chopped
140 g	Shallots, finely sliced
60 ml	Fish sauce (*nam pla*)
60 ml	Lime juice
Salt and pepper to taste	
16–20	Small lettuce leaves

PREPARATION
Wash the sardines and pat dry with paper towels.
Steam for 7–10 minutes, remove from heat and leave to cool on a tray, covered with a moist kitchen cloth.
When cool, remove the skin and bones, crumble the meat to the size of small sweet peas and leave covered with a moist kitchen cloth.

PRESENTATION
Add the crumbled sardines to the remaining ingredients except the lettuce leaves, mix well and adjust the seasoning to taste. Place a spoonful of the sardine salad on each lettuce leaf and arrange on a plate to serve.

SPICY CRISP FISH WITH SPARKLING LIME RIND
Yaam Pla Grob Gub Piw Som-Sa (opposite, right)

Serves 4

800 g–1 kg	Dry-smoked sweet water perch
10–12	Fresh small chillies, crushed
90 ml	Fish sauce (*nam pla*)
90 ml	Lime juice
2 tbsp	Sparkling lime juice
2–3 tsp	Sugar syrup
120 g	Soft-cooked pork skin, cut into fine strips
4 tbsp	Finely sliced, peeled and pickled garlic
4 tbsp	Crisp-fried shallots
4 tbsp	Crisp-fried sliced garlic
4 tbsp	Crisp-fried sliced boiled peanuts
3–4 tsp	Finely sliced sparkling lime rind

PREPARATION
Steam the perch for 5–7 minutes until the flesh is quite tender and can be easily detached from the bones. Remove, place on a tray covered with a moist kitchen cloth and leave to cool. Remove the bones, without crumbling the flesh, and fry the fish in hot vegetable oil until crisp and golden brown. Remove with a perforated spoon and drain on paper towels.

PRESENTATION
Place the crushed chillies in a bowl, add the fish sauce, lime juice, sparkling lime juice and sugar syrup, stir well and leave for a few minutes, then add remaining ingredients and crispy fried fish. Toss well, taking care not to break up the fish. Serve on 4 individual plates or on a single serving plate.

SOFT-SHELL CRAB SALAD WITH GREEN MANGO

Plar Poo Nim Gub Mamuang (above, left)

Serves 2

4	Soft-shell crabs (approx. 80 g each)
2–3 tbsp	Rice flour
2½ tbsp	Fish sauce (*nam pla*)
2 tbsp	Lime juice
1 tsp	Small red chillies, crushed
1 tsp	Sugar syrup
3	Shallots, sliced
160 g	Green mango, sliced into thin strips
½ tsp	Chopped garlic
2 tbsp	Chopped mint leaves

Garnish
A few lettuce leaves
A few sprigs coriander leaves
2 large red chillies, seeds removed, cut lengthwise into fine strips

PREPARATION
Coat the soft-shell crabs with rice flour and deep-fry over medium heat for about 3 minutes until golden brown in colour. Remove and drain on paper towels. Keep warm.
To prepare the dressing, combine the fish sauce, lime juice, crushed chillies and sugar syrup into a bowl and mix well. Leave to rest for 1–2 minutes.

PRESENTATION
Add the shallots, mango strips, chopped garlic and mint leaves to the dressing and toss well.
Line a serving dish with lettuce leaves, place the mango-shallot salad in the centre and top with the soft-shell crabs.
Garnish with coriander leaves and red chilli strips, and serve immediately, while the mango strips are still crunchy.

HERBED SOUP OF VEGETABLES AND SHRIMPS
Gaeng Liang Ghoong (opposite)

Serves 4

140 g	Coriander root, chopped
3 g	Small red chillies
80 g	Shallots, sliced
25 g	Dried shrimps
40 g	Lesser galangal, cut up and peeled
3 g	Ground white pepper
20 g	Deep-fried smoked perch meat
10 g	Thai shrimp paste
1 litre	Chicken stock (see recipe on Pg 101)
45 g	String beans, cut into 2-cm pieces
45 g	Baby corn, cut into 1-cm pieces
45 g	Rib gourd, peeled, cut into bite-sized pieces
100 g	Straw mushrooms, cleaned
200 g	Fresh shrimps, peeled and cut in half lengthwise
40 g	Ivy leaves
35 g	Sweet basil leaves
70–80 ml	Fish sauce (*nam pla*)

PREPARATION
Place the coriander root, red chillies, shallots, dried shrimps, lesser galangal, white pepper, smoked perch and shrimp paste into a stone mortar and pound until very fine and emulsified. Scrape out of the mortar and keep chilled. (This can also be made in a blender, although care should be taken not to overblend the paste.)
Bring the chicken stock and the pounded mixture to the boil, add the string beans, baby corn, rib gourd and straw mushrooms, and boil on low heat for about 5 minutes, or until the vegetables are *al dente* (soft but still have a good bite).
Add the shrimps, season with fish sauce and boil for a few seconds. Add the ivy leaves and sweet basil leaves, return the soup to the boil and serve in individual pre-heated soup bowls or in a large serving bowl.

FRIED FISH ROLLS WITH TWO-MANGO SALAD
Yaam Mamuang Gub Pla Foo (Pg 33, bottom right)

Serves 4–5

2–2.2 kg	Whole seabass, cleaned and dried with paper towels
2 litres	Vegetable oil for frying
A few sprigs of fresh coriander leaves	

Two-Mango Salad

200–250 g	Sour green mango, cut into strips
200–250 g	Half-ripe sweet sour mango, cut into strips
2 tbsp	Peanuts, dry-roasted and coarsely chopped
5–6	Shallots, peeled and finely sliced

Salad Dressing

2–3 tbsp	Fish sauce (*nam pla*)
2 tsp	Granulated sugar
2–3 tbsp	Lime juice
4–5	Small red chillies, crushed
1	Garlic clove, finely chopped

PREPARATION
Wrap the fish in plastic film and steam for 25–30 minutes until well cooked. Remove, unwrap fish and leave to cool.
Peel off the skin and debone. Rub the fish meat between your palms until it resembles coarse breadcrumbs and leave to dry on a clean paper towel.
Combine dressing ingredients in a bowl and mix well.
Heat the oil in a wok over a medium fire. When it is hot but not smoking, sprinkle a handful of fish crumbs into the oil in a circular motion (you should do this while the fish is still slightly damp), to create a disk approx. 10 cm in diameter (the crumbs will stick to form a disk when they touch the oil).
Remove the disk when it turns light brown and shape it into a roll approx. 2.5 cm in diameter whilst it is still hot.
Repeat the procedure until all the fish crumbs are cooked.

PRESENTATION
Combine the salad ingredients, add the dressing and toss well. Place the salad on a serving plate, top with the fried fish rolls, and garnish with the coriander sprigs to serve.

BRAISED SHIITAKE MUSHROOM CUPS FILLED WITH CRABMEAT AND MINCED PORK

Gaeng Khiaw Waan Hed Hom Sod Sai Moo Gub Poo

Serves 4

20–25	Large fresh shiitake mushrooms, stems removed

Crabmeat and Minced Pork Filling

200–250 g	Fresh crabmeat
100–120 g	Lean pork meat, minced
1 tbsp	Thai green curry paste
2	Shallots, peeled, chopped and sautéed
1	Garlic clove, finely chopped
2	Eggs
10–12 tbsp	Coconut cream (see recipe on Pg 42)
A big pinch of salt to season	

Curry Sauce

600 ml	Coconut milk (see recipe on Pg 42)
1½ tbsp	Thai green curry paste
1 tbsp	Palm sugar
2 tsp	Lesser galangal, peeled and finely chopped
2–3 tbsp	Fish sauce (*nam pla*)

Garnish

2–3 pcs	Young kaffir lime leaves, finely shredded
10–15 pcs	Thai sweet basil leaves

PREPARATION

Crabmeat and Minced Pork Filling

Combine all the filling ingredients into a bowl and mix well. Avoid breaking up the crabmeat while mixing.

If the filling becomes too firm, just add a little coconut milk to loosen the mixture.

Clean the mushrooms with a damp cloth, fill each one with a mound of the mixture, cover with plastic film and refrigerate.

Curry Sauce

Bring the coconut milk to a gentle boil and simmer until the oil rises to the surface.

Stir in the curry paste, palm sugar and lesser galangal, and simmer for 20–25 minutes. Season with some fish sauce to taste and cook for a few more minutes.

PRESENTATION

Place the filled mushroom cups in a large frying pan and pour over the prepared curry sauce. Cover and simmer over low heat for 8–10 minutes.

Arrange the cooked mushroom cups on a warm serving dish, return the sauce to a boil, and adjust the seasoning with more fish sauce if necessary. Pour the sauce over the mushroom cups and garnish with the shredded kaffir lime leaves and basil leaves. Serve very hot with steamed jasmine rice.

Chef's note: This dish should be sweet, salty and a little spicy.

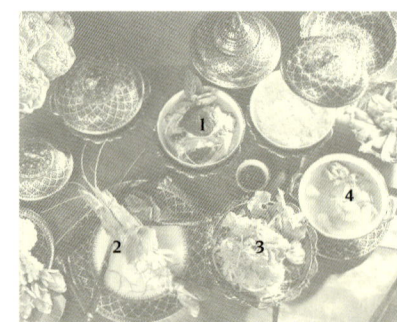

1. Braised Shiitake Mushroom Cups filled with Crabmeat and Minced Pork
2. Steamed White Prawns with Chilli and Lime
3. Fried Fish Rolls with Two-Mango Salad
4. Clear Shrimp Soup

FISH DUMPLINGS WITH CUCUMBER-CHILLI DIP
Jaeng Ron (above)

Serves 7–8

Fish Dumplings

500 g	Fresh fish meat such as snapper, garoupa or seabass, finely minced
2 tbsp	Red curry paste (see recipe on Pg 41)
60 ml	Coconut cream (see recipe on Pg 42)
90 g	Coconut flesh, grated
1 tbsp	Chopped kaffir lime leaves,
1 tbsp	Chopped basil leaves
1	Egg
1½ tbsp	Palm sugar
½ tsp	Ground white pepper
4 tbsp	Fish sauce (*nam pla*)
16–18	Young pandanus leaves

Cucumber-Chilli Dip

250 ml	Distilled white vinegar
85 g	Granulated white sugar
2 tsp	Sea salt
8–10	Seedless large red chillies, finely chopped
2 tbsp	Garlic, peeled and finely chopped
2 tsp	Coriander root, finely chopped
2	Cucumbers, approx. 5–6 cm in length

PREPARATION

Fish Dumplings

Combine the fish and curry paste in a bowl and mix well with a spoon. Add the coconut cream and mix well, then add the coconut flesh, kaffir lime leaves, basil leaves, egg, palm sugar, ground pepper and fish sauce. Stir until the mixture is sticky and translucent. Leave aside for 10–15 minutes.

Cucumber-Chilli Dip

Combine the vinegar, sugar and salt in a saucepan, bring to the boil and simmer for 1–2 minutes. Add the chillies, garlic and coriander root and keep boiling over a low heat until it has the consistency of liquid honey. Remove and leave to cool. Cut the cucumbers lengthwise into 4, then cut into 2-mm pieces. Add to the dip.

PRESENTATION

Roll the dumpling mixture into 6–7 cm long 'sausages' and steam for 2 minutes until they are cooked outside but still raw inside. Let cool, then wrap each 'sausage' with a young pandanus leaf, then slot on a bamboo skewer and charcoal-grill over low heat until golden brown and fragrant. Serve the grilled fish skewers with a bowl of cucumber-chilli dip.

EGG NOODLES WITH CHICKEN CURRY
Khao Soi Gai (above)

Serves 4

1.3 litres	Coconut milk (see recipe on Pg 42)
200 ml	Chicken stock (see recipe on Pg 101)
350 g	Chicken thigh meat, skinned, cut into 3-mm slices
2 tbsp	Light soy sauce
3–4 tbsp	Fish sauce (*nam pla*)
350 g	Finely cut fresh egg noodles
100 g	Pickled Chinese cabbage, cut into cubes
5–6	Green lime wedges
5	Shallots, peeled and cut into medium-sized cubes
10	Fried red chillies, finely chopped and mixed with one tablespoon of the oil used for frying

Curry Paste

4–5	Large dried red chillies, halved, seeded and cored
3	Shallots, peeled and finely sliced
80–100 g	Galangal, peeled and finely sliced
4	Fresh coriander root, finely chopped
1 tsp	Ground cumin
1 tsp	Curry powder
2 tsp	Coriander seeds
2 tsp	Ground turmeric
2 cm	Peeled fresh yellow turmeric, finely sliced
½ tsp	Palm sugar

PREPARATION

Stir-fry all the curry paste ingredients, except the palm sugar, over medium heat until fragrant.
Remove to a stone mortar, add palm sugar and 2–3 tsp cold water. Pound into a fine paste.
Bring 250 ml of the coconut milk to the boil, add the curry paste and cook for 2–3 minutes.
Add the chicken stock, chicken, soy sauce and half the fish sauce and cook gently for 2–3 minutes, stirring occasionally.
Add the remaining coconut milk, bring it to the boil and simmer for up to 4 minutes. Adjust seasoning with remaining fish sauce if necessary, remove and keep warm.

PRESENTATION

Deep-fry about 70 g of the egg noodles until they are light brown and crispy. Remove and drain on a wire rack.
Boil the remaining noodles for 30 seconds, drain and divide into 5–6 pre-warmed bowls.
Top noodles with curry and garnish with the fried noodles. Serve hot with pickled Chinese cabbage, lime wedges, shallots and fried red chillies.

FRIED RED CORAL REEF GAROUPA WITH SWEET-SALTY CHILLI SAUCE
Pla Gao Thod Gub Prik Sam Ros (opposite)

Serves 2–3

700–800 g	Red coral reef garoupa, whole
1.5–2 litres	Vegetable oil for deep-frying
Salt and cracked black pepper to season	
Tapioca flour for dusting	

Chilli Sauce

3–4	Coriander roots, finely chopped
2–3	Garlic cloves, peeled
3–4	Small red chillies, crushed
2 tbsp	Palm sugar
8–10	Pickled garlic cloves
3–4 tbsp	Chicken stock (see recipe on Pg 101)
3–4 tbsp	Vegetable oil
150 ml	Sour tamarind pulp
3–4 tbsp	Fish sauce (*nam pla*)
120–150 g	Cherry tomatoes, cut into quarters

Garnish

1 tbsp	Shallots, sliced and fried until crispy
1 tbsp	Garlic, sliced and fried until crispy
8–10	Dried small red chillies, fried until crispy
A few sprigs of coriander leaves	

PREPARATION

To prepare the chilli sauce, combine the coriander, garlic, red chillies, palm sugar, pickled garlic and chicken stock in a stone mortar and pound until smooth but not too fine.

Heat the oil in a saucepan, add the ingredients from the mortar and stir-fry over a medium heat until fragrant.

Add the tamarind pulp and cook until the sauce turns syrupy. Season with some fish sauce, add the tomato quarters and continue cooking gently until the tomatoes are soft. Remove from the heat, cover with a lid and keep warm.

Scale and clean the garoupa and pat dry with paper towels. Heat the oil for deep-frying in a wok or deep-sided frying pan. Season the fish with salt and plenty of cracked black pepper, then dust lightly with tapioca flour.

Fry until very crisp on the outside and well cooked on the inside. Remove from the oil and drain on paper towels. Keep warm.

PRESENTATION

Bring the chilli sauce to the boil, season with more fish sauce if necessary, and pour the sauce onto a warm serving plate.

Place the fried fish in the centre and garnish with crisp fried shallots, garlic and chillies, and fresh coriander leaves to serve.

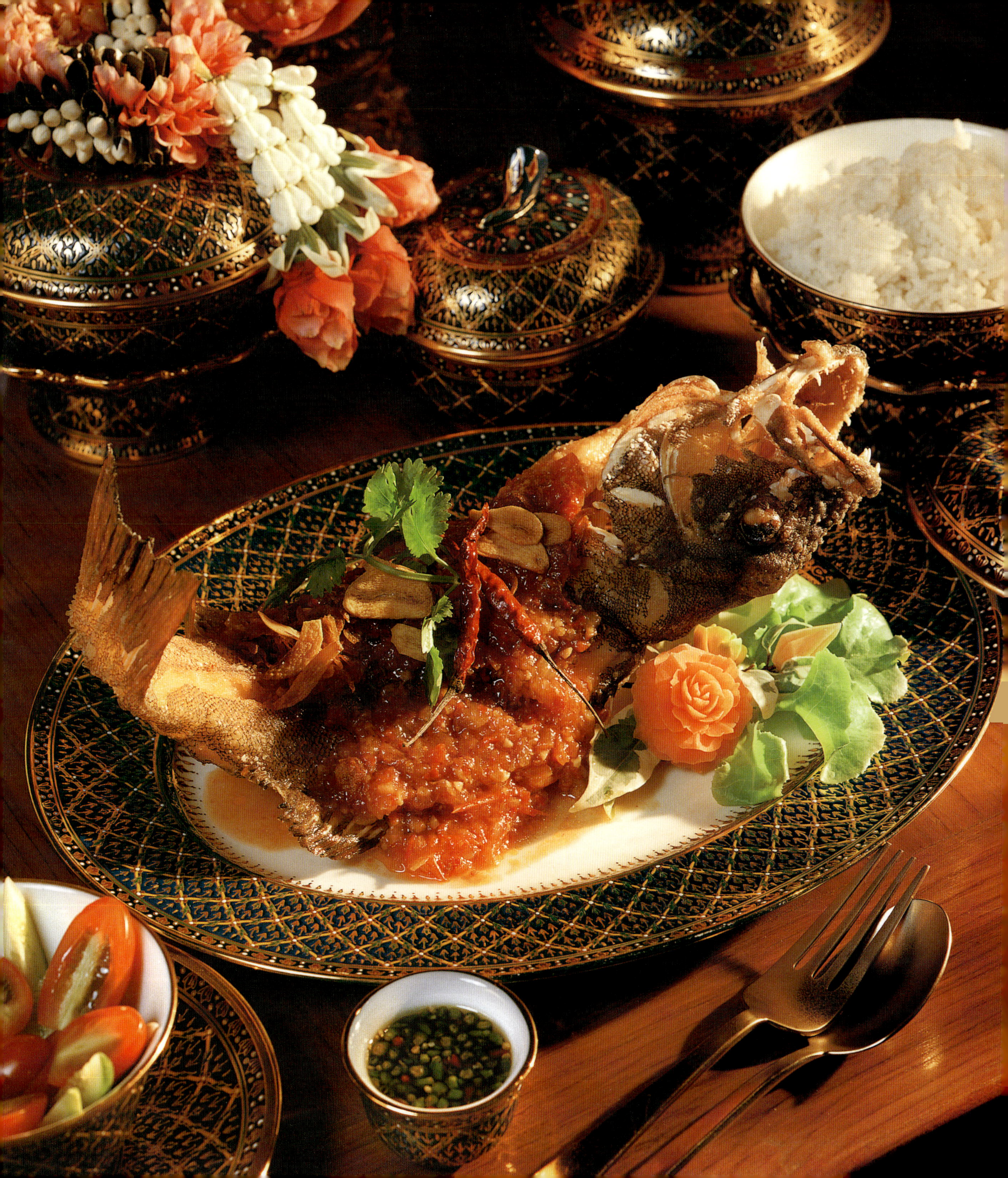

PORK FILLET AND WATER SPINACH CURRY
Gaeng Moo Ta Po (below)

Serves 4

1.25 litres	Medium-thick coconut milk (see recipe on Pg 42)
5 tbsp	Special red curry paste
2 tbsp	Tamarind water
2 tsp	Palm sugar
2–2½ tbsp	Fish sauce (*nam pla*)
320 g	Pork fillet, sliced about ½-cm thick
150 g	Young Thai green water spinach, cut into 2-cm pieces
2	Kaffir lime leaves
3 tbsp	Kaffir lime juice
½	Kaffir lime, seeds removed

Special Red Curry Paste

50 g	Large dried red chillies, cut in half lengthways and seeds removed
10 g	Salt
10 g	Greater galangal, finely sliced
10 g	Lemongrass, finely sliced
3 g	Kaffir lime rind
10 g	Young coriander roots, cleaned and chopped
½ tsp	Dry roasted cumin seeds
30 g	Shallots, peeled and finely sliced
15 g	Garlic, peeled and finely sliced
30 g	Shrimp paste

PREPARATION

Special Red Curry Paste

Soak the dried chillies in warm water for about 10 minutes or until soft. Remove from the water and pat dry with paper towels. Place the chillies and all other ingredients in a stone mortar and pound into a fine paste. This makes 100–120 g of curry paste. Store in an airtight jar and refrigerate until required.

Curry

Boil 250 ml of coconut milk in a heavy-based saucepan, add 5 tbsp special red curry paste and cook, stirring continuously, until the coconut fat separates and the mixture becomes fragrant. Add the remaining 1 litre of coconut milk, tamarind water, palm sugar and fish sauce.
Stir well and simmer slowly for 1–2 minutes, then add the sliced pork and continue to cook for a few more minutes.
Add the water spinach, kaffir lime leaves, kaffir lime juice and kaffir lime. Continue to cook on low heat for 3–4 minutes. Season to taste, adding more fish sauce if required.

PRESENTATION

Before serving, remove the kaffir lime leaves and the kaffir lime, and serve in 4 pre-heated bowls or one large serving bowl.

HERBED BLUE RIVER PRAWNS AND LOTUS STEMS IN COCONUT MILK

Tom Gathi Sai Bou Gub Goong (above)

Serves 4

12	Large blue river prawns (100–120 g each)
1.25 litres	Coconut milk (see recipe on Pg 42)
3 tbsp	Greater galangal, peeled and finely sliced
2 tbsp	Lemongrass, finely sliced
260 g	Lotus stems, peeled and cut into 5-cm pieces
4 tbsp	Shallots, peeled and sliced
5 tbsp	Fish sauce (*nam pla*)
4 tbsp	Freshly squeezed lime juice
4	Kaffir lime leaves, cut in fine threads
2	Large red chillies, seeds removed and finely sliced

Approx. 20 fresh coriander leaves

PREPARATION
Detach the heads from 8 of the prawns, leaving the remaining 4 intact for garnish. Peel the shells from the bodies of all of the prawns and use a knife to cut along the back of each to remove the brown intestinal tract. Wash quickly and pat dry with paper towels. Boil the coconut milk in a medium saucepan. When it starts bubbling, add the galangal and lemongrass and simmer for 3–4 minutes. Add the lotus stems, shallots and prawns. As soon as it starts to boil, lower the heat and simmer for 2–3 more minutes. Season with the fish sauce and lime juice to taste.

PRESENTATION
Ladle into a large pre-heated bowl, arrange the prawns with heads intact in the middle of the bowl, sprinkle with kaffir lime leaves, red chillies and coriander leaves and serve hot.

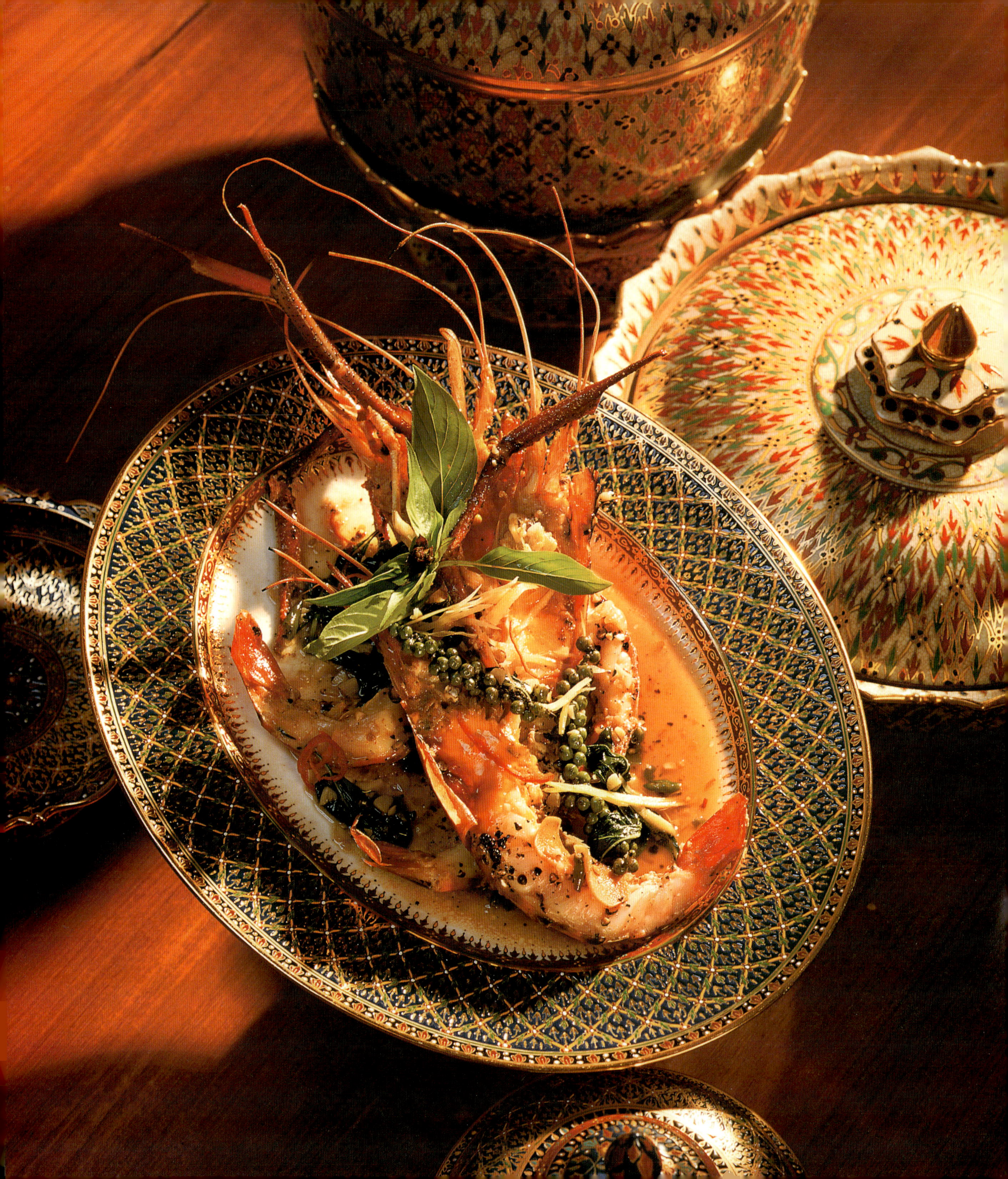

PAN-BRAISED GIANT BLUE RIVER LOBSTERS WITH SWEET THAI BASIL

Goong Mae Naam Ob Bai Horapa Gub Gachai (opposite)

Serves 4

4	Fresh giant-sized blue river lobsters
2–3 tbsp	Vegetable oil
4	Garlic cloves, peeled and finely chopped
2–3	Small red chillies, crushed
2–3 bunches	Thai basil with stems
2 tbsp	Lesser galangal, peeled and cut into fine strips
2 tbsp	Light soy sauce
2 tbsp	Oyster sauce
3–4 tbsp	Chicken stock (see recipe on Pg 101)
2 tbsp	Thai rice whisky
5–6 clusters	Fresh green peppercorn (each about 3–4 cm long)
2–3 tbsp	Fish sauce (*nam pla*)
Fresh ground black pepper to season	
20	Thai sweet basil leaves, fried until crispy

Marinade

2–3	Garlic cloves, peeled and crushed
1 tbsp	Peeled fresh ginger, cut into fine strips
2 tbsp	Light soy sauce
2–3	Small red chillies, crushed
1 tbsp	Oyster sauce
1 tbsp	Thai rice whisky
2 tbsp	Vegetable oil
Freshly ground black pepper to season	

PREPARATION

Combine all the marinade ingredients in a bowl and mix well.
Cut each giant blue river lobster in two lengthwise, remove the brown gut and pat clean with a damp kitchen cloth.
Marinate the lobsters in the mixture for 45 minutes – 2 hours.
To cook the lobsters, heat oil in a large heavy-based frying pan, add the garlic and fry over a low heat for about 30 seconds.
Remove the pan from the heat and add in the lobster halves, shell side facing down.
Add the chillies, basil stems, galangal, soy sauce, oyster sauce and chicken stock.
Shake the pan a little to spread the ingredients evenly, cover and cook for 3–4 minutes over a low heat.
Remove lid to allow some moisture to evaporate, then *flambé* with Thai whisky.
Add the peppercorn clusters, cover and boil for 20–30 seconds.
Remove the lobsters and arrange on a pre-warmed serving plate, cover and keep warm.
Allow the sauce to reduce a little more, and adjust the seasoning with more fish sauce if necessary (very little sauce is needed, but the flavour must be concentrated).
Remove from heat and discard the basil.
Season with pepper to taste and pour the sauce over the warm lobster tails.
Garnish with crisp-fried Thai sweet basil leaves to serve.

RED CURRY PASTE *Naam Prig Gaeng Ped*

Makes 300 g

50 g	Dried large red chillies, cut in half lengthwise and seeded
3 g each of dry-roasted bay leaves, coriander and cumin seeds	
50 g	Greater galangal, peeled and finely sliced
30 g	Lemongrass, peeled and finely sliced
50 g	Lesser galangal, peeled and finely sliced
10 g	Shrimp paste
50 g	Shallots, peeled and finely sliced
50 g	Garlic, peeled and finely sliced
3 g	Coriander roots, finely sliced
15 g	Kaffir lime zest
1 tsp	Salt

PREPARATION

Soak the dried chillies in warm water until soft.
Remove from the water and pat dry with a kitchen cloth.
Pound the bay leaves, coriander seeds and cumin seeds in a stone mortar until pulverised.
Add all remaining ingredients and continue pounding until the paste is very fine, smooth and homogenised.
Keep the paste chilled until ready to use.
The curry paste will keep for 3–4 days refrigerated.

BANANA BLOSSOM SALAD
Yaam Hao Plee

Serves 2–4

250 ml	Coconut cream (see recipe below)
4 tbsp	Chilli jam (*naam prig pow*)
1 tbsp	Fish sauce (*nam pla*)
2 tsp	Lime juice
½ tbsp	Sugar syrup
½ tbsp	Bird's eye chillies (*prik kee noo*), crushed
1	Fresh banana blossom, whole
40 g	Chicken meat, poached and shredded
40 g	Shrimps, poached
25 g	Crushed peanuts, toasted
6 g	Sweet basil leaves
40 g	Shallots, peeled and sliced
20 g	Lemongrass, finely sliced

Coriander leaves, red chilli slices and shredded kaffir lime leaves to garnish

PREPARATION

Place the coconut cream in a heavy-based saucepan and heat until the oil floats to the top.
Add the chilli jam and mix well. Remove from the heat and leave aside to cool.
As soon as the mixture is cool, add the fish sauce, lime juice, sugar syrup and the crushed chillies, stir well and leave aside.
Remove the hard outer leaves of the banana blossom, then cut it lengthwise into quarters. Remove the hard core with a sharp knife, then slice the quarters across into very thin strips and place them in a medium mixing bowl.
Add the shredded chicken, poached shrimps, peanuts, basil leaves, shallots, lemongrass and the coconut mixture to the bowl and toss gently until well-coated.
Transfer to a serving dish and garnish with the coriander leaves, chilli slices and shredded kaffir lime leaves.

CRISPY PERCH AND HERB DIP *Prig Khing Grob*

Serves 10

100 g	Coriander roots
100 g	Lemongrass, sliced
100 g	Ginger, sliced
30 g	Dried large red chillies, seeds removed and sliced
100 g	Shallots, sliced
100 g	Garlic, sliced
100 g	Peanuts, skin removed
10 g	Kaffir lime leaves
100 g	Fluffy deep-fried sundried salted sea perch
100 ml	Fish sauce (*nam pla*)
100 g	Palm sugar
100 ml	Tamarind water

PREPARATION

In separate batches, deep-fry the coriander roots, lemongrass, ginger, red chillies, shallots, garlic, peanuts, kaffir lime leaves and sea perch until crispy. Drain off excess oil and put aside.
Mix the fish sauce, palm sugar and tamarind water in a small saucepan and bring to the boil. Lower the heat and reduce the sauce until it becomes viscous.
Roughly chop the fried herbs and fish, then combine in a mixing bowl with the cooled sauce. Add seasoning to taste.
Serve as a dip for fresh vegetables.

COCONUT MILK / COCONUT CREAM *Gathi*

Makes 800 ml milk
300 ml cream

1 kg	White coconut pulp, freshly grated
800–900 ml	Warm water

PREPARATION

Place the grated coconut pulp in a large kitchen bowl and pour the warm water over it.
Using both hands, knead the coconut mixture vigorously for 8–10 minutes.
Strain through a sieve, pressing the pulp with a small ladle so as to extract as much milk as possible.
If the recipe asks for coconut cream, let the milk rest for 1 hour to allow the cream to separate from the milk. (The longer you rest the milk, the thicker the cream becomes.) Use a flat ladle to scoop off this layer of cream.
Use the coconut milk within one day of making, otherwise freeze it to preserve.

MINIATURE YELLOW BEAN MARZIPANS
Loog Choob (Pg 45)

Serves 6

400 ml	Water
40 g	Jasmine flower blossoms
500 g	Dried yellow beans
300 g	White coconut meat, finely grated
500 g	Granulated sugar
400 ml	Coconut milk (see recipe on Pg 42)

Choice of food colouring

Agar Agar Coating

25 g	Agar-agar powder
30 g	Granulated sugar
600 ml	Cold water

PREPARATION

Infuse the water with the jasmine blossoms, cover tightly with a kitchen cloth, and leave in the refrigerator for 24 hours.
Soak the yellow beans in warm water for 40–50 minutes, strain and then steam for 30 minutes until tender and well cooked.
Process the beans and grated coconut in a blender until you get a fine smooth paste. Leave aside.

Remove the jasmine, add sugar and bring water to the boil. Reduce heat and boil until the mixture resembles a thick syrup. Add the coconut milk, continue to cook for 10–15 minutes, then add the bean paste, stirring constantly until the mixture is firm enough to be shaped into little balls.
Remove from heat, transfer onto a tray and leave to cool, then mould the mixture into the shape of small fruit such as cherry, mango, mangosteen and banana.
Use a toothpick to hold each mini bean fruit and paint all the fruit with food colouring.
To prepare the agar-agar coating, boil the agar-agar powder with sugar and water, stirring well with a wire whisk.
Reduce heat and boil gently until the quantity is reduced by half (keep stirring to prevent the agar-agar from sticking and burning). Still holding it with a toothpick, dip the miniature fruit into the warm agar-agar coating.
Let the coating cool and set slightly, then repeat the procedure to get a nice shiny coating.
Place onto a tray lined with baking paper, and remove the toothpicks carefully.
Arrange in small bowls or on a serving platter in groups of colours or in rows, and serve.

CRISPY THAI PANCAKE
Kanom Bieng Thai

Serves 4

Batter

50 g	Fine-milled lentil flour
100 g	Rice flour
5 g	Salt
50 g	Granulated white sugar
3	Egg yolks
500 ml	Alkaline water (red lime water)

Sweet Topping Paste

200 g	Palm sugar
1	Egg white

Dry Topping

50 g	Dried persimmon fruit, cut in fine flakes
50 g	Candied orange peel, finely shredded
50 g	Sweet egg yolk, cut into 3-cm-long threads
50 g	Freshly grated coconut

PREPARATION

Sift the lentil flour with the rice flour and salt. Add the sugar, egg yolk and alkaline water and mix well. Strain through a fine-mesh sieve. Combine the palm sugar with the egg white and beat until it starts foaming.
Warm a cast-iron griddle or frying pan over low heat (there are iron pans, flat spoons and charcoal stoves designed for this), pour 1 tbsp batter onto it, and spread in a circular motion to make a small disk approx. 5–6 cm in diameter. (You can make 4–5 pancakes at a time.)
Top the lentil batter disk with 1 tsp palm sugar paste, then top this with a pinch of the dry topping ingredients. Fold each pancake into half, then remove from pan and keep warm.
Repeat this procedure until the batter and toppings are used up.

EMERALD TAPIOCA SWEETS *Yok Manee*

Serves 6–8

250 g	Fine tapioca grains
600 ml	Water
12	Young pandanus leaves, finely chopped
270 g	Granulated white sugar
400–500 g	Freshly grated white coconut

PREPARATION

Put the tapioca grains in a sieve and wash them well under cold running water. Shake off excess water.

Bring 500 ml of the water to the boil, and gradually add the tapioca grains, stirring slowly but constantly with a wooden spoon to prevent the tapioca grains from sticking to the bottom of the saucepan. Cook gently over low heat for 20–25 minutes. Blend the chopped pandanus leaves and the remaining 100 ml of water until very smooth. Strain through a very fine-mesh sieve, keeping the green water and discarding the pulp.

Add the sugar to the tapioca mixture, mix well and continue to cook for about 20 minutes, strirring constantly until the mixture is very sticky. Add the green pandanus leaf water and stir well until the mixture starts to boil.

Transfer to a tray, cover with plastic film and leave aside to cool. To finish, roll the mixture into small balls, then coat each ball with grated white coconut.

BABY PUMPKIN CUSTARD *Sangkhaya Fak Thong*

Serves 10

5	Small pumpkins (approx. 250 g each)
500 ml	Coconut cream (see recipe on Pg 42)
500 g	Chicken and duck eggs, in equal quantity
400 g	Palm sugar
3–4	Fresh pandanus leaves, cut into 5 cm lengths

PREPARATION

Using a small sharp kitchen knife, cut open the top of each pumpkin, making an opening of about 6–7 cm. With a spoon, scoop out the seeds, core and filaments. Wash the pumpkins and pat them dry with a paper towels. Place the coconut cream, eggs, palm sugar and pandanus leaves in a bowl and mix and squeeze the ingredients with your hands for at least 5 minutes (this process helps to give the custard a good pandanus flavour). Pass the custard through a fine-mesh sieve.

Fill the pumpkin shells with the custard and steam over a gentle heat for 1 hour 15 minutes. Remove and leave to rest at room temperature for at least 45 minutes before serving.

CHEWY COCONUT COOKIES *Khow Tu*

Serves 6–8

380 ml	Coconut cream (see recipe on Pg 42)
560 g	Palm sugar
50 g	Sticky rice flour
190 ml	Water
340 g	Ground toasted rice
520 g	Finely grated white coconut meat

PREPARATION

Bring the coconut cream and palm sugar to the boil and allow to simmer gently over medium heat for 20–30 minutes until the mixture becomes syrupy. Combine the sticky rice flour with the water and add it to the coconut-sugar mixture.

Boil gently, stirring constantly for 5–7 minutes, then add the ground toasted rice and coconut meat. Continue cooking over low heat until the mixture is firm enough to be shaped into small balls (stir constantly or the mixture will burn). Transfer it to a tray and let it cool down to room temperature.

Use cookie cutters to shape the cookies, or roll the mixture into little balls between your palms and flatten them slightly.

Cover and keep at room temperature until ready to serve.

Chef's note: Ground toasted rice can be bought ready-prepared in markets, but to prepare it at home, dry-roast the raw rice grains in a wok until brown, spread out on a tray to cool, then blend until very fine.

1. *Egg Yolk Sweets*
2. *Miniature Yellow Bean Marzipans*
3. *Egg Yolk Sweets*
4. *Egg Yolk Sweets, Chewy Coconut Cookies and Pandan Coconut Custard*
5. *Centre: Pandan Coconut Custard; middle: Emerald Tapioca Sweets; outside: Egg Yolk Sweets*
6. *Baby Pumpkin Custard*
7. *Crispy Thai Pancakes*

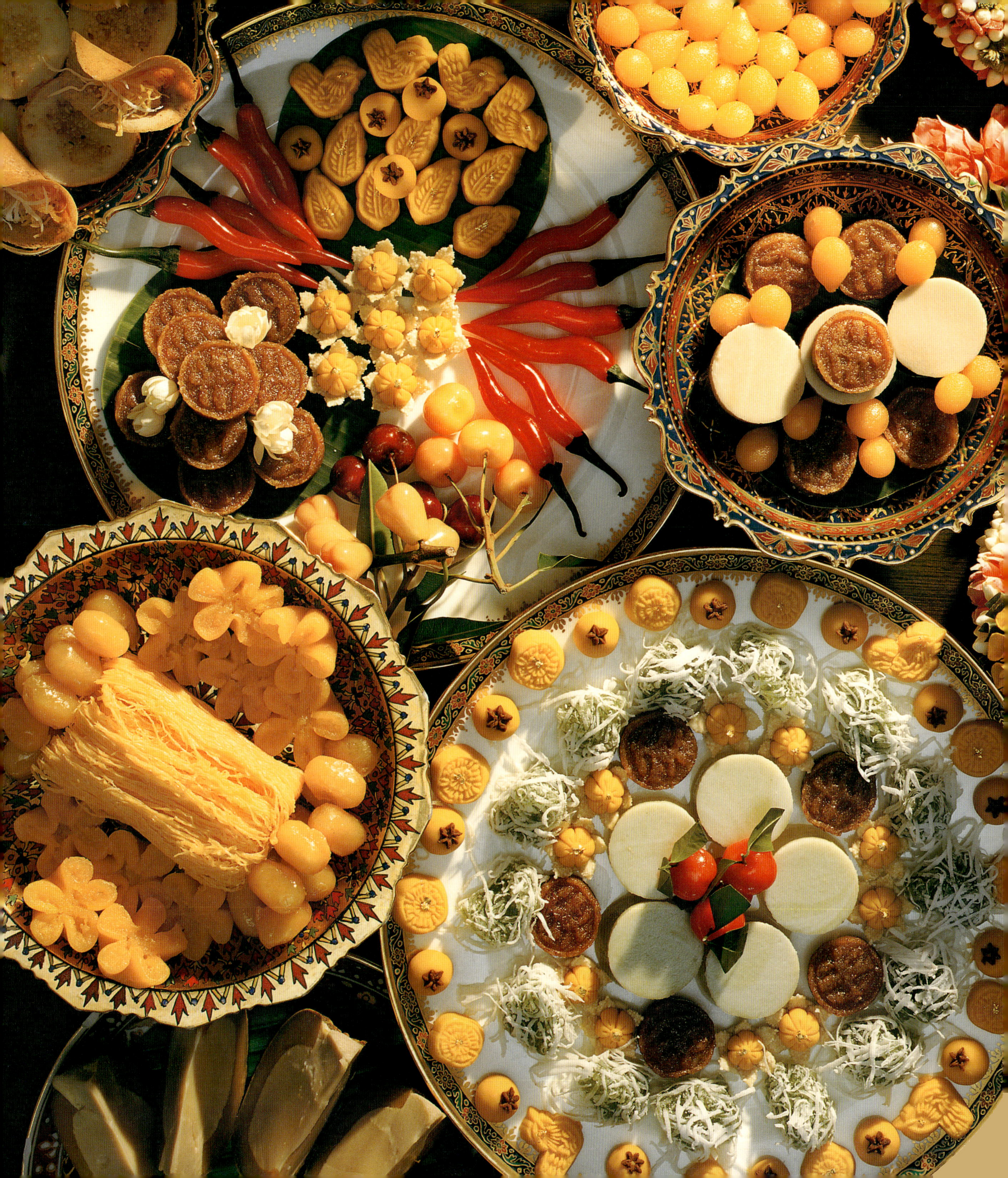

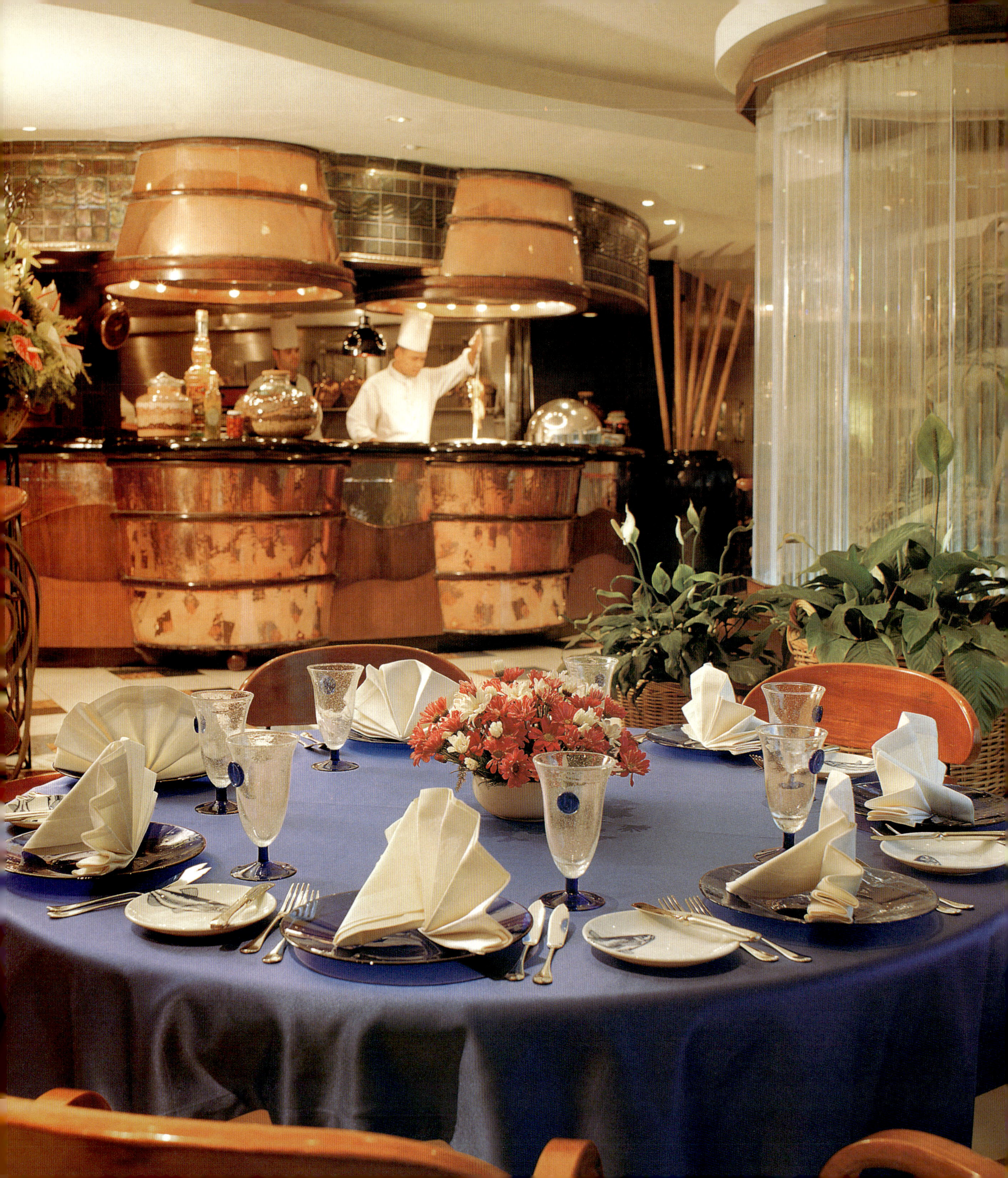

LORD JIM'S

Lord Jim is the hero of Joseph Conrad's famous novel, a sailor who acquires a kingdom of his own in an exotic Eastern land (inspired by the real-life White Rajah of Sarawak). The writer is honoured with a suite at The Oriental, as well as another named after the ship he commanded. It seemed only suitable, then, to give the name of his most celebrated character to a restaurant specialising in creations based on the bounty of the sea.

While Lord Jim's does offer such items for meat lovers as Rosemary-roasted Rack of Lamb with Garlic Potatoes, and Grilled Striploin of Grain-fed U.S. Beef with Yorkshire Pudding, as well as a vegetarian selection, its menu is predominantly devoted to seafood of all kinds, prepared in a variety of imaginative ways. Some cold-water ingredients are imported, like fresh oysters and Tasmanian salmon; most of them, though, come from the abundant waters off Thailand's long southern coast, brought in daily at the peak of freshness.

Experienced diners have learned to look for the little fish logo that marks the restaurant's signature dishes. Under starters and soups, for example, these include the delectable Thai-style Crisp Rainbow Trout Salad with Spicy Cashew Nuts and Exotic Herbs, and Seafood Tartare with Cucumber and Capsicum Salsa, as well as Crabmeat Timbal with Sweet Corn and Red Capsicum Soup. Among the entrées are Char-grilled Spiced Salmon Tournedos on Sweetcorn-Potato Mousseline and Char Siu Garoupa with Star Anise and Szechuan Pepper Sauce. A popular favourite is the scrumptious Crispy Gnocchi Salad with Rock Lobster in Lobster-Vanilla Essence.

With expansive views of the broad Chao Phraya River, where Joseph Conrad anchored more than a century ago, Lord Jim's offers an unforgettable dining experience for true lovers of the finest seafood.

Joseph Conrad's seafaring hero is immortalised in this outlet, where fresh seafood, as well as a wide selection of meat and vegetarian dishes, prepared in the most innovative ways, adorn the dinner table

CRABMEAT CAKE WITH MANGO BEURRE BLANC (opposite, back)

Serves 4–5

Balsamico Dressing

30 ml	Balsamic vinegar
90 ml	Extra virgin olive oil
2	Garlic cloves, flattened

Crabmeat Cakes

90 g	Toast bread, crusts removed and cut into cubes
70 g	Cold milk
1	Egg
60 ml	Thick mayonnaise
70 g	Shallots, chopped and blanched
50 g	Leek, finely diced and blanched
20 g	Ginger, finely chopped
10 g	French mustard
	Salt and freshly ground black pepper to season
20 g	Chopped parsley
450 g	Chunky crabmeat
1 cup	Breadcrumbs

Mango Beurre Blanc

40 ml	White wine vinegar
50 ml	Chicken stock (see recipe on Pg 101)
200 g	Mango flesh
40 ml	Whipping cream
80 g	Cold unsalted butter, cut into cubes
	Salt and freshly ground black pepper to season
4 handfuls	Mixed salad leaves
4 sticks	Chives (16–18 cm each), blanched

PREPARATION

Combine all the balsamico dressing ingredients and mix well.
Tie the salad leaves into 4 bouquets with the chives (insert some carrot sticks and beansprouts into the bouquet if you wish to add more colour).
Soak the cubes of bread in milk for 10 minutes.
Mix the egg with mayonnaise, shallots, leek, ginger and French mustard. Season with salt and a good pinch of coarsely ground black pepper. Add the chopped parsley and the soaked bread cubes and mix well.
Carefully fold in the crabmeat chunks, taking care not to break up the chunks too much.
Shape mixture into patties (40–50 g each), and coat them with breadcrumbs.
Gently pan-fry the patties on both sides for 2–3 minutes. Drain excess oil on paper towels.
To prepare the mango beurre blanc, bring the vinegar and chicken stock to the boil in a saucepan. Add the mango and let simmer for 10 minutes. Process with a blender until smooth.
Add the cream and bring to the boil again. Remove from heat and whisk in the cold butter cubes one at a time. Continue whisking until the butter emulsifies in the sauce.
Season with salt and pepper and remove from heat.

PRESENTATION

Lightly coat each salad bouquet with some balsamico dressing and place it in the centre of a plate.
Arrange three crabmeat patties around and spoon the mango sauce in between the patties (drizzle some chilli oil over the sauce for more colour).

SEAFOOD TARTARE (opposite, front)

Serves 4–6

100 g	Salmon fillet, sashimi grade, skin and fat removed
100 g	Tuna fillet, sashimi grade
100 g	Scallops, sashimi grade
100 g	Snapper fillet, sashimi grade
50 g	Shallots, chopped
30 g	Chives, finely chopped
20 ml	Hazelnut oil
	Salt and freshly ground pepper to season
10 ml	Tabasco sauce
100 g	Cucumber, peeled, seeded and cubed
100 g	Red capsicum, peeled and seeds removed
100 ml	Extra virgin olive oil
50 ml	Freshly squeezed lemon juice

PREPARATION

Cut the salmon, tuna, scallops and snapper fillet into 5-mm cubes. Add the chopped shallots, chives and hazelnut oil. Mix well and season with salt, pepper and the Tabasco sauce.
To prepare the salsa, cut the cucumber and red capsicum into 3-mm cubes. Add the olive oil and lemon juice and season with salt and pepper to taste. (This can be prepared a few hours in advance and left to marinate.)

PRESENTATION

Place a 4-cm stainless steel ring in the centre of a plate and fill with the seafood tartare. Spoon the salsa around. Remove ring to serve. (Optional: Garnish with bread sticks, chive flowers, fresh coriander leaves and a carrot butterfly.)

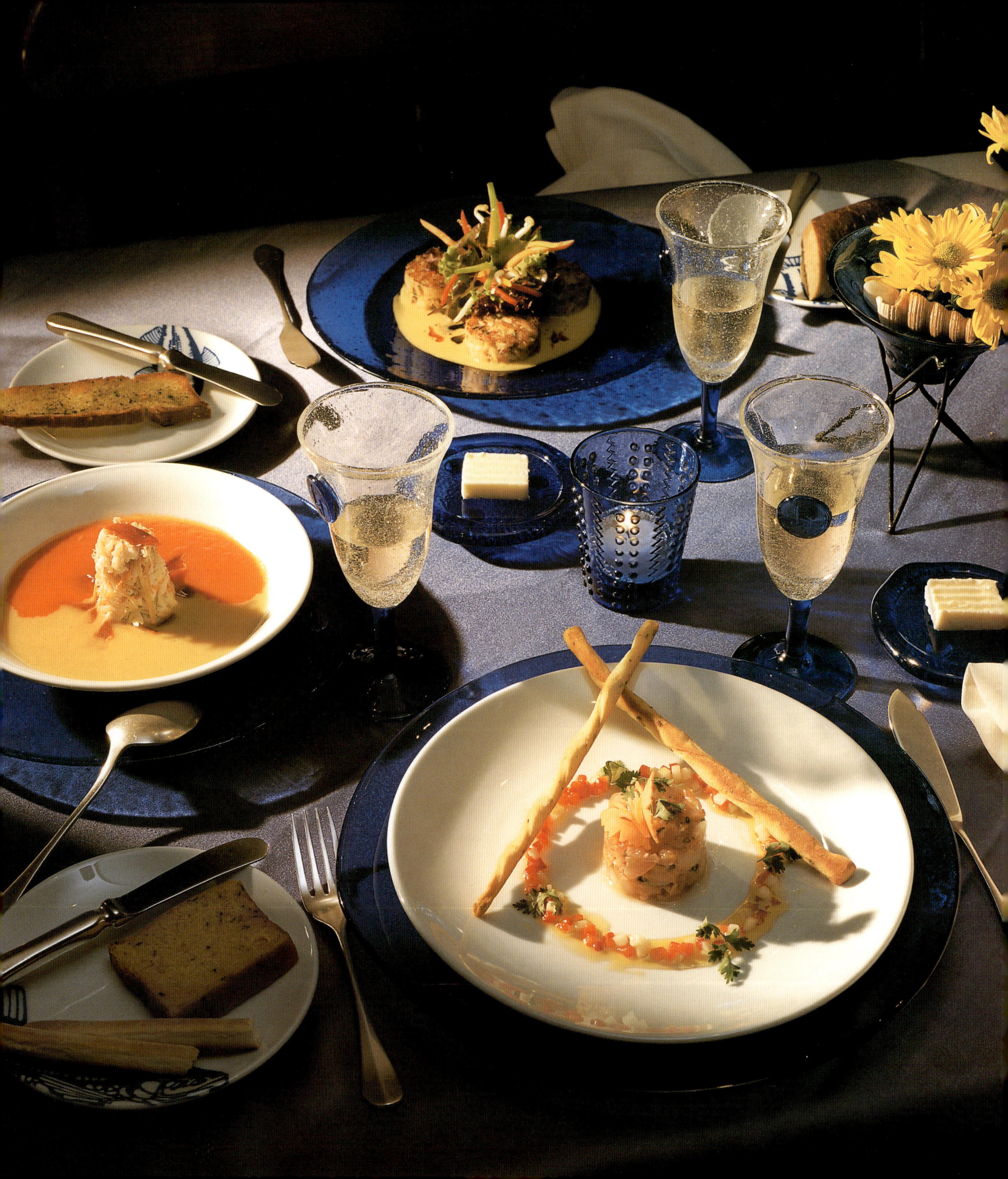

CRABMEAT TIMBAL WITH SWEET CORN AND RED CAPSICUM SOUP (Pg 49, left)

Serves 4–5

30 g	Carrots, julienned
30 g	Leek, julienned
150 g	Crabmeat
Salt and pepper to season	
50 g	Thinly sliced Parma ham

Sweetcorn Soup

40 g	Onion, chopped
40 g	Leek, sliced
30 g	Unsalted butter
200 g	Sweetcorn kernels
80 g	Potatoes, peeled
1 litre	Chicken stock (see recipe on Pg 101)
100 ml	Cream

Red Capsicum Soup

40 g	Onion, chopped
20 g	Garlic, chopped
40 g	Leek
30 g	Unsalted butter
200 g	Red capsicum, peeled and seeded
80 g	Potatoes, peeled
800 ml	Chicken stock (see recipe on Pg 101)

PREPARATION
For the sweetcorn soup, sauté the chopped onion and leek with the butter. Add the sweet corn, potatoes and chicken stock. Bring this to the boil and then simmer until the potatoes are very soft.
Pour into a blender and purée mixture until it is very fine. Return soup to the pot and bring it to the boil again.
Add cream and season to taste.
For the red capsicum soup, sauté the chopped onion, garlic and leek with the butter. Add the peeled red capsicums, potatoes and chicken stock. Bring this to the boil and allow to simmer until all ingredients are soft. Blend until very fine and return soup to the pot. Bring to the boil again and season with salt and pepper to taste.

PRESENTATION
Sauté the julienned carrots and leek with some butter, add the crabmeat and season with salt and pepper.
Bake the sliced Parma ham for 2–3 minutes at 120°C, then cut into 1-cm squares.
Fill a cone-shaped mould with the crabmeat mixture, and place in the centre of a soup plate. Remove the mould. Pour in both soups, each from a different side, without mixing them.
Garnish with the Parma ham and serve.

CLAM, BACON AND OKRA CHOWDER

Serves 6

50 ml	Vegetable oil
1 kg	Very fresh clams
50 g	Shallots, peeled and sliced
2–3	Garlic cloves, whole
2–3	Fresh thyme sprigs
5	Parsley stems
100 ml	Dry white wine
40 g	Unsalted butter
150 g	Mildly salted bacon, diced
70 g	White onion, diced
200 g	Okra (lady's fingers), cut into 1-cm lengths
50 g	Celery, diced
50 g	Leek, diced
50 g	Carrots, diced
200 g	Potatoes, diced
1	*Bouquet garni* (combine bay leaf, thyme and parsley)
2 tbsp	All-purpose flour
700 ml	Fish stock (see recipe on Pg 65)
200 ml	Fresh cream
Salt and freshly ground pepper to season	

PREPARATION
To make the clams expel sand, place them in a kitchen bowl, cover them in cold water and add 2 tbsp salt.
Heat 2 tbsp oil in a saucepan, add the clams, shallots, garlic cloves and thyme and stir-fry for a little while. Deglaze with wine and cover. Leave to cook for 2–3 minutes until the clams all open. (Note: Discard the clams which did not open. This means they are not fresh.)
Remove the clams, strain the cooking juice through a fine sieve; remove the clam flesh from the shells; and keep both aside.
Melt the butter in a stockpot, add bacon and onion and sauté until translucent. Add the other vegetables and *bouquet garni* and continue cooking until most of the liquid has evaporated. Add the clam juice and boil for 2–3 minutes, stirring occasionally. Add flour and stir well.
Add the fish stock gradually, stirring with a wooden spoon, and bring to the boil. Simmer for 15–20 minutes, stirring occasionally. Then add the cream, stir well and cook for 15–20 minutes.
Add the clam flesh, bring the soup to the boil and season with salt and freshly ground pepper to taste. Serve hot.
(Optional: garnish with chopped parsley or celery leaves.)

THAI-STYLE HERBED RAINBOW TROUT SALAD (below)

Serves 4

4	Rainbow trout fillets, deboned and skinned
40 ml	Soy sauce
120 ml	Fish sauce (*nam pla*)
100 ml	Fresh lime juice
80 g	Granulated sugar
60 g	Shallots, finely sliced
60 g	Lemongrass, finely sliced
80 g	Green mango, cut into thin strips
4-6	Bird's eye chillies (*prik kee noo*), finely chopped
20 g	Spring onion, sliced
20 g	Kaffir lime leaves, cut into very fine shreds
1	Banana leaf
3-4	Lettuce leaves
2	Large red chillies, cut into strips
80 g	Fried unsalted cashewnuts
20 g	Fresh mint leaves

Vegetable oil for frying

PREPARATION
Marinate the rainbow trout fillets in the soy sauce and leave to stand for 5 minutes.

Heat the vegetable oil over a medium heat and fry the trout fillets until they are golden brown. Remove the fish fillets from the oil and drain on a wire rack.

Combine the fish sauce, lime juice and sugar in a mixing bowl, stirring until the sugar has completely dissolved.

Add the sliced shallots, lemongrass, green mango, chopped bird's eye chillies, spring onions and finely shredded kaffir lime leaves. Break the trout fillets into bite-sized pieces and add them to this salad. Mix gently, making sure that the fish is well coated with the other ingredients.

PRESENTATION
Cut the banana leaf into a square. Place it on a serving plate with the lettuce leaves in the centre. Place the trout salad on the lettuce leaves and sprinkle with the red chilli strips, unsalted fried cashew nuts and fresh mint leaves. Decorate with carrot carved into leaves or a leek flower.

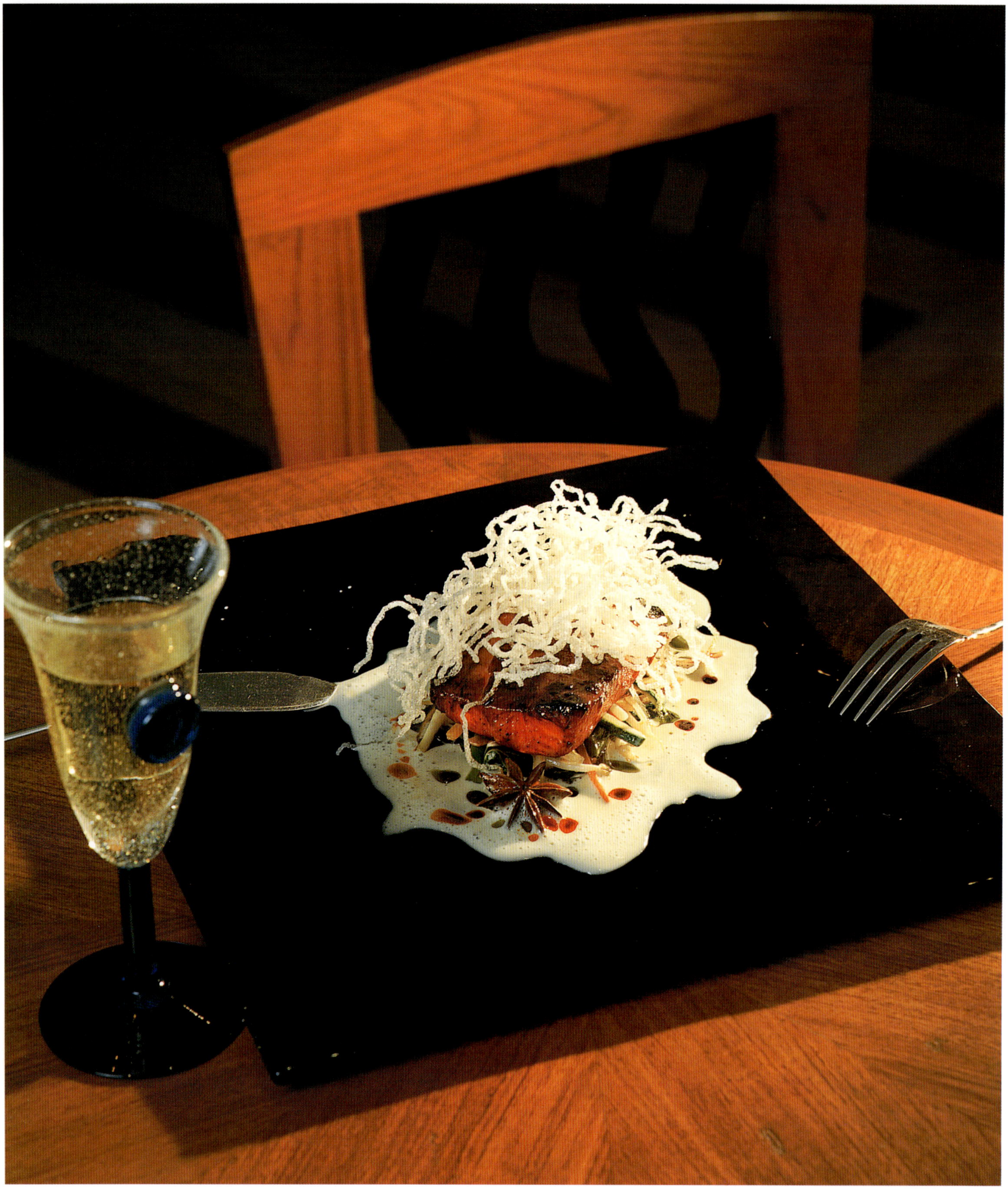

CHAR SIU GAROUPA WITH STAR ANISE AND SZECHUAN PEPPER SAUCE (opposite)

Serves 4

200 ml	Char siu marinade
4	Garoupa fillet (approx. 160 g each)
	Oil for frying
600 ml	Fish stock (see recipe on Pg 65)
20 g	Star anise
20 g	Szechuan pepper
100 ml	Cream
	Salt and pepper to taste
60 g	Green asparagus
60 g	Carrots, cut into thin strips
60 g	Red peppers, cut into thin strips
60 g	Yellow peppers, cut into thin strips
60 g	Green peppers, cut into thin strips
80 g	Baby bok choy
60 g	Beansprouts, with tails removed
60 g	Spring onion
30 ml	Sesame oil
50 g	Dry glass noodles for decoration

Char Siu Marinade

280 g	Sugar
2	Eggs
100 g	Garlic
100 g	Shallots
100 g	Ginger
100 g	Coriander
180 ml	Hoisin sauce
3 g	Red food colouring
50 ml	Chinese rice wine
210 g	Preserved yellow bean paste
150 ml	Water

PREPARATION

To prepare the char siu marinade, combine all the marinade ingredients in a large bowl and mix well. (This will yield about 1 litre of marinade.) Keep refrigerated for about three days.

To prepare the fish, coat the garoupa fillets with 200 ml char siu mixture and leave for about 1 minute.

Sear both sides of the fish in a skillet over medium heat for 15 seconds. Transfer to a tray and bake in the oven until done. Keep warm, but without over-cooking the fish.

Pour the fish stock into a saucepan and bring to the boil. Add the star anise and Szechuan pepper, and allow to reduce by half. Strain into another saucepan containing the cream and leave to simmer for about 15 minutes.

Season with salt and pepper to taste.

Blanch the vegetables, except the beansprouts and spring onion, in boiling water for 1 minute. Drain, then plunge the vegetables into ice water. Drain and pat dry with paper towels.

Quickly sauté the vegetables in sesame oil and season with salt and pepper to taste.

Deep-fry the glass noodles in very hot oil for about 10 seconds until they expand and become crispy. Drain off excess oil on a wire rack.

PRESENTATION

Arrange the vegetables in the centre of a serving plate, top with the roasted garoupa fillet and drizzle the sauce around the vegetables. Top the fish with some deep-fried glass noodles and garnish with two star anise pods. Give the sauce some colour with a few drops of chilli oil and coriander oil.

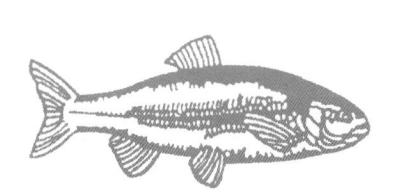

CRISPY GNOCCHI SALAD WITH ROCK LOBSTER IN LOBSTER-VANILLA ESSENCE (opposite)

Serves 4

20 g	Shallots, chopped
10 g	Garlic, chopped
80 g	Red peppers, peeled and with seeds removed
80 g	Yellow peppers, peeled and with seeds removed
80 g	Cured black olives, pitted and cut into sixths
50 ml	White wine

Spinach Gnocchi

500 g	Potatoes, peeled
250 g	Spinach, blanched
1	Egg yolk
Salt, pepper and nutmeg to season	
75 g	Plain flour

Lobster-Vanilla Essence

300 ml	Lobster stock (see recipe below)
1	Vanilla pod
100 ml	Cream
Salt and pepper to season	

Rock Lobster

6	Rock lobster tails, cut in half lengthways
2 tbsp	Extra virgin olive oil

Salad

200 g	Small mixed lettuce leaves
A handful of Italian parsley, basil, tarragon and chervil leaves	
60 g	Cherry tomatoes, cut in half
80 ml	Balsamico dressing (see recipe on Pg 48)

PREPARATION

Spinach Gnocchi
Cut potatoes into small cubes and boil until soft. Strain and let the potatoes dry in an oven at 100°C for about 20 minutes.
Process the spinach in a blender and remove excess water by squeezing through a kitchen towel.
Mash the potato, add the egg yolk, spinach purée, salt, pepper and nutmeg, followed by adding a small amount of flour at a time and checking the consistency of the gnocchi dough before adding more. Only add more flour if the dough is still wet.
Roll the dough into 3-cm-thick 'sausages', then cut them into 3-cm-thick slices and roll them over a fork to form small grooves on the dough. (This makes 800 g of gnocchi.)
Boil a large pot of water, add some salt and boil 320 g of gnocchi until they float to the surface.
Refresh them in cold water, drain and toss in some olive oil to prevent them from sticking together.

Lobster-Vanilla Essence
Boil the lobster stock in a saucepan and reduce by two-thirds. Cut the vanilla pod open and scrape out the seeds. Add the seeds and the cream to the lobster stock. Increase heat and allow to cook for about 2 minutes to let the vanilla infuse the sauce. Season with salt and pepper to taste.

Rock Lobster
Season the rock lobster tail halves with salt and pepper. Pan-fry in 1 tbsp olive oil, remove and keep warm.

PRESENTATION
Heat up 1 tablespoon of olive oil and sauté the gnocchi until they are slightly brown. Add the chopped shallots, garlic, peppers and black olives. Deglaze the pan with white wine and cook until the wine has evaporated. Place the spinach gnocchi in the centre of a serving plate with 3 rock lobster tails.
Combine the salad ingredients and toss with balsamico dressing. Arrange the salad on top of the gnocchi and drizzle the lobster sauce around to serve.

LOBSTER STOCK

Makes 500 ml

1 kg	Fresh lobster shells, cut into 2–3-cm chunks
50 ml	Vegetable oil
80 g	Carrots, peeled and sliced
80 g	Leek, cleaned and sliced
60 g	Celery stalks, sliced
3–4	Garlic cloves, unpeeled and crushed
100 g	Fennel, cleaned and sliced
150 g	Ripe tomatoes, cut in quarters
70 g	Shallots, peeled and sliced
1 tsp	Cracked white peppercorns
30 ml	Brandy
100 ml	White wine
30 ml	Tomato paste
2–3	Bay leaves
1 litre	Cold water

PREPARATION
Stir-fry the lobster shells until they turn red in colour and the moisture has evaporated. Add the vegetables and peppercorns. Mix well. Flambé the mixture with the brandy and white wine. Add tomato paste, stir well and remove from heat. Leave ingredients to cool, then add water and slowly bring to the boil. Boil gently for 1 hour. Skim off the substance that floats to the surface regularly. Remove from heat and rest it for 15–20 minutes, then strain through a fine-mesh sieve. Let cool, then refrigerate or use immediately.

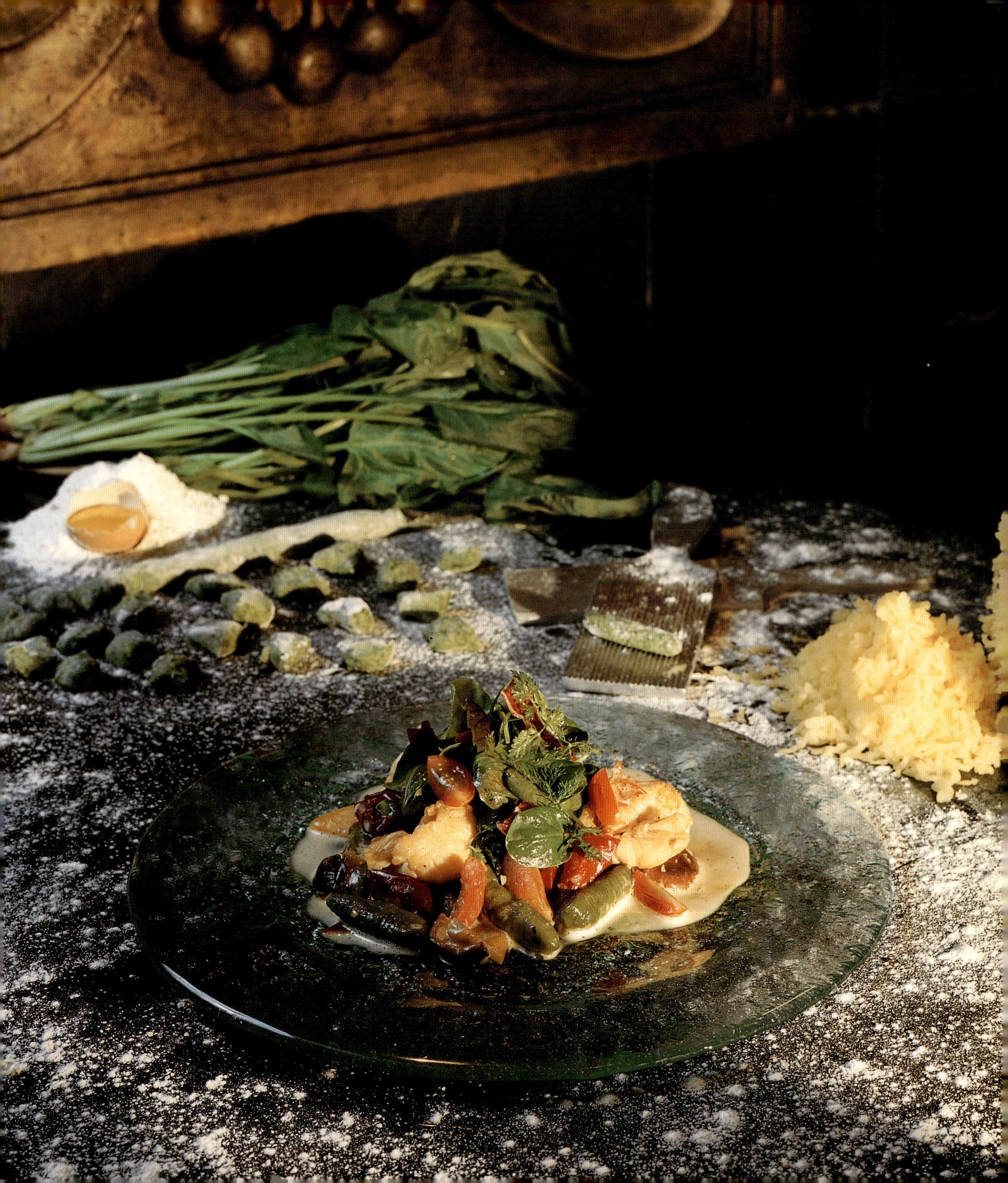

CHAR-GRILLED SPICED SALMON TOURNEDOS WITH EGGPLANT MARMALADE (opposite)

Serves 4

Corn-Potato Mousseline

270 g	Potatoes, peeled and cut into 2-cm cubes
60 ml	Chicken stock (see recipe on Pg 101)
130 g	Corn kernels, fresh or canned
50 ml	Cream, heated but not boiling
20 g	Butter

Salt, freshly ground pepper and nutmeg to season

Eggplant Marmalade

400 g	Eggplants, peeled
200 g	Tomatoes, peeled and seeded
35 g	Black olives, drained and pitted
20 ml	Extra virgin olive oil
10 g	Garlic, chopped
15 g	Shallots, chopped
10 g	Sweet basil leaves
3 g	Thyme leaves
200 ml	Chicken stock (see recipe on Pg 101)

Salt and freshly ground black pepper to taste

Sauce

100 g	Shallots, sliced
2 g	Thyme leaves
30 g	Unsalted butter
200 ml	White wine
600 ml	Fish stock (see recipe on Pg 65)
170 ml	Cream

Salt and freshly ground pepper

10 ml	Lemon juice

Some fresh dill, parsley, basil leaves and tarragon

120 g	Unsalted butter, cut into small cubes

Salmon Tournedos

8	Salmon tournedos (approx. 80 g each)
5 g	Cajun spice

PREPARATION

Corn-Potato Mousseline

Boil the potatoes until soft. Strain and leave to rest for 1–2 minutes until they are dry.
Boil the chicken stock, add the corn kernels and purée in a blender. Mash the potatoes, add the hot cream and corn purée. Mix well. Add the fresh butter and mix thoroughly. Season with salt, pepper and some freshly-ground nutmeg. Keep warm.

Eggplant Marmalade

Cut the peeled eggplants and tomatoes into 1-cm cubes. Slice the black olives.
Heat up the olive oil in a large pot and sauté the chopped garlic and shallots until translucent. Add the eggplants and sauté for 1–2 minutes, then add the tomatoes, black olives, basil and thyme leaves. Stir well, then add the chicken stock. Let the stock evaporate over a slow fire, taking care not to let the marmalade mixture burn. Season with salt and black pepper. Remove from the heat when all ingredients are tender. Keep warm.

Sauce

Sauté the sliced shallots and the fresh thyme leaves in butter until translucent.
Add the white wine and let it reduce by half. Then add the fish stock and cream and let it reduce again by half.
Strain and season with salt, pepper and lemon juice.
Chop the fresh herbs, keeping some sprigs whole for garnishing. Bring the white wine sauce to the boil, and add half the chopped herbs. Process mixture in a blender until the sauce turns green. Return to a saucepan and bring to the boil again. Slowly whisk the cold butter cubes into the sauce. Add the remaining herbs and adjust the seasoning.

Salmon Tournedos

Season the two salmon tournedos with the Cajun spice, taking care to cover their sides completely.
Grill the salmon on a charcoal grill until medium-well.

PRESENTATION

Reheat the corn-potato mousseline and the eggplant marmalade.
Place 2 tbsp corn-potato mousseline next to each other in the centre of a plate.
Form quenelles with the eggplant marmalade using two spoons, and then place them between the mousseline.
Top the corn-potato mousseline with the two salmon tournedos.
Spoon the sauce around the spiced salmon tournedos.
Garnish with a bouquet of fresh herbs and some drops of chilli oil on the sauce.

Lord Jim's

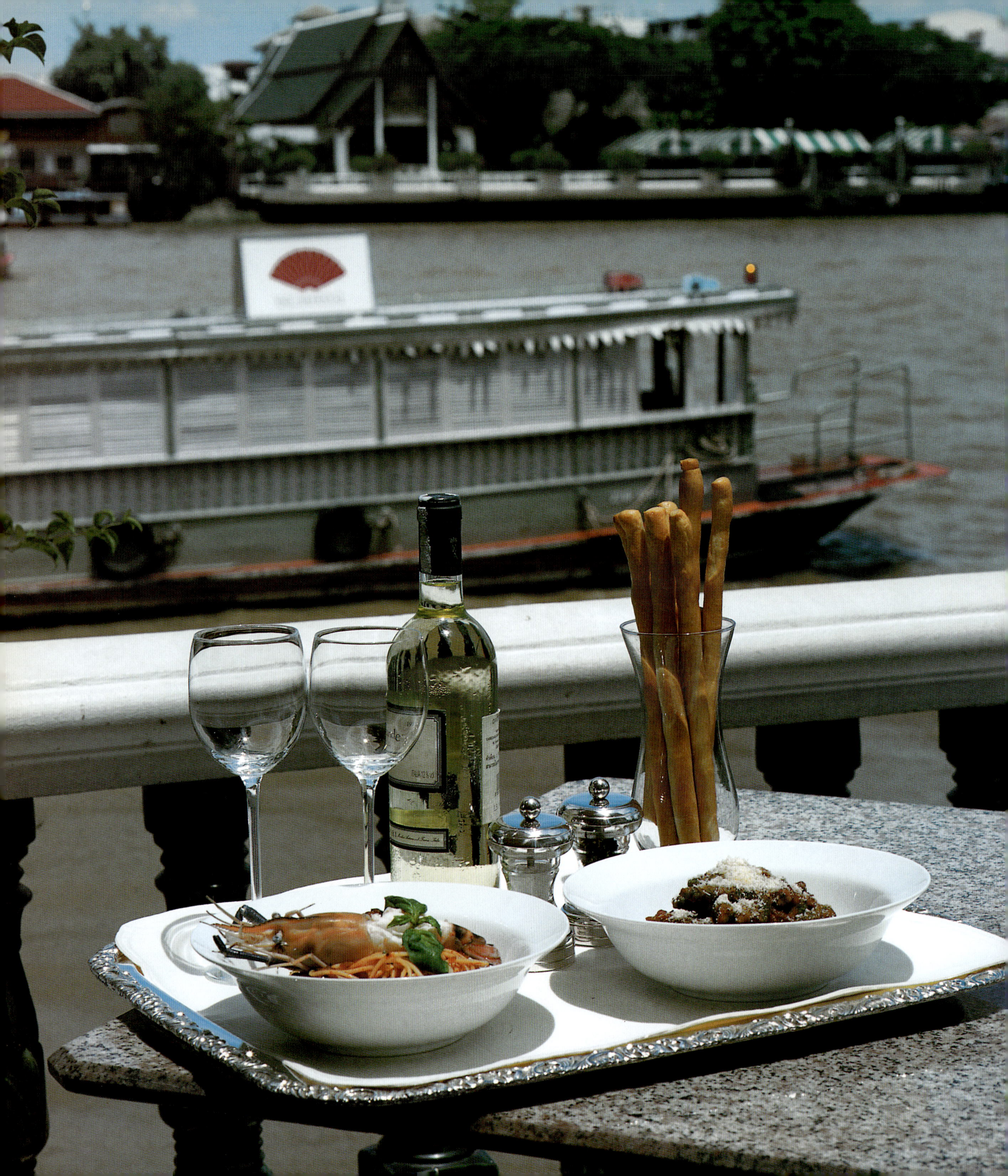

CIAO AND THE VERANDAH

The timeless Chao Phraya is one of The Oriental's greatest attractions. By day or night, the river presents a continuous pageant that never fails to enchant and often surprise. Nowhere is this more apparent than when dining at Ciao or The Verandah, both of which offer 'front-row' seats for an unencumbered view.

Ciao is Bangkok's only *al fresco* Italian restaurant, open during the dry months with candle-lit riverside tables and a menu that covers most of the classic fare. Signature dishes include Carpaccio of Fresh Salmon and Red Snapper, Seafood Salad with Citrus Segments, Spinach, Ricotta and Silver Beet Gnocchi with Gorgonzola and Grappa Sauce, Pan-sautéed Tiger Prawns with Fresh Mushrooms, Oven-Roasted Whole Seabass. All, of course, with that fascinating river view literally at one's elbow.

Open for breakfast, lunch and dinner, The Verandah is a casual, all-day affair, specialising in food that blends the familiar with the exotic in various innovative ways. Among the appetisers, for instance, is a salad composed of fresh local crabmeat and green papaya, while other offerings include a Roast Pumpkin Soup with a drizzle of coconut cream, a Whole Wheat Pita Pocket with Tandoori Chicken and Green Papaya Slaw, Rosemary Focaccia layered with Roasted Vegetables, Mozzarella and Herb Pesto, and, for dessert, Chocolate and Ginger Tart with Kumquat Marmalade Ice Cream. The Verandah also has heartier fare like veal sausage, steak and lamb chops, as well as low-calorie 'natural cuisine' and a selection of popular Thai and Chinese dishes.

Ciao, Bangkok's only al fresco Italian restaurant, offers a 'front-row' view to the legendary Chao Phraya River. For those seeking the complete 'Oriental' experience, don't miss breakfast at The Verandah

CORN-FED CHICKEN AND SLIPPER LOBSTER WITH FENNEL RAGOUT (opposite, back)

Serves 4

4	Slipper lobsters (approx. 100 g each)
25 g	Mixed fresh herbs, chopped
4	Chicken breasts with skin (approx. 180 g each)
Butter and oil for frying	
300 ml	Aged Armagnac lobster bisque

Fennel Ragout

300 g	Fennel, sliced
70 ml	Olive oil
80 g	Onion, chopped
20 g	Garlic, chopped
100 g	Tomatoes, cubed
10 g	Dill, chopped
Salt and pepper to taste	

Aged Armagnac Lobster Bisque

30 ml	Vegetable oil
500 g	Fresh lobster and prawns, cut into 2-cm chunks
50 g	Carrots, sliced and peeled
100 g	Leek and celery stalks (100 g each), sliced
100 g	Ripe fresh tomatoes, quartered
30 g	Shallots, sliced and peeled
1	Bay leaf
30 ml	Armagnac brandy
40 g	Tomato paste
20 g	All-purpose flour
100 ml	White wine
50 ml	Dry white vermouth
500 ml	Fish stock (see recipe on Pg 65)
150 ml	Whipping cream
A squirt of lemon juice	
Salt and pepper to taste	
70 g	Butter, cut into cubes

PREPARATION
Remove the shell from the slipper lobster tails and roll the tails in the chopped herbs. Keep the shells for the bisque.
Insert one of the tails inside each chicken breast, and add salt and pepper to taste.
Melt the butter with the oil in a frying pan, add the chicken breasts, skin-side down, and cook until the skin is crispy. Then bake the breasts in a pre-heated oven at 165°C for 10–12 minutes.

Fennel Ragout
Sauté the sliced fennel in olive oil, onion and garlic for 4 minutes, then add the tomatoes, dill, and salt and pepper.

Aged Armagnac Lobster Bisque
Heat the vegetable oil in a saucepan, add the cut-up lobster and prawn chunks and stir-fry until the shells turn red.
Add the vegetables, shallots and bay leaf, continue frying then flambé with the brandy. Add the tomato paste and flour, stir, then add the white wine, dry vermouth and the fish stock. Bring to the boil and simmer for 1 hour.
Strain through a fine-mesh sieve.
Reduce the liquid to about 200 ml and add the fresh cream. Bring to the boil again and simmer for about 15 minutes. Season with salt, pepper and a squirt of lemon juice and then add the cold butter cubes, a few at a time, whisking vigorously with a wire whisk.

PRESENTATION
Place the fennel ragout in the centre of 4 pre-heated plates, put the sliced chicken breasts on top of the fennel and spoon the lobster bisque around.

Chef's note: This is a classic creation of The Oriental Hotel by Chef Dominique Bugnand. You can substitute the lobster with an equal quantity of fresh-river prawns or white sea prawns.

COLD TOFU AND JELLY MUSHROOM TOURNEDOS (opposite, front)

Serves 1

50 g	Beansprouts
10 g	Carrots, sliced into thin strips
10 g	Shiitake mushrooms, sliced
10 g	Spring onions, sliced
1 tsp	Oyster sauce
1 tsp	Soy sauce
½ tsp	Pepper
100 ml	Vegetable oil

Jelly Mushroom Tournedos

60 g	Finely chopped tofu, boiled
25 g	White jelly mushrooms
25 g	Black jelly mushrooms
40 g	Chilli sauce
10 g	Roasted ground rice
10 g	Shallots, sliced
5 g each of spring onions and kaffir lime	

PREPARATION
Fill a cone-shaped mould with the tournedo mixture, place it in the centre of a serving plate and remove the mould. Arrange the stir-fried vegetables around and serve.

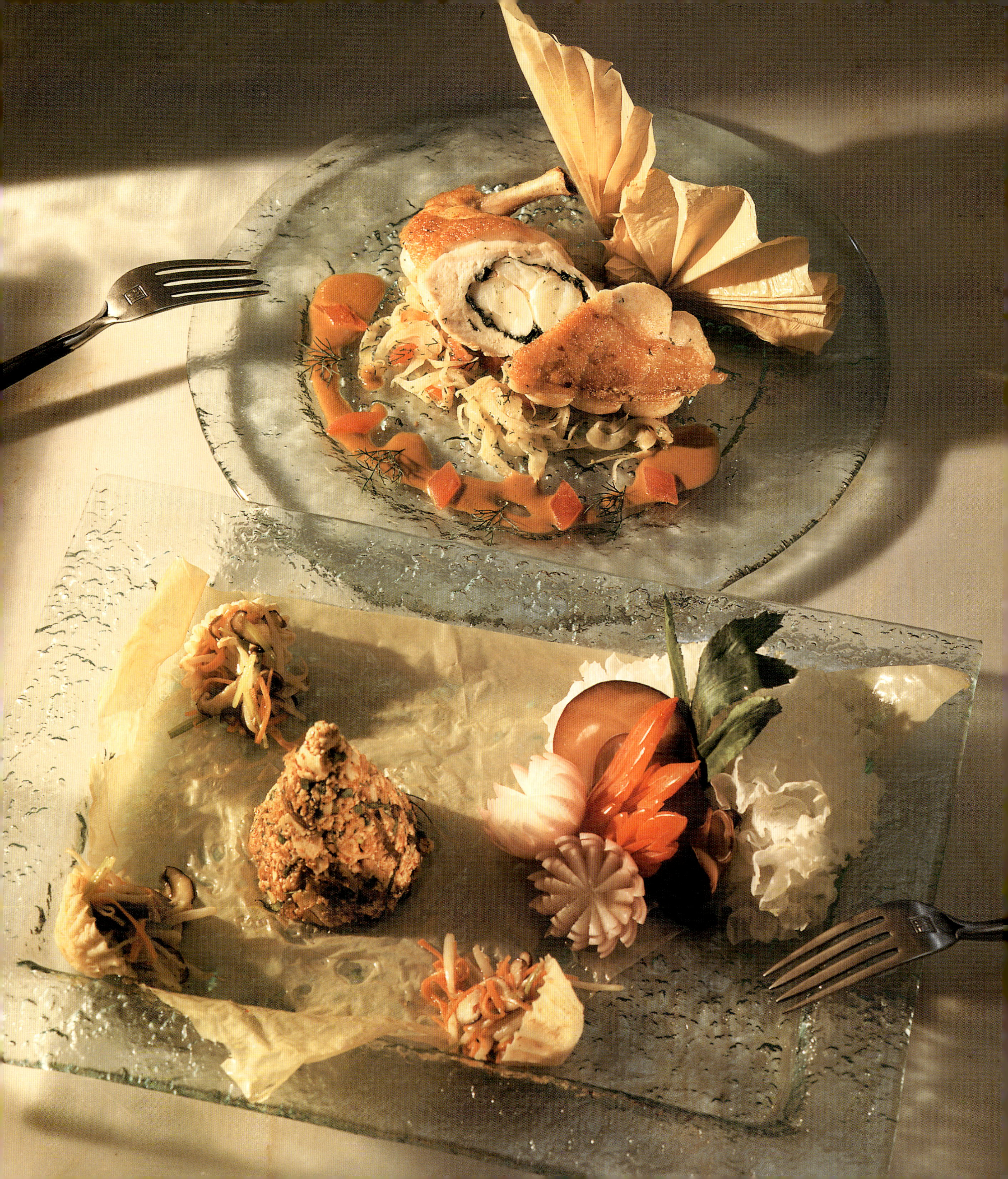

CIAO'S SEAFOOD SOUP

Serves 4–5

750 g	Fish bones (of fish such as mullet, garoupa, pomfret)
100 g	Carrots, diced
100 g	Potatoes, cubed
100 g	Onion, peeled and diced
3–4 cloves	Garlic, peeled and sliced
100 g	Leek, sliced
50 g	Shallots, peeled and diced
100 ml	Olive oil
300 g	Ripe tomatoes, diced
50 g	Tomato paste
150 g	White prawns, chopped
12	Medium-sized prawns, peeled
2	Bay leaves
3 sprigs	Fresh or dried thyme
4 sprigs	Parsley
A pinch of saffron threads	
Salt and freshly ground white pepper to season	
1½ litres	Cold water
180 g	Fresh red snapper, cut into 3-cm cubes
180 g	Fresh garoupa, cut into 3-cm cubes
12	Fresh large scallops
160 g	Lobster meat, cut into 3-cm cubes
12	Fresh mussels, scrubbed and beards removed

PREPARATION
Rinse the fish bones in cold running water thoroughly, pat dry with paper towels, then chop roughly.
Sauté the carrots, potatoes, onion, garlic, leek and shallots in olive oil, add the tomatoes and tomato paste. Mix well.
Add the fish bones, prawns, bay leaves, thyme, parsley and saffron. Season with some salt and pepper, and pour in cold water. Cook on medium heat for about 45 minutes. Pass the soup through a fine-mesh sieve. (It should have a velvety consistency.) If the soup is too thin, bring back to the boil and reduce slightly. Adjust the seasoning with salt and pepper.

PRESENTATION
Just before serving, bring the soup to the boil, add the seafood and simmer for about 4 minutes.
Remove the seafood and mussels and place in 4 pre-heated serving soup plates.
Slowly pour the hot soup over and serve immediately.

Chef's note: This seafood soup was created at Ciao's and is only served on special occasions. It is best served with toasted farmhouse bread slices rubbed with garlic.

PAN-FRIED GAROUPA STEAK WITH MORNING GLORY AND CARROT SAUCE (opposite)

Serves 4

4	Garoupa steaks with skin (approx. 150 g each)
50 g	Flour
Salt and pepper to taste	
Vegetable oil for frying	
320 g	Morning glory
20 g	Garlic, chopped
40 ml	Oyster sauce
40 ml	Soya sauce

Carrot Sauce

1.25 litres	Fresh carrot juice
100 g	Fresh ginger, peeled
60 ml	Whipping cream
100 g	Butter
100 g	Brown chicken sauce (see recipe on Pg 75)
100 ml	Fish stock (see recipe on Pg 65)
Salt and pepper to taste	

PREPARATION
Score the skin of the garoupa steaks, sprinkle the flour, salt and pepper onto a plate and coat the skin side of the steaks with this mixture. Shake off any excess. Heat 2 tbsp oil in a frying pan, add the fish, with skin facing down, and fry over high heat for 3–4 minutes until the skin is crispy. Transfer to oven and bake the fish until it is cooked but not dry. Sauté the morning glory in 1 tbsp oil for 1 minute, add the garlic, oyster sauce, soya sauce, salt and pepper to taste.

Carrot Sauce
Combine the carrot juice and ginger in a saucepan and bring to the boil. Turn down the heat and reduce the mixture until about ½ cup of liquid remains. Add the cream, butter and chicken sauce, and reduce again over medium heat until the sauce thickens. Adjust seasoning with salt and pepper if necessary.

PRESENTATION
Place the morning glory in the centre of a serving plate, top with the garoupa steak and spoon the carrot sauce around.

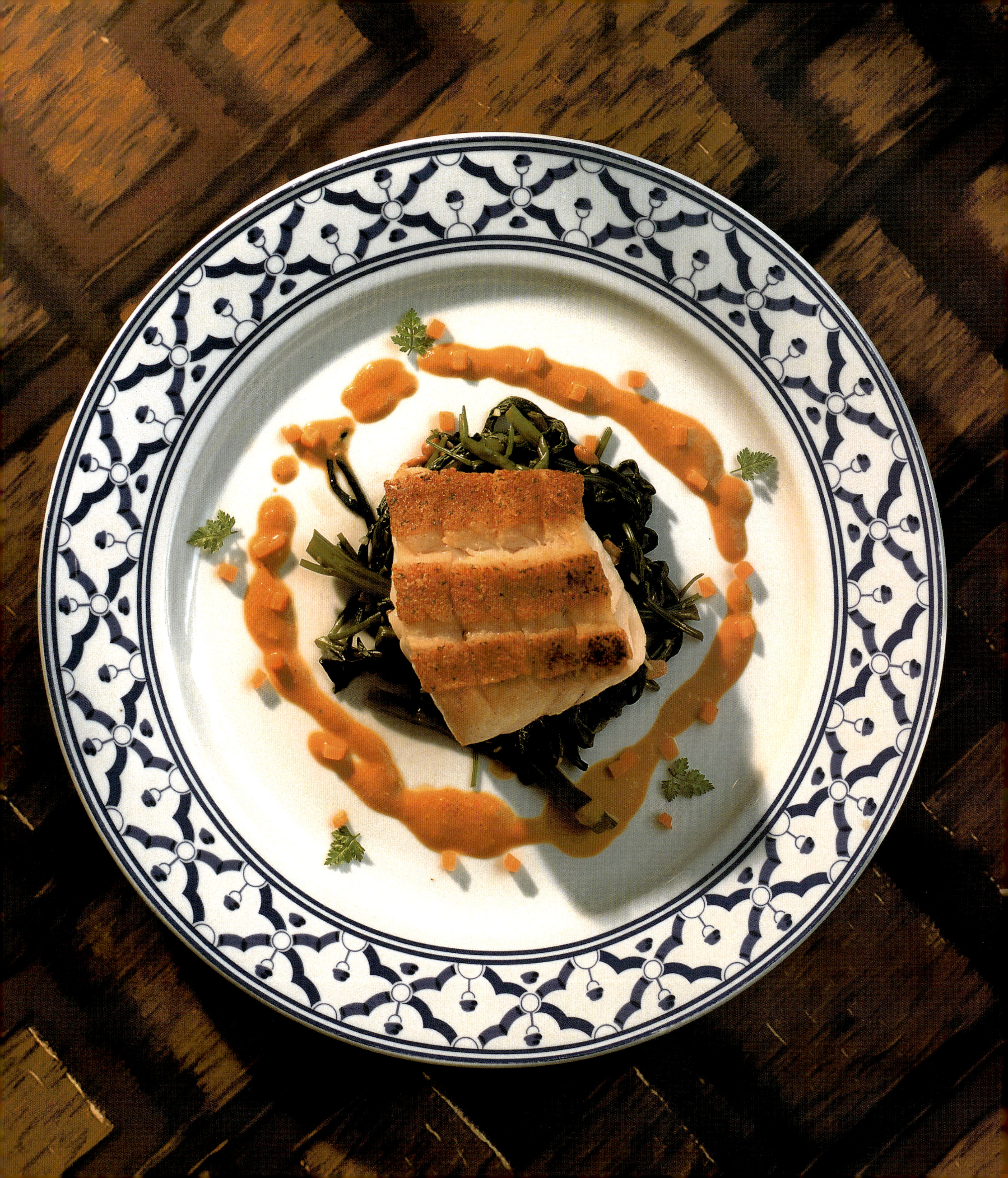

CRABMEAT AND GREEN PAPAYA SALAD (above)

Serves 1

100 g	Crabmeat
30 g	Green papaya, peeled and julienned
10 g	Tomatoes, cubed
5 g	Green onion, sliced
80 g	Thousand Island dressing

A few drops of Tabasco sauce to taste

10 ml	Lime juice
10 ml	Olive oil
20 g	Cherry tomatoes
20 g	Asparagus, peeled and cooked for garnish
10 g	Lemon segments for garnish

Salt and freshly ground pepper to season

3 slices	Papaya, carved or sliced for decoration
20 g	Mixed lettuce leaves, made into a bouquet

PREPARATION

Mix the crabmeat, green papaya, cubed tomatoes, onion, Thousand Island dressing and Tabasco sauce. Set aside. Mix the lime juice and olive oil, then add the cherry tomatoes, asparagus and lemon segments. Season with salt and pepper to taste.

PRESENTATION

Place a 4-cm stainless steel ring in the centre of a serving plate and fill with the crab salad. Arrange the carved or sliced papaya as shown, garnish with the bouquet of mixed lettuce leaves and spoon the lime and olive oil vinaigrette around.

EGG NOODLE DOUGH

Serves 2–4

500 g	All-purpose flour, sifted
5	Large fresh eggs (65–70 g each)
1 tbsp	Olive oil

PREPARATION
Place the flour in a mound on a work surface or in a large bowl. Make a well in the centre, add the eggs and oil into the well. Use your fingertips to gradually work the flour from inside the well into the eggs, taking care not to allow the liquid to run out. Continue mixing the egg and flour together until the mixture is quite thick, then knead the dough for 10–15 minutes until smooth. Wrap the dough in kitchen film and leave to rest for about 20 minutes. Unwrap the dough and knead again for 1–2 minutes. Roll the dough out manually or pass it through a pasta machine to make sheets of desired thickness.
Let the sheets dry for a while, then roll them up and cut with a knife or cut them using the machine. This dough is suitable for all types of ravioli, tortelli or any filled pasta.

Chef's note: If you don't have a pasta machine but would still like to make your own noodles, you can roll out the dough by hand using a heavy wooden or stone rolling pin. When using this method, make sure that both the rolling pin and the work surface you are using are lightly floured at all times to prevent the dough from sticking.

PESTO GENOVESE

Serves 2

60 g	Fresh basil leaves
15–20 g	Pinenuts, toasted
250 ml	Extra virgin olive oil
3	Garlic cloves, peeled
40–50 g	Sardinian pecorino cheese or parmesan cheese

Finely grated sea salt and freshly ground black pepper to taste

PREPARATION
Process the basil leaves, pinenuts, olive oil and garlic in a blender until smooth. Add the cheese and blend well. Transfer the pesto into a bowl, adjust seasoning with salt and pepper, cover with clear kitchen film and refrigerate until required.

Chef's note: This is a classic Genovese recipe.

PICKLED LEMONS

Serves 10–12

8–10	Yellow lemons, unwaxed, with no bruises or spots
300 g	Coarse sea salt
30 g	Granulated sugar
10	Almonds, peeled
100 ml	Water

PREPARATION
Wash the lemons thoroughly.
Boil a pot of water, remove from heat, then add the lemons. Cover and leave to rest for approx. 10 minutes.
Remove the lemons and place in a bowl of cold water (not iced) to cool. When the lemons are cool, cut each lengthwise into 8 wedges and put in a bowl.
Add salt, sugar and almonds and mix, squeezing the lemon wedges to extract the juice. Add water and mix once more. Transfer to a sterilised jar and seal tightly. Allow the lemons to macerate and ripen for 7–12 days at room temperature. Shake the jar once every two day to distribute the salt and juice evenly. Continue the pickling process for 3 weeks in the refrigerator. The lemons will then be ready for use. If you wish to store them further, add a few sprigs of thyme, 2–3 bay leaves and good quality olive oil to cover and refrigerate. The lemons will then keep for several months.

FISH STOCK

Makes 700 ml

80 g	Shallots, peeled and finely sliced
150 g	Mushrooms, sliced
120 g	White onion, peeled and finely sliced
80 g	Leek, finely sliced
50 g	Celery, finely sliced
1	*Bouquet garni* (parsley, thyme, bay leaf)
50 ml	Vegetable oil
1 kg	Fish bones, washed and chopped roughly
Salt to season	
100 ml	White wine
1.2 litres	Water

PREPARATION
Place all the vegetables, *bouquet garni* and the oil in a saucepan and cook slowly for about 5 minutes over medium heat.
Add the fish bones and leave to cook for another 5 minutes. Add a little salt and the white wine, bring to the boil for a few seconds, then add the water.
Bring to the boil again and simmer for 30–40 minutes.
Skim off the substances that have collected on the surface. Remove from heat and rest for 10 minutes. Strain the fish stock through a fine-mesh sieve. The stock keeps well in the refrigerator for a few days, or longer if frozen.

BIGOLI WITH ANCHOVY TUNA SAUCE (opposite, left)

Serves 4

Bigoli (Home-made Spaghetti)

300 g	All-purpose flour
120 g	Finely ground semolina
2	Large eggs
40 ml	Water

Anchovy-Tuna Sauce

100 g	White onion, coarsely chopped
50 ml	Good quality olive oil
50 g	Anchovies, drained and chopped
50 g	Canned tuna, drained and flaked
50 ml	White wine
450 g	Tomatoes, peeled, deseeded and chopped
100 ml	Fish stock (see recipe on Pg 65)

Salt and freshly ground black pepper to season

2 tbsp	Chopped parsley

PREPARATION

Bigoli

Place the flour and semolina in a mound on a working surface. Make a well in the centre of the flour, and add the eggs and water. Using your fingertips, gradually work the flour into the egg-water mixture. Continue mixing until the mixture is quite thick, then knead the dough for 10–15 minutes until smooth and elastic.

Wrap the dough in kitchen film and rest for 30–40 minutes. Then, remove the film and knead the dough for 5–6 minutes. Pass this through a bigoli-pressing machine, little by little. Dust the resulting bigoli with flour to prevent them from sticking together. Cover with a clean kitchen cloth.

Anchovy-Tuna Sauce

Fry the onion in olive oil until it becomes pale golden in colour. Add the anchovies and tuna, and fry gently for 1–2 minutes. Add the white wine and let it evaporate for a few seconds, then add the tomatoes and fish stock. Reduce the heat and simmer gently for about 20 minutes, until the tomatoes are well-cooked and the sauce becomes a silky consistency. Season with salt and pepper. Remove from heat, cover with a lid to keep warm.

PRESENTATION

Cook the bigoli in salted water for 5–6 minutes, then drain. Re-heat the sauce, season with black pepper and salt if necessary, then add the parsley and boiled bigoli. Toss well until the bigoli are well-coated with the sauce. Transfer to pre-heated plates and serve immediately.

Chef's note: This is a classic Venetian dish.

SAFFRON SEAFOOD RISOTTO WITH ARUGULA AND MUSHROOMS (opposite, right)

Serves 4

600–700 ml	Fish stock (see recipe on Pg 65)
40 g	White onion, finely diced
40 g	Unsalted butter
150 g	Risotto rice (Vialone or Arborio)
50 ml	White wine
100 g	Seasonal market mushrooms, cut into 2-cm cubes
250–300 g	Fresh seafood (lobster, prawns, squid, fish, scallops), cut into cubes

A pinch of saffron soaked in 3 tbsp warm water

60 g	Arugula leaves
30–40 g	Unsalted butter, cut into 1-cm cubes

Salt and freshly ground pepper to season

2 tbsp	Chopped flat leaf parsley

PREPARATION

Heat the stock and simmer. Fry the onion in butter until translucent. Add the rice and cook over low heat for a minute, stirring often, until the rice turns slightly translucent.

Turn up the heat and add the white wine. When the wine has been absorbed, add just enough stock to cover the rice, stir well, and reduce the heat. Keep the rice at a gentle simmer and keep adding stock, about $\frac{1}{2}$ cup at a time, stirring often (let the stock be almost completely absorbed by the rice before adding more). After 10 minutes, stir in the mushrooms and the seafood. Continue to ladle in more stock, stirring before and after each addition. After about 7 minutes, add the strained saffron water and arugula leaves, stir, then add the cold butter cubes and stir to mix well. Adjust the seasoning as required and add more stock if necessary. Finally, add the parsley, stir and serve warm.

Chef's note: In Italy, seafood pastas and risotto don't usually come with grated parmesan cheese so this is a serving option.

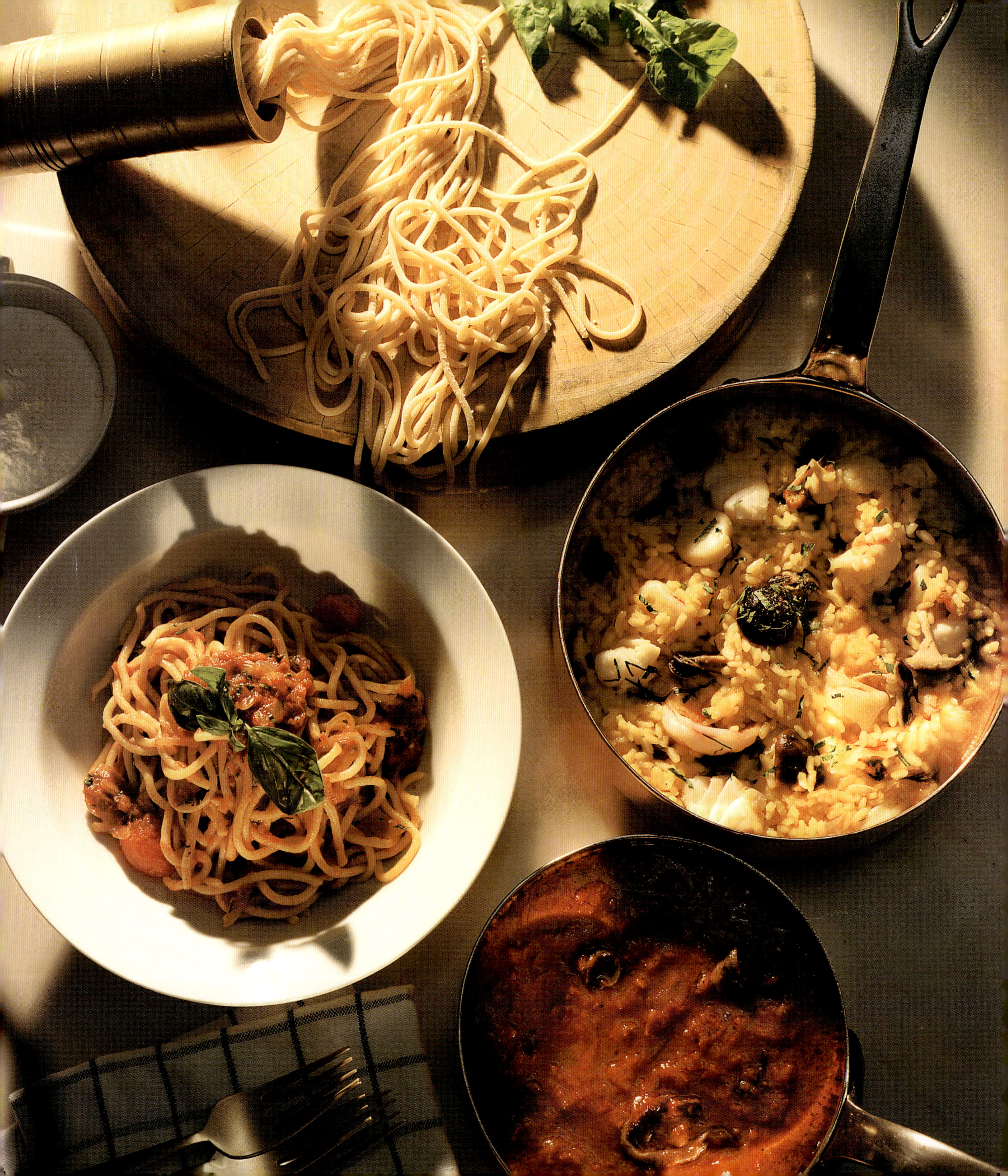

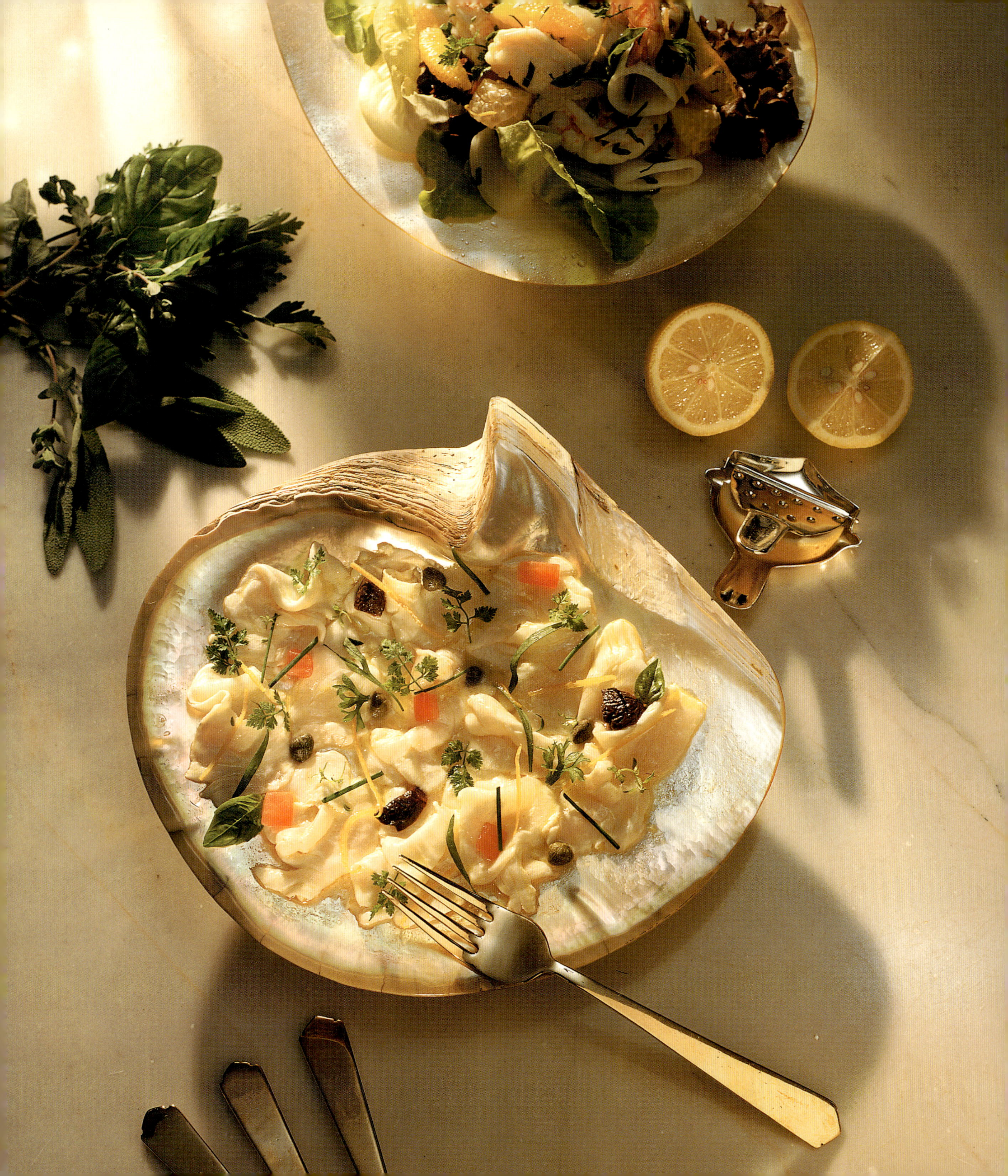

SHELLFISH SALAD WITH ORANGE AND RED ONION (opposite, top)

Serves 4

1 tbsp	Lemon juice
100 ml	White wine
300 ml	Water
50 g	White onion, sliced
A few parsley stems and fennel sprigs	
150 g	Fresh prawns, peeled
150 g	Slipper lobster tails, shells removed, cut into 2-cm pieces
150 g	Fresh scallops, with roe removed
150 g	Squid, cleaned and cut into ½-cm thick rings
12–16	Mussels, scrubbed in half-shell
120 g	Mixed salad leaves (butterhead, arugula, radicchio, cos lettuce and oakleaf lettuce)
25	Orange segments
60 g	Red onion, sliced
Italian parsley sprigs	

Dressing

100 ml	Good quality extra virgin olive oil
50 ml	Lemon juice
2 tbsp	White wine
Salt and freshly ground white pepper to season	

PREPARATION
Combine the lemon juice, white wine, water, white onion, parsley and fennel sprigs in a pot and bring to the boil. Simmer for about 10 minutes then add the shellfish and simmer for 4–5 minutes. Transfer the cooked seafood into a bowl. Pour enough stock into the bowl to cover the seafood, then cover and chill by placing the bowl into a tub of ice water.

Dressing
Combine the dressing ingredients and whisk until it is well mixed. Drain the liquid from the chilled seafood and pat the seafood dry with paper towels. Toss the shellfish in half of the dressing, then toss the salad leaves in the remaining dressing.

PRESENTATION
Arrange the salad leaves on individual serving plates and then add the shellfish. Garnish with orange segments, sliced onion and parsley sprigs to serve.

Chef's note: This is an original creation by a chef of Ciao.

CARPACCIO OF CORAL REEF TROUT WITH MEDITERRANEAN HERBS (opposite, bottom)

Serves 4

500–600 g	Coral reef trout fillet, skin removed
15	Young basil leaves
20	Small fresh tarragon leaves
20	Flat leaf parsley sprigs
20	Fennel sprigs
30	Tomatoes, peeled, seeded and cut into 1-cm cubes
30	Capers in brine
30	Black olives, each cut into 8 pieces
1 tbsp	Pickled lemon rind, cut into very fine strips

Marinade

150 ml	Extra virgin olive oil
60 ml	Lemon juice
25 g	Dijon mustard
Salt and freshly ground white pepper to season	

PREPARATION
Clean the fish fillets and cut into fine slices. Cover with kitchen film and keep cool.
Combine all marinade ingredients and whisk vigorously until it is well mixed. Adjust the seasoning if necessary. (The marinade should taste sour and quite salty.)
Dip the fish slices into the marinade, one by one, and arrange them next to one another on a shallow dish. Pour the remaining marinade over and cover with kitchen film.
Refrigerate and leave to marinate for at least 3 hours.

PRESENTATION
Spread a little of the marinade on individual serving dishes, sprinkle with some salt and pepper, then line the plate with slices of carpaccio. Decorate each plate with the fresh herbs, tomatoes, capers and olives as shown. Pour a little more of the marinade over the carpaccio and serve chilled.

RICOTTA AND SILVER BEET GREEN GNOCCHI WITH GORGONZOLA AND GRAPPA (opposite, left)

Serves 4–5

Gnocchi

150 g	Potatoes, peeled and cut into large cubes

Nutmeg and salt to season

180 g	All-purpose flour
150 g	Dry ricotta cheese, finely crumbled
90 g	Silver beet, boiled, squeezed dry and finely chopped

Gorgonzola and Grappa Sauce

200 g	Fresh cream
200 g	Gorgonzola cheese, crumbled
2	Garlic cloves, crushed and peeled
2	Fresh thyme sprigs

A few parsley stems

30 ml	Grappa

Salt and freshly ground black pepper to season

PREPARATION

Gnocchi
Cover the potatoes with cold water in a saucepan, add a pinch of salt and bring to the boil.
Simmer for 15–20 minutes until the potatoes are soft.
Transfer potatoes to a tray and dry in a pre-heated oven (180–200°C) for 7–8 minutes.
Remove and force them through a potato press.
Add the flour, ricotta cheese, silver beet and nutmeg and quickly knead into a dough. (This must be done as quickly as possible, as overworking the dough will make it rubbery.)
Roll a little dough at a time on a lightly floured board to make a rope approx. 2 cm in diameter.
Cut this into 2-cm thick pieces, then imprint each gnocchi with the back of a fork.

Gorgonzola and Grappa Sauce
Combine the cream, gorgonzola, garlic, thyme and parsley stems in a saucepan and bring slowly to the boil, stirring frequently with a wooden spoon. Boil gently for 5–6 minutes. Strain through a sieve into a second saucepan and add the grappa. Season with salt and black pepper, cover and keep warm.

PRESENTATION
Boil a pot of salted water and cook the gnocchi. They will rise to the surface when cooked.
At the same time, bring the gorgonzola sauce back to the boil. Remove the cooked gnocchi and add to the gorgonzola sauce. Toss well so that the gnocchi are evenly coated and serve very hot on pre-heated plates.

PENNE PASTA WITH STRACCHINO CHEESE AND SPINACH LEAVES (opposite, right)

Serves 4–5

100 ml	Whipping cream
1	Garlic clove, peeled and crushed
250 g	Stracchino cheese

Salt and freshly ground black pepper to season

3 litres	Water
400 g	Penne pasta or any other kind of short, dried pasta

A big handful of spinach leaves, stems removed and washed

40 ml	Cherry grappa

A small pinch of grated nutmeg

40–50 g	Grana Padano cheese, grated

PREPARATION
Pour the cream into a saucepan, add the crushed garlic and bring it to the simmering point.
Add the Stracchino cheese and stir with a wooden spoon until the cheese has melted and the sauce has a velvety consistency. Remove from the heat and season with a little salt and black pepper. Cover and keep warm.
In a large pot, bring the water to the boil, add half a handful of salt, and cook the penne pasta for 9–10 minutes until *al dente*. At the very end of the cooking, plunge the spinach leaves into the water, let boil for 15 seconds and then strain the spinach and penne.
Keep 2–3 tbsp of the water used to cook the pasta, add it to the cheese sauce and reheat the sauce.
Remove the garlic, add the grappa and nutmeg, and whisk well. Add the sauce to the pasta, and mix well until the pasta is coated with the sauce. Adjust the seasoning if necessary.

PRESENTATION
Transfer to pre-warmed soup plates and sprinkle with Grana Padano cheese and some black pepper to serve.

Ciao and The Verandah

FILLET OF RED MULLET AND OVEN-ROASTED VEGETABLES (opposite, right)

Serves 4

2	Purple eggplants
	Salt and fresh ground black pepper to season
100 ml	Extra virgin olive oil
2	Large yellow capsicums
2	Large red capsicums
	A few fresh thyme sprigs
8	Red mullet fillets (approx. 40 g each), bones removed
4	Medium tomatoes, cut into 16 slices
6–8 tbsp	Pesto
12–16	Basil leaves

PREPARATION
Pre-heat the oven at 190–200°C.
Cut each eggplant into 4 slices approx. 1.5-cm thick. Season with a little salt and pepper, and drizzle oil generously on both sides. Arrange the eggplant on a baking tray and roast until tender. Remove from the oven and keep warm, keeping all the baking juices.
While the eggplants are roasting, grill the capsicums over an open flame until charred all over. Cool, then scrape off as much charred peel as possible with a small paring knife.
Cut the capsicums in quarters, and remove the core and seeds.
Arrange the capsicum on a roasting tray, season with salt, black pepper, thyme and 2–3 tsp olive oil, and roast in the oven for 10 minutes or until tender.
Remove and keep warm next to the eggplant.
Season the red mullet with salt and pepper. Pan-fry them with a little olive oil, then remove and keep warm.
Using the same frying pan, quickly warm the tomato slices which have been seasoned with a little salt and black pepper.

PRESENTATION
Place a slice of eggplant on each of 4 pre-warmed serving plates, followed by two capsicum wedges, two slices of tomato and two red mullet fillets. Cover the red mullet with two more slices of tomato, two capsicum slices and top off with a slice of eggplant. Drizzle some juices from baking the eggplant and capsicum on the eggplant and spoon 2 tbsp pesto around each dish. Garnish with a few basil leaves to serve. This dish should not be served too hot.

Chef's note: Once a guest asked for a Mediterranean dish with fish and lots of vegetables. Coincidentally, we were preparing vegetables to be marinated at the time, and quickly assembled this dish for our guest, who later expressed great satisfaction.

SAUTÉED KING PRAWNS WITH LEMON AND CAPSICUM (opposite, left)

Serves 4

	Rind from 1 lemon, finely shredded
3	Garlic cloves, finely sliced
2	Small red chillies, finely chopped
5	Bay leaves
100 ml	Extra virgin olive oil
250 g	Capsicums, cored, seeded and cut into 2-cm cubes
60 ml	White wine
500–600 g	King or white sea prawns, peeled and de-veined
	Salt and freshly ground black pepper to season
	2 big pinches of dry marjoram
3 tbsp	Lemon juice
1 tbsp	Flat leaf parsley, coarsely chopped
1	Lemon, cut into 6–8 wedges

PREPARATION
Place the lemon rind in a small saucepan filled with some water and bring to the boil for 1–2 minutes.
Strain and rinse under cold, running water. Leave aside.
Sauté the sliced garlic, chillies and bay leaves in olive oil for 30 seconds, then add the capsicums and cook for a few minutes.
Deglaze the pan with the wine and let the wine evaporate for about 20 seconds.
Season the prawns with salt, pepper and marjoram and add them to the pan, stirring for 2–3 minutes until the prawns are just cooked and have turned pink in colour. Adjust the seasoning.
Stir in the lemon juice and rind, and remove from the heat.
Transfer to a pre-warmed serving dish, sprinkle with the chopped parsley, and garnish with the lemon wedges to serve.

Ciao and The Verandah

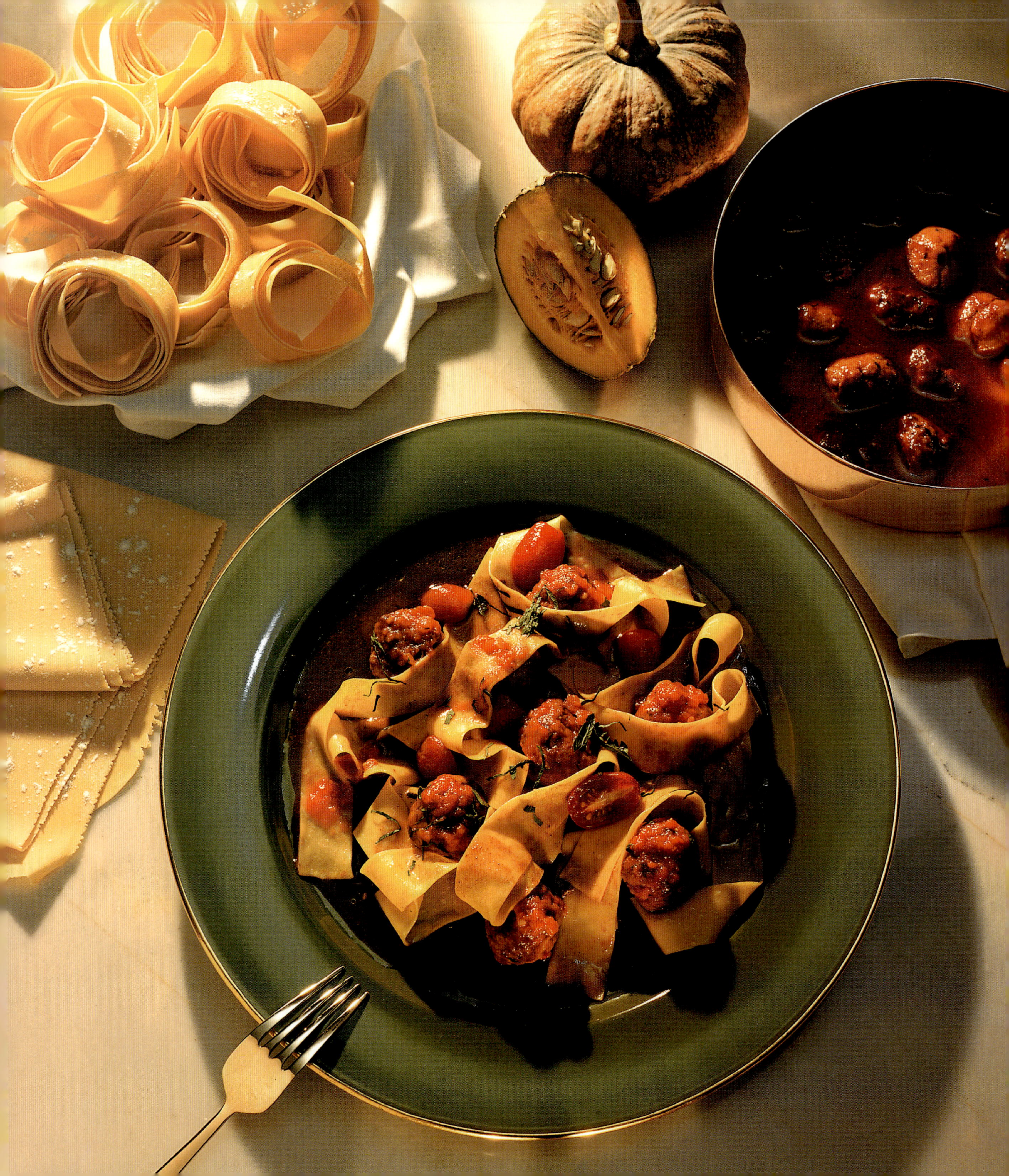

PUMPKIN PAPPARDELLE WITH MEATBALLS (opposite)

Serves 4

100 ml	White wine
500 g	Tomatoes, peeled, seeded and chopped
4–5	Fresh basil leaves (or a pinch of dried basil)
100 ml	Brown pork sauce (see recipe below)
60–80 g	Parmesan cheese, grated

Pappardelle

130 g	Pumpkin, cut into 2-cm cubes
300 g	All-purpose flour
4	Egg yolks
70–80 g	Unsalted butter
2 tbsp	All-purpose flour

Meatballs

400 g	Pork meat, finely minced
2 cloves	Garlic, finely chopped
3 tbsp	Fresh bread crumbs
2 tbsp	Flat leaf parsley, chopped
1 tsp	Dried marjoram
3 tbsp	Parmesan cheese, grated
2	Eggs
45 ml	Whipping cream

Grated rind from 1/4 of a lemon
Salt, freshly ground pepper and nutmeg to season
Butter for frying
Flour for dusting

PREPARATION

Pappardelle

Cover pumpkin cubes with cold water in a pot, bring to the boil, then simmer until tender for about 10 minutes. Drain, place on a tray and dry in a pre-heated oven for about 10 minutes. Remove and pass the pumpkin through a fine-mesh potato press or vegetable mill. Place the flour in a mound on a working surface. Make a well in the centre and add the eggs and pumpkin. Use your fingers to work the flour from the outside of the mound into the egg-pumpkin mixture. Continue until the mixture is quite thick. Knead the dough for 10–15 minutes until it is smooth and elastic. Wrap it in kitchen film and leave for 20–30 minutes.
Then unwrap and knead the dough for another 1–2 minutes. Flatten this until it is about 5-cm thick, then cut into 2-cm thick portions. Run the dough, one at a time, through a pasta machine on progressively finer settings to make thin pasta sheets. Lay them flat on a kitchen cloth and allow them to dry slightly for easy handling. Roll each sheet up and slice (about 2-cm thick) with a sharp knife. Dust with a little flour.

Meatballs

Combine all the meatball ingredients in a bowl, except the butter and flour, season with salt, pepper and nutmeg and mix thoroughly. Shape into small meatballs weighing about 20 g each.

PRESENTATION

Dust the meatballs with flour and sauté in butter until light brown on all sides. Deglaze with the white wine and reduce liquid by half. Add the tomatoes, basil leaves and pork brown sauce, bring to the boil and simmer for about 20 minutes, half-covered. Adjust the seasoning if necessary, and keep warm.
Cook the pappardelle in boiling salted water for 3–4 minutes, drain, add to the meatballs and mix well. Transfer to pre-heated plates, sprinkle with Parmesan cheese and serve immediately.

BROWN SAUCE (pork, beef or chicken)

Makes 800–900 ml

100 ml	Vegetable oil
1 kg	Pork spare ribs, cut in small pieces
200 g	White onion, cubed
150 g	Carrots, peeled and cubed
100 g	Celery stalks, washed and chopped
100 g	Leek, washed and chopped
5–6	Garlic cloves, flattened
1 tbsp	Cracked black pepper
3–4	Bay leaves
10	Parsley stems
1 tsp	Thyme, dried
200 g	Ripe tomatoes, cubed
60 g	Tomato paste
40 g	All-purpose flour
1.5 litres	Water

Salt and freshly ground pepper to season

PREPARATION

Heat the oil, add the ribs and cook slowly until they are dark-brown in colour. Or, roast them in the oven at 180–200°C. When the bones are brown, add the vegetables, herbs and spices except the tomatoes and tomato paste, and continue roasting until the vegetables are translucent and fragrant. Drain any oil from the mixture, add the flour and roast for a few minutes until the flour absorbs all the moisture.
Add the tomatoes, tomato paste and half of the water. Scrape the bottom of the saucepan to loosen any particles attached to the bottom and bring to the boil. Add the remaining water, bring to the boil and simmer for 1 1/2 hours. Remove any substance that appears on the surface during cooking.
If too much sauce evaporates, just add more water. Season if necessary. Strain the sauce through a fine-mesh sieve, leave to cool and store refrigerated until needed. The sauce can also be kept frozen (below minus 18°C) for up to one month.

TANDOORI CHICKEN IN PITA POCKET SANDWICHES (opposite, left)

Serves 4

500 g	Chicken
50 ml	Vegetable oil for frying
240 g	Lettuce leaves, mixed
120 g	Tomatoes, sliced
20 g	Spring onions
100 g	Green papaya
200 g	Pita sauce
4	Pita pockets

Pita Sauce

100 g	Mayonnaise
25 g	Lemon juice
60 ml	Hoisin sauce
10 g	French mustard
50 g	Garlic, chopped
250 g	Yoghurt, plain

Salt and pepper to season

Yoghurt-Cucumber Dip

250 g	Large cucumbers, peeled and cut in half lengthwise
5 g	Rock salt
200 g	Yoghurt, plain
40 g	Garlic, peeled and chopped

5 g each of pepper, cumin powder and chopped mint

First Tandoori Marinade

5 g	Red chilli paste
10 g	Lemon juice
6 g	Cumin powder
10 g	Coriander and mint leaves, chopped
4 g	Garam masala

10 g each of ginger paste and garlic paste
Salt and pepper to season

Second Tandoori Marinade

200 g	Plain yoghurt
50 g	Cream
5 g	Red chilli paste
3 g	Ginger powder
1 g	Cinnamon
30 ml	Mustard oil
1	Egg yolk
10 g	Chat masala

10 g each of ginger and garlic paste
2 g each of cumin, garam masala, fennugreek seeds, black and green cardamom and nutmeg powder
A pinch of red colour powder

PREPARATION

Pita Sauce
Mix the pita sauce ingredients and keep chilled until needed.

Yoghurt-Cucumber Dip
Scoop out the seeds of the cucumber and discard. Grate cucumber coarsely. Place the grated cucumber in a sieve over a bowl, add rock salt and leave to drain for 10 minutes. Finally, press the cucumber to extract all the juice. Combine the dry-pressed grated cucumber with the remaining dip ingredients.

Tandoori Chicken
Mix the chicken with the first Tandoori marinade ingredients and leave for $1\frac{1}{2}$ hours. Then, mix the ingredients for the second marinade and pour over the chicken. Refrigerate overnight. Remove the chicken from the marinade and pan-fry it in a little vegetable oil. Cut the cooked chicken into 1-cm cubes. Set aside.

PRESENTATION
Combine the lettuce, tomatoes, spring onion and green papaya, then add the chicken cubes and pita sauce. Warm the pita pockets, cut open and fill with the mixture. Serve with yoghurt-cucumber dip on the side.

VEGETABLE STOCK

Makes 1.2 litres

100 ml	Vegetable oil for frying
200 g	White onion, peeled and cut in cubes
300 g	Carrots, peeled and cut in cubes
250 g	Daikon, peeled and cut in cubes
100 g	Celery sticks, coarsely chopped
200 g	White leek, sliced
5–6	Garlic cloves, peeled and crushed
10	Parsley stems
4–5	Bay leaves

a few sprigs fresh thyme or a big pinch of dried thyme

2 tsp	White peppercorn
300 g	Tomatoes, cut in half
400 g	White Chinese lettuce, coarsely cut
1.5 litres	Cold water

PREPARATION
Sauté all the vegetables and herbs, except the tomatoes and Chinese lettuce, until translucent and fragrant. Leave to cool for 10–15 minutes. Add the cold water, lettuce and tomatoes, then bring to a gentle boil. Simmer for 1 hour, skimming off the foam that floats to the surface regularly. Remove from heat and leave to rest for 30 minutes. Strain the stock through a sieve.

ROAST PUMPKIN SOUP (above, right)

Serves 4

500 g	Pumpkin, peeled
5 g	Grated nutmeg
2	Bay leaves
100 ml	Olive oil
50 g	Butter
50 g	Carrots, peeled
70 g	Onion, peeled
20 g	Potatoes, peeled
500 ml	Vegetable stock (see recipe on Pg 76)
110 g	Coconut milk (see recipe on Pg 42)
4	Small pumpkins, in which to serve the soup
Salt and pepper to season	
5 g	Chives, chopped
10 g	Roasted pumpkin seeds

PREPARATION

Peel the pumpkin and cut the flesh into 3-cm cubes, discarding the seeds and fibres. Add the grated nutmeg, bay leaves and olive oil. Wrap in foil and roast until tender.
Melt the butter in a large saucepan, add the carrots, onion, potatoes, cover and cook very gently for 10 minutes until soft. Add the vegetable stock and roasted pumpkin, then bring to the boil. Cover and simmer for 30 minutes.
Purée the soup in a blender until smooth.

PRESENTATION

Remove the flesh from the small pumpkins to make soup bowls. Return the soup to the pan and stir in the coconut milk, adjust seasoning to taste, heat through and transfer the soup to the pumpkin bowls. Sprinkle with chopped chives, roasted pumpkin seeds, or drizzle with coconut milk to serve.

Chef's note: This soup, served at The Verandah, was created by Chef Dominique Bugnand.

CHOCOLATE AND GINGER TART WITH KUMQUAT MARMALADE ICE CREAM (opposite)

Serves 8

Pastry

100 g	Flour
70 g	Butter
30 g	Icing sugar
2	Eggs
½	Vanilla pod

Chocolate Tart Filling

75 g	Butter
500 ml	Cream
500 g	Dark chocolate, chopped
125 g	Candied ginger

Kumquat Marmalade Ice Cream (½ litre)

5	Egg yolks
60 g	Sugar
190 g	Milk
300 g	Cream
15 g	Milk powder
30 g	Glucose
10 g	Kumquat juice
100 g	Kumquat marmalade (see recipe below)
240 g	Orange sauce
40 g	Whipping cream

PREPARATION

Pastry
Put the flour into a large bowl, add butter and work in until the mixture resembles fine bread crumbs. Stir in the sugar, eggs and vanilla seeds scraped from the pod, form a dough, then wrap in cling film and chill for 30 minutes.

Put the pastry on a floured work surface and flour the rolling pin. Roll out from the centre and give it a quarter-turn occasionally. To line the pie dish, roll the pastry into a circle diameter 2 cm longer than the diameter of the dish, roll it loosely around the rolling pin and unroll over the dish. Gently ease the pastry into the pie dish, pressing it into the dish corners, but do not overstretch the pastry. Carefully trim away the excess pastry with a table knife. Prick the pastry shell all over with a fork, chill for 30 minutes and press a piece of foil or greaseproof paper into the pastry shell, then fill the shell with beans or uncooked rice. Bake in a preheated oven at 200°C for 15 minutes. Remove the foil and bake for 15 more minutes.

Chocolate Tart Filling
Boil the milk and cream, then add to the chopped chocolate. Stir until the chocolate is melted, and add the candied ginger. Pour into the pastry shell and refrigerate overnight.

Kumquat Marmalade Ice Cream
Place the egg yolks and sugar in a bowl and whisk until it turns light in colour. Heat the milk, cream, milk powder and glucose to just below boiling point, then add a little of this to the egg yolk mixture. Mix well, then pour in the remaining milk.
Return mixture to the saucepan and heat gently, stirring until the froth disappears and the mixture coats the back of a spoon. Do not boil. Leave the custard to cool before adding the kumquat juice and strain the mixture into an ice cream maker.
Freeze until the mixture starts to become stiff. Remove from the machine and fold in the kumquat marmalade, creating a marbled effect. Keep in the freezer until needed.
Serve chocolate and ginger tart with kumquat ice cream and garnish with whipped cream and orange sauce.

KUMQUAT MARMALADE

Makes 4.7 kg

60 g	Pectin
100 g	Granulated castor sugar
2.5 kg	Chinese kumquats (with no bruises or dark spots)
250 g	Water
1 litre	Tangerine or orange juice
2.3 kg	Granulated sugar

PREPARATION

Mix the pectin and castor sugar.
Wash the kumquats thoroughly in very warm water and pat dry with a kitchen towel. Remove a little of both ends of each fruit and then cut them in half. Remove all the pips by pressing each half-fruit between two fingers and by loosening them with a fork.

Strain the resulting juice through a sieve and discard the pips. Bring the kumquats, collected juice and water to the boil and simmer for 30–35 minutes, stirring occasionally to prevent the mixture from sticking. By now the kumquats will be tender. Add the sugar, stir well, and continue cooking for another 20–25 minutes, stirring frequently.
When the marmalade is nice and shiny, add the tangerine or orange juice and continue the slow-cooking procedure for another 20 minutes. When you see that the marmalade is clear and shiny once again, add the sugar-pectin mixture, mix well and let cook for 10 more minutes. Skim off any foam that has accumulated on the surface and remove from the heat. Pour the marmalade into sterilised jam jars, seal the jars and sterilise in a boiling water bath for 45 minutes.
Allow to cool and keep refrigerated.

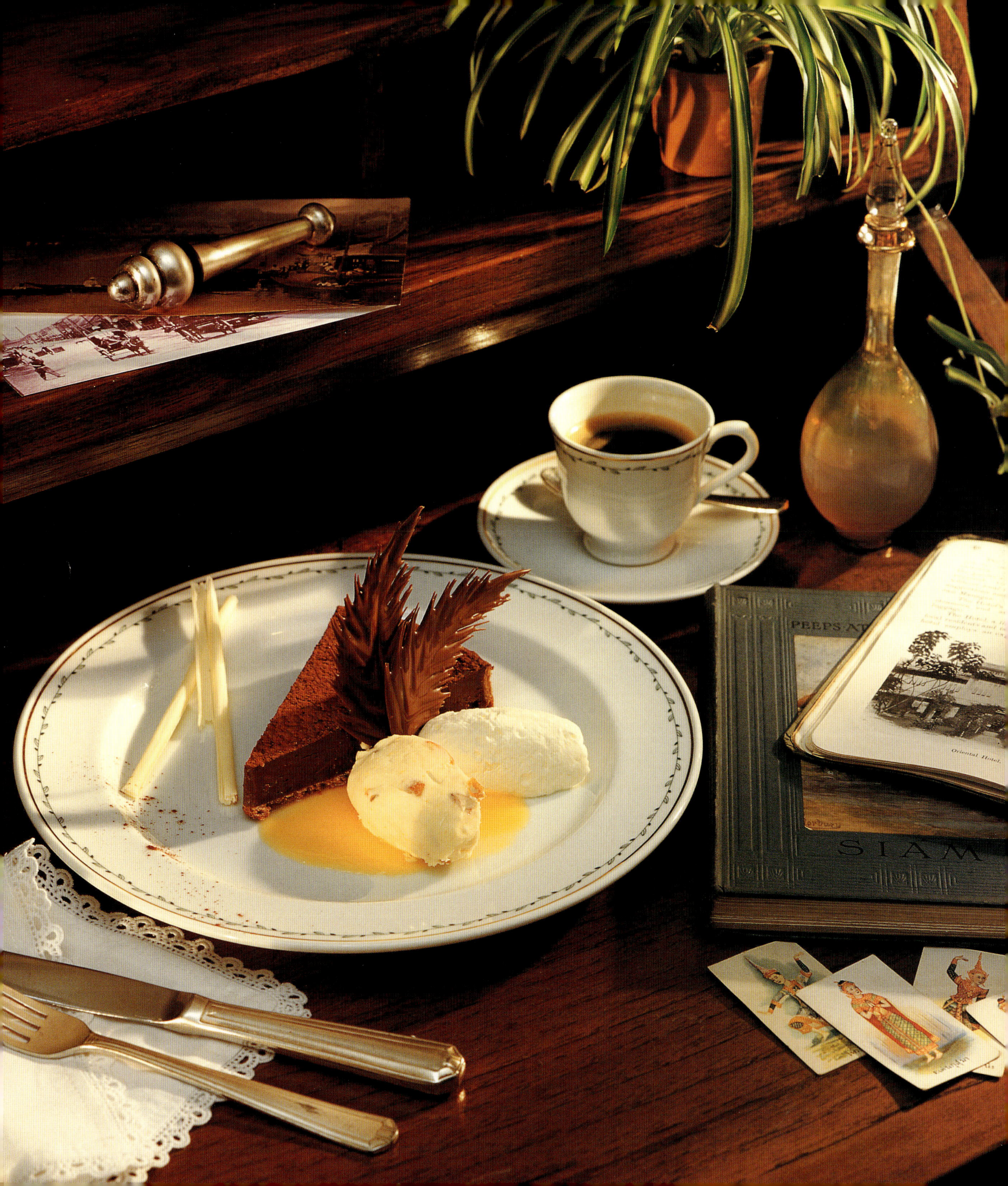
SIAM

EGGPLANT, TOMATO AND CAPSICUM FLAN (above)

Serves 10

250–300 g	Shortcrust pastry
1 tbsp	Parmesan cheese, grated
60–70 g	Gruyère cheese, or other soft cheese, cut into cubes
5–6	Fresh basil, shredded (or a pinch of dry basil)

Shortcrust Pastry
150 g	All-purpose flour
A pinch each of salt and sugar	
110 g	Unsalted butter, cut into 1-cm cubes
50 ml	Cold water

Filling
400 g	Firm purple eggplants, cut into 2-cm cubes
Salt and freshly ground black pepper to season	
40 g	Unsalted butter
150 g	White onion, peeled and chopped
2–3	Garlic cloves, peeled and finely chopped
4–5	Bay leaves
A few sprigs of fresh thyme or a large pinch of dried thyme	
200 g	Tomatoes, peeled, seeded and coarsely chopped
30 ml	Olive oil
300 g	Capsicums, cored and cut into 3-mm strips

Custard
2	Medium-sized fresh eggs
100 ml	Whipping cream
50 ml	Milk
15 g	All-purpose flour
Salt, ground white pepper and grated nutmeg to season	

PREPARATION

Shortcrust Pastry

Sift the flour with salt and a little sugar into a large bowl.
Work the butter cubes into the dry mixture with your hands until it resembles fine breadcrumbs.
Add the cold water and combine the mixture with the tips of your fingers. Do not over-knead the pastry, just work it as much as necessary to form a dough. Wrap the resulting pastry in plastic film and keep refrigerated for at least 1 hour.
You will need a 23-cm tart tin, about 3-cm deep.
Remove the pastry from the refrigerator and roll evenly to a thickness of 2 mm and refrigerate until required.
Brush the inside of the tart tin with a little butter, then line it with the prepared pastry.

Filling

Sprinkle the eggplant generously with salt, mix with your hands and leave to rest for up to 30 minutes.
Rinse under running water and press dry between your palms.
Heat the oven to 190–200°C.
Melt the butter in a medium-sized heavy-based saucepan and sauté the chopped onion, garlic, bay leaves, thyme and a pinch of black pepper until golden brown.
Add the tomatoes and a little salt and cook gently until the tomatoes have disintegrated and all the moisture has evaporated.
The tomato mixture should be fairly dry.
Heat the olive oil in a medium-sized frying pan, and sauté the dry pressed eggplant cubes until golden brown and tender.
Drain and leave to rest on absorbent paper towels.
Place the capsicum strips in a saucepan, cover with a little water, and bring to the boil. Simmer for 2–3 minutes, strain and pat dry with a clean kitchen towel.
Add the eggplant cubes and capsicum strips to the tomato mixture, return to the heat and adjust seasoning. Then transfer to a kitchen tray and leave to cool to room temperature.
Remove the lined tart tin from the refrigerator and pour the capsicum-eggplant mixture over the base of the tin.

Custard

In a bowl, combine the eggs, cream and milk. Add the flour.
Season with salt, pepper and nutmeg, then pour this topping over the tart base.
After pouring in the custard, sprinkle Parmesan cheese, Gruyère cheese and basil leaves over the filling.
Place the tart tin on a baking sheet and bake it in the pre-warmed oven for 30–35 minutes, until it is firm in the centre and the surface has turned golden brown.
Remove the baked flan from the oven and rest for 10 minutes before serving (this will make the tart easier to cut and serve).

TIRAMISU

Serves 12–14

250 ml	Espresso
100 ml	Kahlua liqueur
500 g	Mascarpone cheese
125 g	Icing sugar
3	Egg yolks
300 ml	Whipped cream
50 ml	Rum
25–28	Sponge fingers
Cocoa powder to dust	

PREPARATION

Mix the espresso and Kahlua liqueur. Leave aside.
Mix the cheese and the icing sugar in a bowl until smooth (it is best to do this on a bowl of ice to keep the cheese cool).
Add the egg yolks one by one, mixing well after each addition.
Fold in the whipped cream and rum.
Take a serving bowl and place a layer of the Mascarpone cream in the bottom about 2-cm deep. Dip the sponge fingers in the coffee-Kahlua mixture and place on top of the cream; continue until you have covered the cream completely.
Add another layer of Mascarpone cream (about 2-cm thick) and repeat process with the sponge fingers two more times.
Cover with a layer of cream. Smooth flat and cover with food wrap. Place in the refrigerator until ready to serve.
To serve, sprinkle generously with cocoa powder.

PANNA COTTA

Serves 14–16

150 g	Sugar
140 ml	Water
2	Vanilla pods
1 litre	Fresh whipping cream
250 g	Sugar
15 g/5	Gelatine powder/
	Gelatine leaves soaked in cold water for 10–15 mins

PREPARATION

Bring the sugar and 80 ml of water to the boil and simmer until the mixture turns to a brown caramel. Immediately add the remaining water. Return to the heat to dissolve any lumps, and pour the caramel into moulds. Put aside.
Cut the vanilla pods open and scrape the seeds out.
Add both the pod and seeds to the cream along with the sugar, and heat this mixture to a simmer. Do not boil. Add the gelatine to the hot cream mixture and whisk to dissolve.
Strain this custard mixture through a fine-mesh sieve and leave to cool a little. While still warm, pour the cream into the prepared moulds and keep refrigerated for a few hours until set.
To remove the panna cotta from the moulds, dip the moulds quickly in hot water and turn over onto serving plate.
Serve chilled.

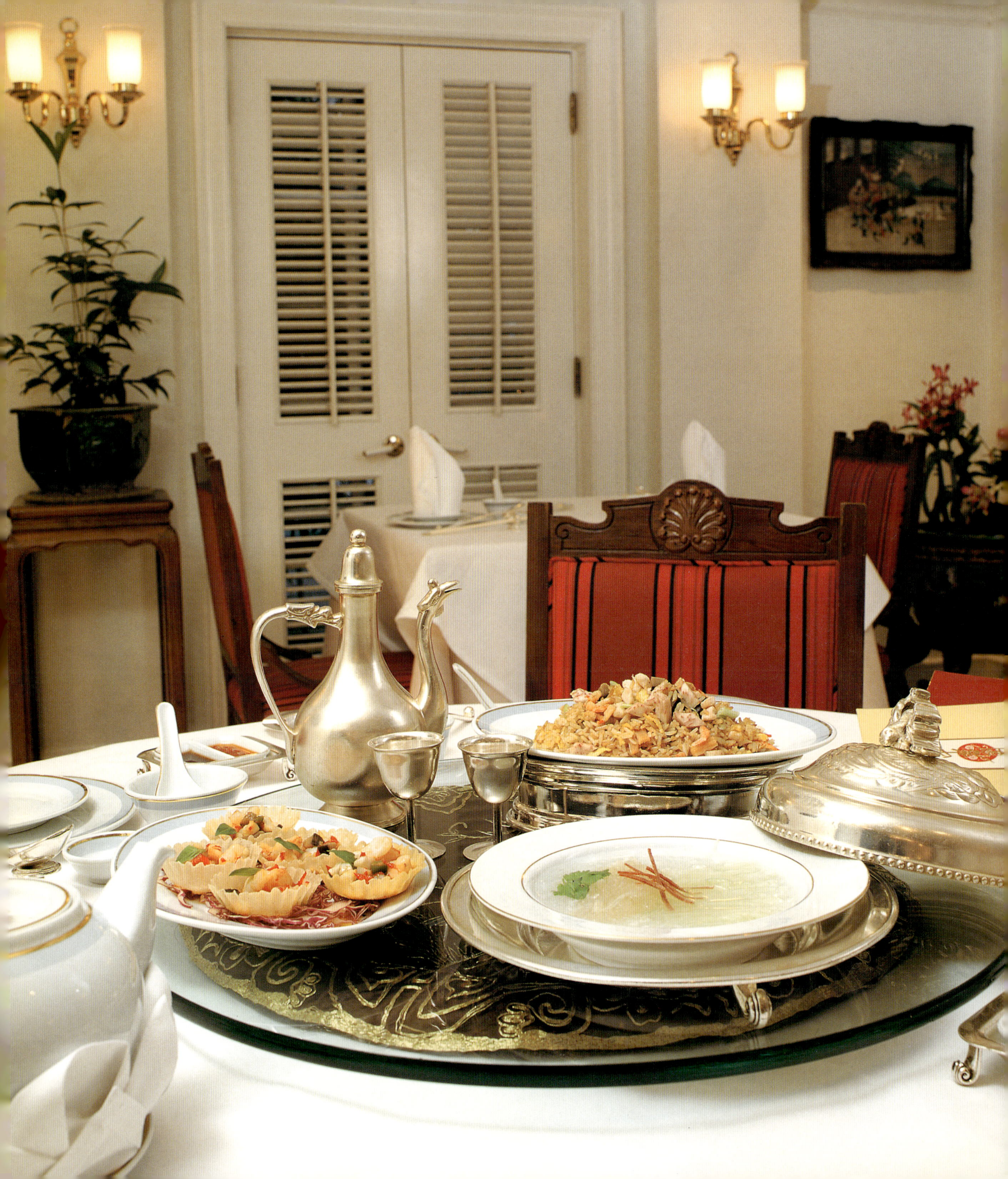

THE CHINA HOUSE

A relatively recent addition to The Oriental's group of food outlets, The China House occupies one of the hotel's oldest buildings. It and a similar one next door were among a number of residences erected in the late nineteenth century by Captain H.N. Andersen, soon after he opened Oriental Avenue leading to both the hotel and his East Asiatic Company. With its assorted rooms, suitable for both large and intimate gatherings, as well as its atmosphere of an elegant private home, it provides the perfect setting for enjoying superb Cantonese cuisine.

Most of the early Chinese emigrants to Thailand and elsewhere were Cantonese, and their cooking came to be the most familiar of China's regional foods to outsiders. With an emphasis on steamed and stir-fried dishes, using the freshest of ingredients, Chinese cooking is also perhaps the lightest and the most appealing to the eye.

The China House is particularly well known for its dim sum luncheon, when a wide range of tempting delicacies is offered in a succession of little bamboo containers. These include such steamed dishes as Glutinous Rice with Assorted Meat in Lotus Leaves, Water Chestnut and Shrimp Dumplings, and Spare Ribs with Black Bean Sauce, as well as deep-fried dishes such as Crispy Barbecued Pork Rolls and Thousand-Year Egg and Seafood wrapped in Rice Paper.

More substantial fare is available in the evening. Among the dishes on the menu are Superior Shark's Fin Soup with Ham-flavoured Sauce, Imperial Bird's Nest Soup with Shredded Winter Melon, Prawns with Curry Leaves and Cream Sauce, Chilled Sliced Abalone with Vinegar Sauce, Sautéed Beef Tenderloin with Black Pepper Sauce, Steamed Garoupa with Soy Sauce, and Claypot Fried Rice with Meat and Yam.

The restaurant's chefs are masters of the Chinese banquet, and equally adept at planning special events such as weddings and private parties.

The China House's culinary brigade specialises in dishing out fine Cantonese dishes from the casual dim sum luncheon to a lavish banquet Pg 92–93: Succulent dim sum treats; a highlight of the extensive menu

COLD-MARINATED CHICKEN WITH PEANUT SAUCE
(opposite, back)

Serves 4–6

800 g	Chicken breasts, deboned
30 g	White sugar
120 g	Sesame paste
120 g	Peanut butter
5 g	Salt
100 g	Hot bean paste
45 ml	Vegetable oil for frying
150 g	Cucumber, shredded
100 g	Carrots, shredded
80 g	Spring onion, shredded

Peanut Sauce

220 g	Sesame paste
250 g	Peanut butter
120 g	Soya sauce
120 g	Chilli sauce
60 g	Salt

PREPARATION

Steam the chicken breasts for 6–10 minutes. Remove the cooked chicken from the steamer and allow to cool. Shred the chicken into long thin strips and place them on a serving platter. Combine all the sauce ingredients in a bowl and mix well. Add a little water or chicken broth to thin the sauce if necessary, then pour over the chicken strips, or put in a small bowl and serve alongside the chicken. Garnish the chicken with shredded cucumber, carrots and spring onion and serve immediately.

SUPERIOR SHARK'S FINS WITH YUNNAN HAM FLAVOURED BROTH (opposite, left)

Serves 5–6

600–700 g	Pre-cooked frozen superior shark's fins
200 g	Ginger, peeled and sliced
1.5 litres	Water
120 g	Yunnan ham, cooked and shredded
120 g	Bean sprouts
100 g	Yellow Chinese chives
50 ml	Vegetable oil

Yunnan Ham-flavoured Broth

500 g	Yunnan ham
400–500 g	Pork ribs, cut into pieces
600–700 g	Old chicken with bones, cut into 5-cm pieces
2.1 litres	Water
40 g	White peppercorns
60–70 g	Tapioca flour
8 g	Salt

PREPARATION

To prepare the broth, rinse the Yunnan ham, pork ribs and chicken under running water for 10 minutes, then place them in a soup pot. Add the water and peppercorn and let boil gently for 2 hours. Strain and keep aside.

Place the defrosted shark's fins and ginger slices in a bowl, add 1.5 litres water, then cover with cling film and steam for 1 hour or until the fins are soft.

Transfer the shark's fins to a serving plate, cover with a clean, damp kitchen cloth and keep warm.

Bring the broth to the boil, mix the tapioca flour and salt with 100 ml water and add to the boiling broth. Stir with a small ladle and let boil gently for 15 seconds. Pour the broth over the shark's fins and top with the Yunnan ham.

Quickly sauté the bean sprouts and yellow Chinese chives and serve separately with the warm shark's fins.

PRAWNS WITH CREAM SAUCE AND CURRY LEAVES
(opposite, right)

Serves 4

600 g	White prawns
5 g	Salt
2	Egg whites
150 g	Tapioca flour
	Vegetable oil for frying
120 g	Green curry leaves
80 g	Garlic
100 g	Small chillies
80 g	Pandanus leaves
	Salt and freshly ground white pepper to season
150 ml	Mayonnaise

PREPARATION

Shell the prawns and remove the intestinal track, then cut them in half lengthwise. Marinate them in a mixture of salt, egg whites and tapioca flour.

Heat the oil in a wok. When hot, deep-fry the curry leaves until crispy. Remove them from the oil and deep-fry the prawns until golden brown and crispy. Remove and drain off excess oil on paper towels.

Heat 3 tbsp oil in the wok and sauté the garlic, small chillies and pandanus leaves for 1 minute. Add the prawns and season with salt and white pepper. Transfer to a plate, garnish with crispy curry leaves and serve with mayonnaise.

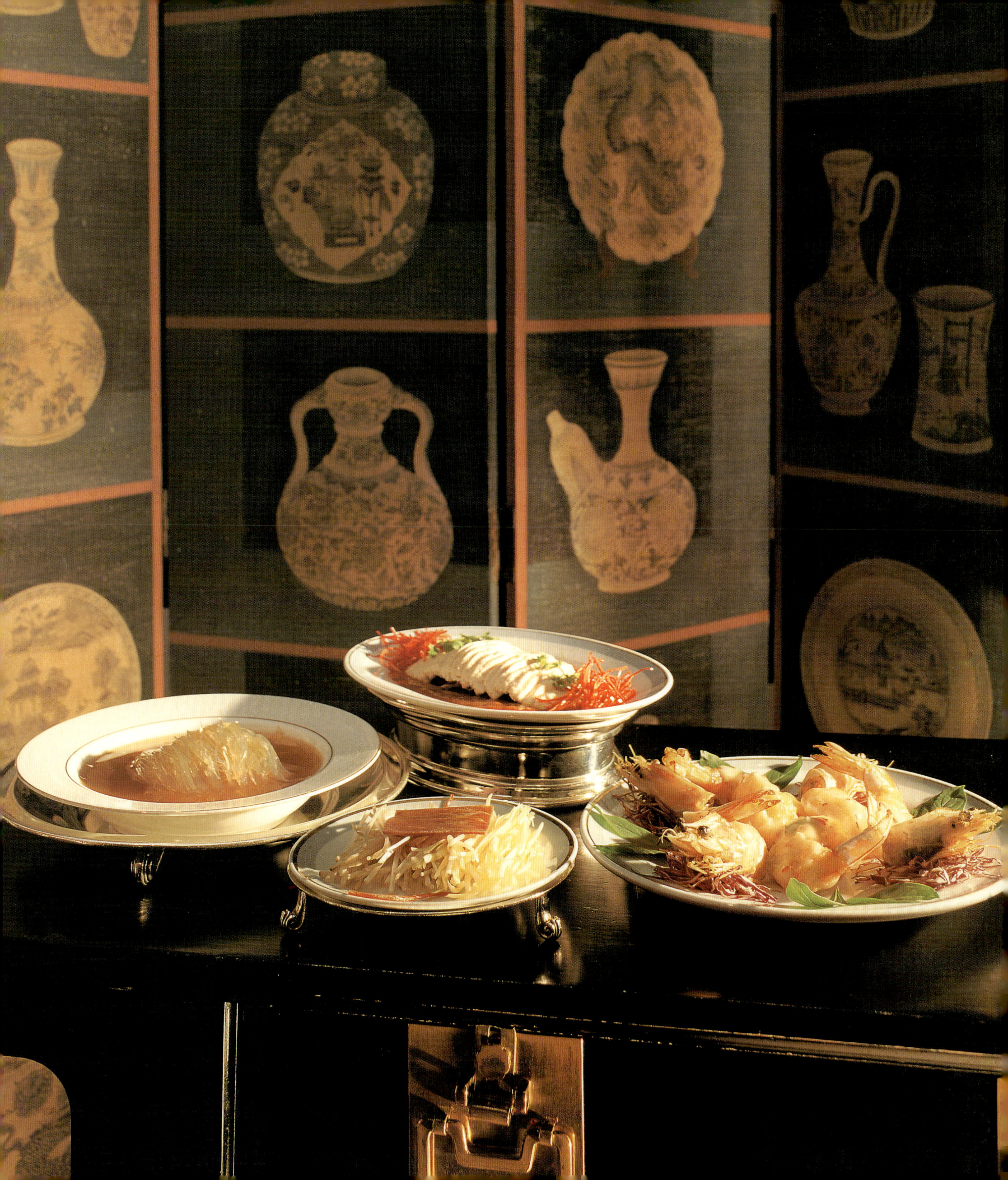

SAUTÉED FRESH SCALLOPS WITH CRAB ROE AND POTATOES (Opposite)

Serves 4–6

450 g	Fresh scallops
8 g	Salt
300 g	Potatoes, cleaned and peeled
150 g	Crab roe
4 tbsp	Vegetable oil for frying
70 g	Garlic

PREPARATION

Rinse the scallops, then marinate them with salt for 20 minutes.
Shred the potatoes to resemble noodles and stir-fry for 1 minute.
Sprinkle with salt and a little water, and leave aside.
Poach the crab roe in boiling water for 50 seconds. Drain.
Heat oil in a wok and stir-fry the scallops for about 2 minutes until they become opaque. Add the garlic, then add the shredded potato and seasoning, and stir-fry for 1 minute.
Place on a serving platter and top with the crab roe.
Serve immediately.

STIR-FRIED MINCED SEAFOOD IN GOLDEN CUPS (Pg 82, front left)

Serves 4–6

10 sheets	Spring roll skin
150 g	Prawn meat, finely chopped
150 g	Fresh scallop meat, finely chopped
150 g	Yam, finely chopped
70 g	Water chestnuts, peeled and chopped
50 g	Shallots
50 g	Yellow chives
70 g	Celery, sliced
50 g	Fresh black fungus
70 g	Hot bean paste
4 g	Salt
40 g	Sugar
1 tsp	Dark soy sauce
3 tbsp	Vegetable oil for frying

PREPARATION

Cut the sheets of spring roll skin into circles approx. 6 cm in diameter.
Place a circle inside a small tart mould then place another tart mould on top to form a cup.
Heat oil to 180°C and fry the cups inside the two moulds until golden brown. Drain and keep warm until required.
Pour some vegetable oil in a wok, and quickly stir-fry the seafood mixture over medium heat. Remove the mixture from the wok, drain off some of the oil and stir-fry the water chestnuts, shallots, yellow chives, celery and black fungus for a few minutes. Add the seafood mixture, hot bean paste, salt, sugar and dark soy sauce, mix well and spoon the mixture into the warm spring-roll cups to serve.

Chef's note: You can also serve the seafood mixture in lettuce cups.

IMPERIAL BIRD'S NEST SOUP WITH WINTER MELON (Pg 82, front right)

Serves 2

50 g	Superior bird's nest, soaked in cold water
320 g	Shredded winter melon
350 ml	Chicken stock (see recipe on Pg 101)
30 g	Ginger, sliced
3 g	Salt
50 g	Tapioca flour
100 g	Yunnan ham, shredded

PREPARATION

Drain the bird's nest.
Remove the peel and pith from the winter melon and shred.
Bring the chicken stock to the boil, add the sliced ginger and winter melon, and simmer for 10 minutes. Cover for a further 10 minutes, then discard the ginger.
Add the bird's nest and bring to the boil again. Add the salt and tapioca flour and cook for a further 2 minutes.
Place in a serving bowl, garnish with shredded Yunnan ham, and serve immediately.

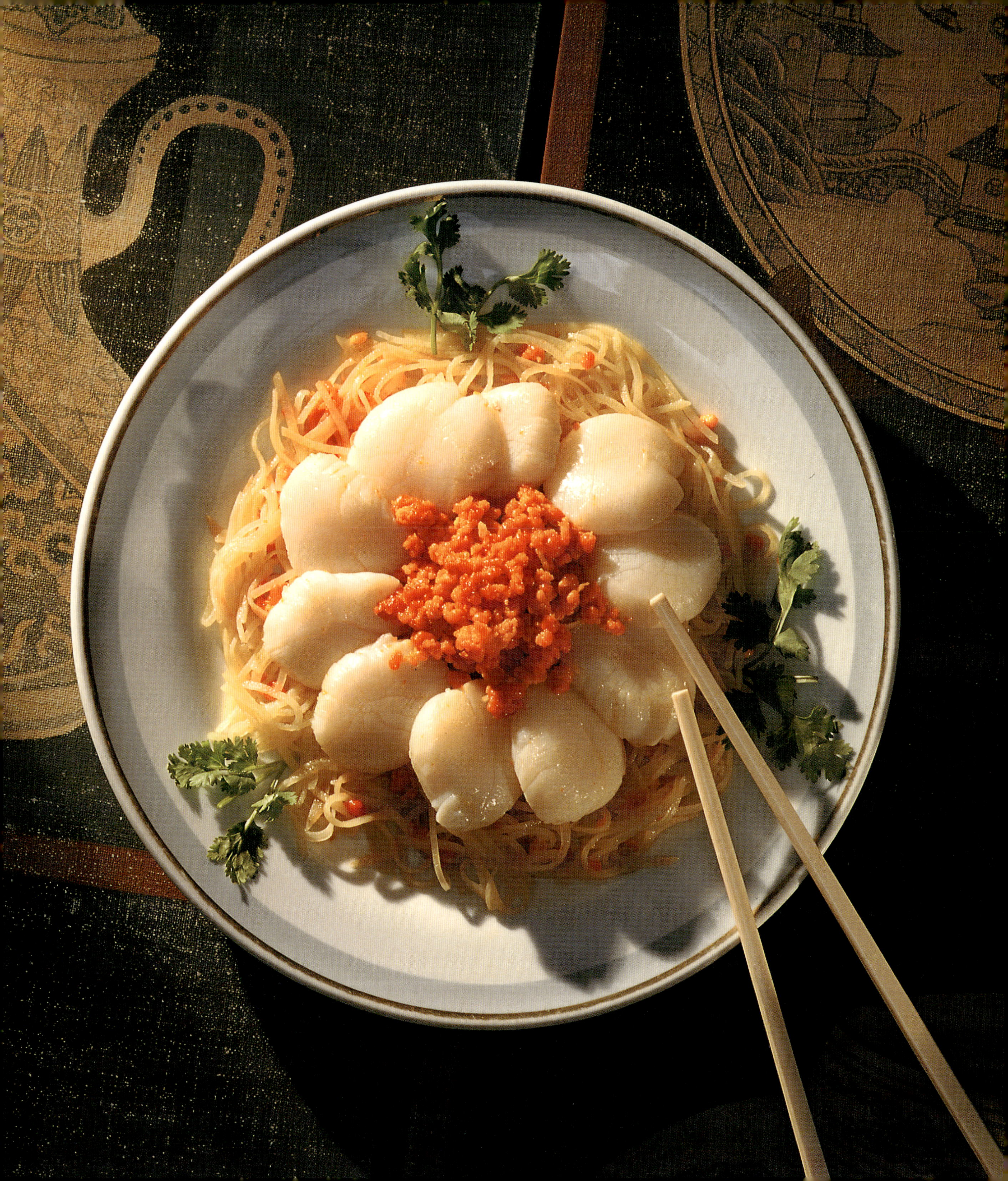

SLICED CHILLED ABALONE WITH VINEGAR SAUCE (opposite)

Serves 4–6

2 x 410 g cans	Abalone
250 g	Iceberg lettuce

Vinegar Sauce

150 ml	Rice vinegar
120 g	Sugar
9 g	Salt
1 tbsp	Oyster sauce
1 tbsp	Sesame oil
10 g	Garlic
5 g	Chinese parsley
5 g	Spring onion
5 g	Small chillies

PREPARATION
Slice the abalone very finely. Place the lettuce on a serving platter, and arrange the abalone slices on top. Chill for 10 minutes before serving.

Vinegar Sauce
Mix all the sauce ingredients together and pour in a sauce bowl. Serve abalone chilled with sauce on the side.

CLAYPOT FRIED RICE WITH MEAT AND YAM (Pg 82, back)

Serves 4–6

60 ml	Vegetable oil for frying
120 g	Yam, cut in cubes
120 g	Chicken meat, cut in cubes
2	Eggs, beaten
500 g	Steamed rice
150 g	Shrimp meat
120 g	Black mushrooms
120 g	Scallops
120 g	Shrimps
100 g	Spring onion
10 g	Salt
1 tbsp	Dark soy sauce
1 tbsp	Oyster sauce
1 tbsp	Chinese cooking wine

PREPARATION
Heat the oil in a wok and sauté the yam and chicken until golden brown. Remove and drain.
Retain some of the oil and fry the beaten egg until set, and break into small pieces.
Add the cooked rice and all other ingredients and fry for 10 minutes, then transfer to the claypot. Bake for a further 10 minutes in a pre-heated oven at 180°C and serve immediately.

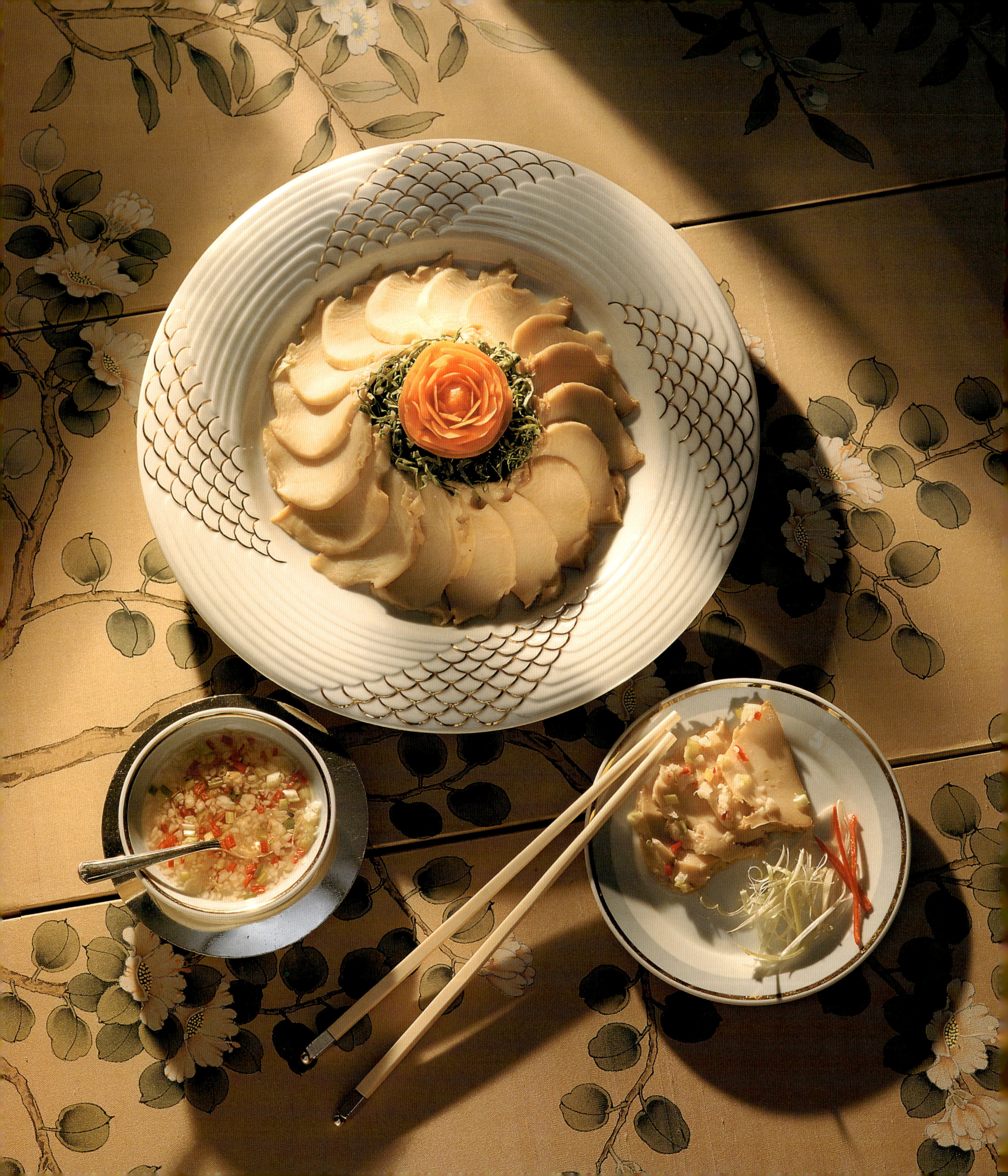

SAUTÉED BEEF TENDERLOIN WITH BLACK PEPPER SAUCE (above)

Serves 4

450 g	Beef tenderloin
Vegetable oil for frying	
250 g	Taiwanese green baby vegetables
Salt to season	
120 g	Bombay onion
170 g	Garlic
70 g	Shallots
1 tsp	Fried sliced garlic for garnish

Marinade

120 ml	Water
9 g	Salt
90 g	Tapioca flour

Black Pepper Sauce

3 tbsp	Tomato paste
1 tbsp	Soy sauce
1 tbsp	Dark soy sauce
50 g	Freshly ground black pepper
80 g	Sugar

PREPARATION

Cut the tenderloin into 2-cm cubes and mix with marinade ingredients. Leave to marinate for 20 minutes.
Quickly sauté the beef for 1 minute until lightly cooked. Remove and drain. Stir-fry the vegetables, then sprinkle some water and season with salt to taste. Remove and drain.
Heat 3 tbsp oil in a wok and stir-fry the onion, garlic and shallots until translucent, then add the tenderloin and sauce ingredients. Stir well. Garnish with sliced garlic to serve.

STEAMED GAROUPA WITH SOY SAUCE (above)

Serves 4–6

800 g	Fresh spotted garoupa
3 tbsp	Vegetable oil
Salt and pepper to taste	
A pinch of tapioca flour	
150 g	Spring onion, shredded
100 g	Ginger, peeled and shredded

Seasoning

120 ml	Light soy sauce
80 ml	Dark soy sauce
150 ml	Fish stock (see recipe on Pg 65)
100 g	Sugar
5 g	Salt
A pinch of ground white pepper	

PREPARATION

Scale, cut and wash the fish. Pat dry with a kitchen towel.
Rub the fish inside and out with oil, salt and pepper. Sprinkle with tapioca flour, then add some oil.
Arrange some shredded spring onion on a steaming plate. Place fish on top and sprinkle a few shreds of ginger over it.
Steam for 8 minutes over high heat.
Discard the used ginger and spring onion, and drain.
Garnish with remaining fresh shredded ginger and spring onion.
Heat oil in a wok, add the seasoning ingredients and when the oil is hot, pour it over the fish. Serve immediately.

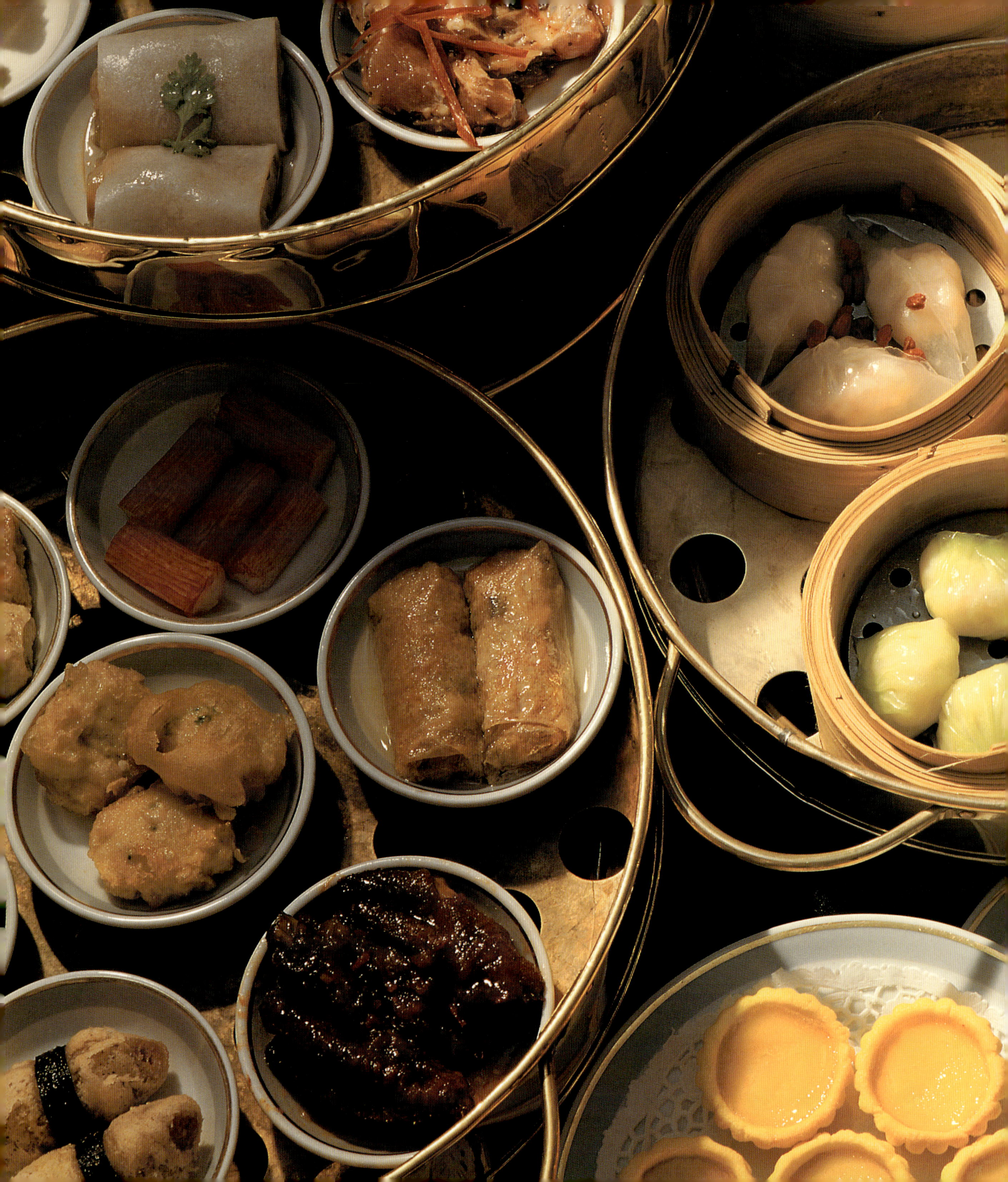

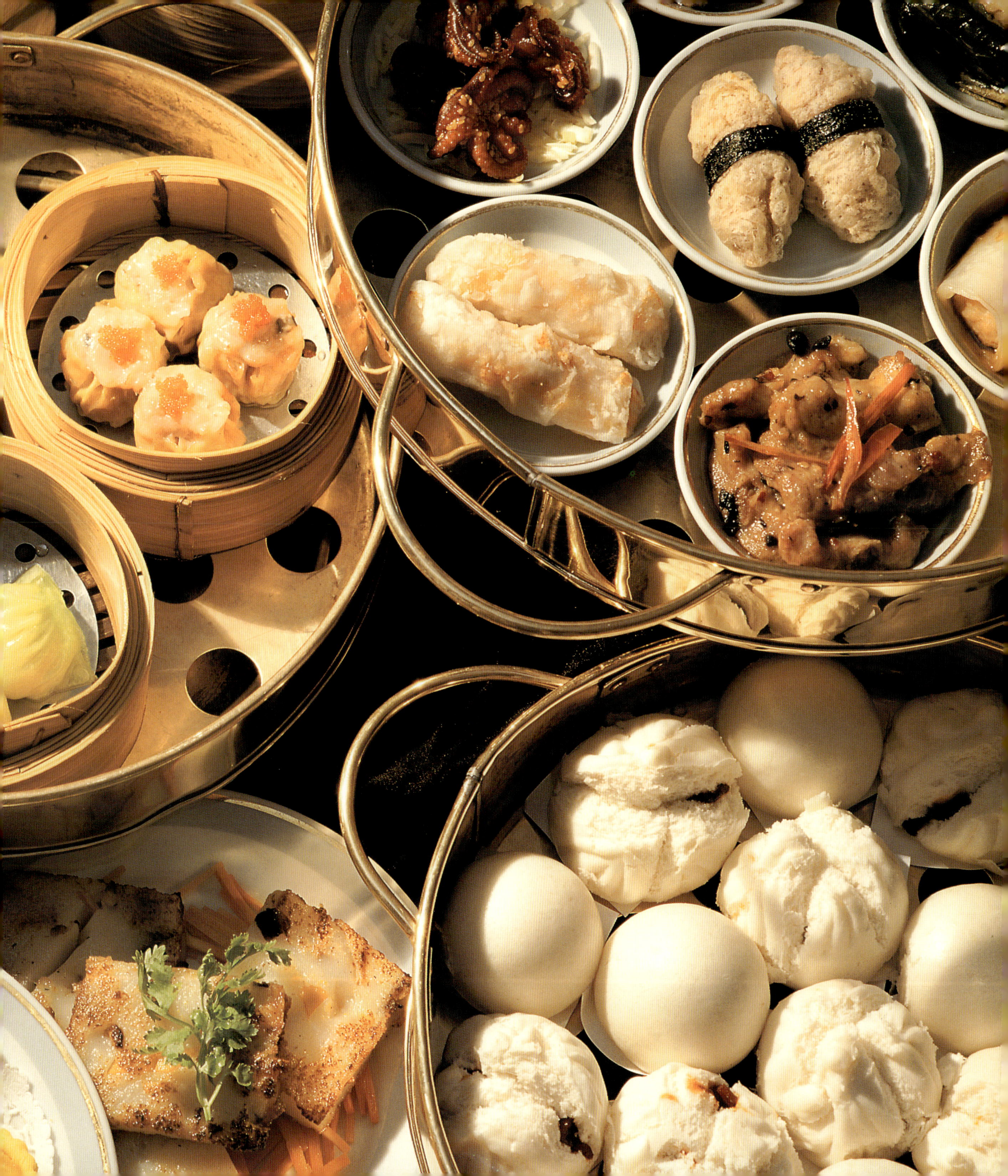

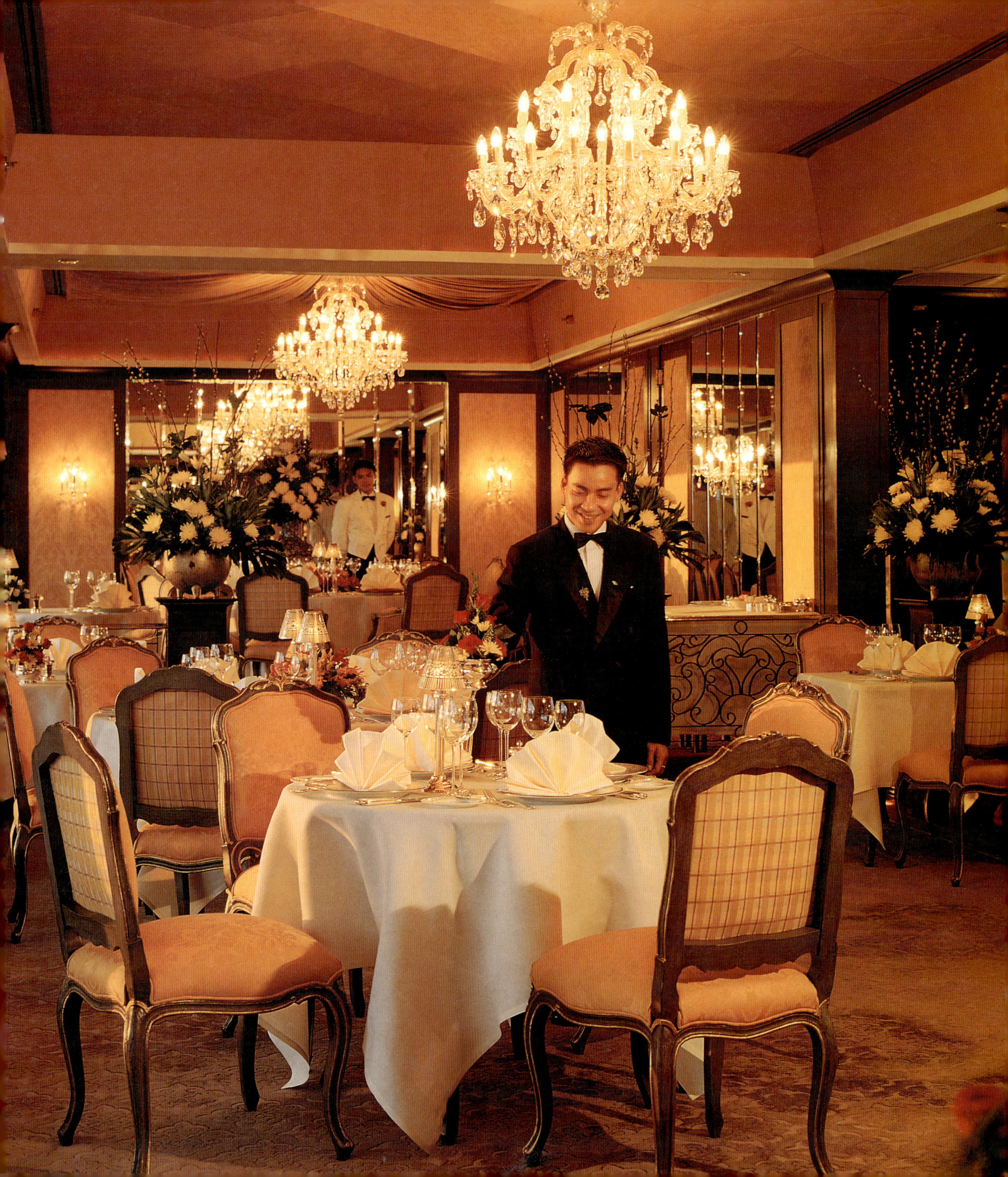

LE NORMANDIE

For more than forty years, Le Normandie at The Oriental has been virtually synonymous with fine French cuisine in Bangkok. The rooftop restaurant set the highest of standards as soon as it was opened by Germaine Krull in 1958 and has maintained them through numerous chefs and changes of décor. It is still Bangkok's ultimate place to lunch or dine with its atmosphere of hushed elegance, its unobtrusive but expert service, its sweeping views of the city and of the Chao Phraya River.

Its head chefs come from the top restaurants of Europe, staying for varying lengths of time and working with a skilled team of dedicated assistants. Though some contribute distinctive touches of their own, the basic objective remains "classic French food cooked in the classic way." This means such fare as fresh goose liver with Perigord truffles, crystal clear consommés, perfectly poached fish and roasted meats, and desserts that delight the eye as well as the palate, all accompanied by the finest wines from an extensive cellar.

To offer variety for regular guests, the restaurant changes its luncheon menu every four weeks, its dinner menu every six months, and its Menu Degustation every month, though certain dishes like the Pan-fried Goose Liver with Grapes can be ordered at any time.

Le Normandie sources the finest ingredients and imports many from abroad to ensure a peak of freshness: goose liver and truffles, Dover sole and Britanny turbot, tender lamb and beef, pigeon and smoked salmon, Iranian caviar and French cheese. Some items are obtained locally, such as rainbow trout, strawberries, salad greens, and many fresh herbs, all of which come from the Royal Project in northern Thailand on which The Oriental's Executive Chef, Norbert Kostner, serves as an advisor.

A meal at Le Normandie remains a gastronomic experience to be long remembered.

Le Normandie is one of Asia's best names in fine dining, serving up dishes that express the height of French gastronomy complemented by impeccable service, and a breathtaking view of the Chao Phraya River

GOOSE LIVER DOME WITH PERIGORD TRUFFLES AND CELERIAC (opposite)

Serves 4

Celery scales and truffle scales for decoration, blanched

Goose Liver Mousse

9 g/3	Gelatine powder/gelatine leaves, soaked in water
220 g	Chicken consommé (see recipe below)
260 g	Goose liver terrine
	Salt and freshly ground pepper to season
100 ml	Sauternes wine, reduced to one-quarter
100 ml	Madeira wine, reduced to one-quarter
60 g	Whipped cream
20 g	Perigord truffles, chopped

Port Wine Jelly

200 ml	Chicken consommé (see recipe below)
50 ml	Red port wine, reduced to one-quarter
50 ml	White port wine, reduced to one-quarter
9 g/3	Gelatine powder/leaves, soaked in water
1 tsp	Noilly Prat
	Salt and freshly ground white pepper to season

Garnish

Tomato cubes
Chervil
Caramelised apple, cut into cubes
Small salad bouquet

PREPARATION

Dome Mould

Line a dome mould with kitchen film larger than the mould. Cut the celery and truffles into 1-mm-thin slices with a 2-cm-diameter round cutter. Line the dome mould with the truffle and celery scales to create a checkered effect. Refrigerate until needed.

Goose Liver Mousse

Soak the gelatine leaves in cold water to soften them.
Bring the consommé to the boil, add the goose liver and return to the boil. Remove from the heat and process the mixture in a blender for 1 minute. Pass through a fine-mesh sieve.
Season the mixture with salt, pepper, and the Sauternes and Madeira wine.
Take a little of the goose liver mixture and warm it gently in a saucepan. Remove 3 leaves of the gelatine from the water, squeeze dry and add to the warm goose liver mixture. When the gelatine has melted, add this to the rest of the mixture.
Leave to cool.
Just before the mixture sets, gently fold in the whipped cream. Divide the mixture into two bowls, adding the chopped truffles into one. Remove the dome mould from the fridge and fill half with the truffle mixture. Return to refrigerator and leave to set.

Port Wine Jelly

Bring the consommé to the boil, then add the red and white port wine and the soaked gelatine leaves. Leave to cool.
When cold, pour a 2-mm-thick layer on top of the truffle mousse in the dome mould. Return to refrigerator and set again. Fill the mould nearly to the top with the plain liver mousse and finish with another thin layer of jelly. Return to refrigerator and leave to set for about 1 hour.

PRESENTATION

To serve, remove the mousse from the mould, place in the centre of the plate and garnish with caramelised apple cubes, tomato cubes, chervil and the salad bouquet.

Chef's note: This dish goes very well with toasted brioche.

CHICKEN CONSOMMÉ

Makes 1 litre

1 kg	Chicken leg meat, minced
150 g	Carrots, peeled and minced
150 g	Onion, minced
100 g	Leeks, minced
100 g	Celery
250 g	Tomatoes, cut into large cubes
80 g	Tomato paste
6	Garlic cloves, crushed
1 tsp	Cracked white peppercorns
1	*Bouquet garni* (bay leaves, thyme, parsley)
400 g	Ice cubes
6	Egg whites
2 litres	Chicken stock, chilled (see recipe on Pg 101)
	Salt to season

PREPARATION

Mix the chicken meat with the prepared vegetables.
Add the tomato, tomato paste, garlic, pepper, *bouquet garni*, ice cubes and egg whites and mix well.
Leave to rest in the refrigerator for 30 minutes.
Add the cold chicken stock and bring to the boil, stirring gently to prevent the mixture from sticking to the bottom of the saucepan. Allow to simmer for approx. 2 hours.
Strain the clear consommé through a fine cheese cloth and skim off any fat.
Add seasoning and serve as required.

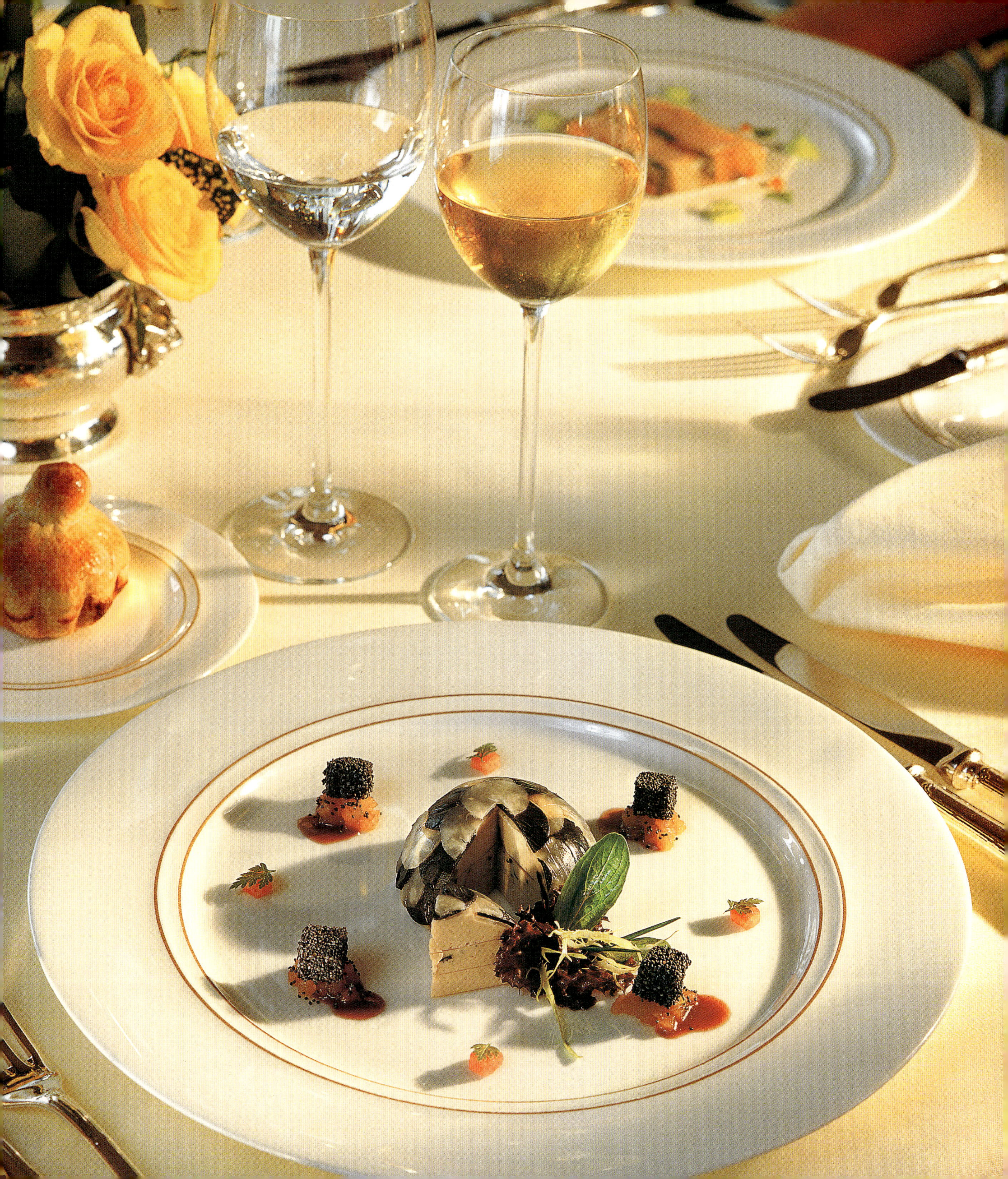

The Oriental Hotel Cookbook

HOME-SMOKED SALMON WITH TOMATO JELLY AND IRANIAN CAVIAR (opposite)

Serves 4

Mixed-herb Sour Cream

2 tbsp	Chopped parsley
2 tbsp	Chopped chervil
2 tbsp	Chopped basil
1 tbsp	Chopped tarragon
2 tbsp	Chopped nettle
90 g	Sour cream
30 g	Whipping cream

Lemon juice to taste
Champagne vinegar to taste
Salt and pepper to taste

Tomato Jelly

15 g/5	Gelatine powder/gelatine leaves
650 g	Tomatoes
2	Egg whites
2	Star anise pods
2 tsp	Salt

Peppercorns, bay leaves and fresh basil to season

90 ml	Noilly Prat, reduced to half

Salmon

600 g	Salmon fillet
100 g	Oak sawdust for smoking

Salt and pepper to season

60 g	Iranian caviar

Tomato cubes and chervil sprigs to garnish

PREPARATION
Mixed-herb Sour Cream
Mix the chopped herbs into the sour cream and whipping cream. Season with lemon juice, champagne vinegar, salt and pepper.

Tomato Jelly
Soak the gelatine leaves in cold water to soften. Clean the tomatoes, cut into smaller pieces and put through a vegetable juicer to extract the juice. Mix the juice with the egg whites in a heavy-based saucepan and bring to the boil. Remove from the heat and season with star anise, salt, peppercorns, bay leaves, fresh basil and Noilly Prat. Leave to infuse for one hour.
Strain through a fine cheesecloth (the liquid should be clear and pale). Strain the gelatine leaves and squeeze out any excess liquid, then gently warm the leaves in a bowl over a low heat to melt the gelatine. Add to the tomato mixture.
Place in the refrigerator for 1 hour until set.
When set, dice the tomato jelly into a very fine cubes.

Salmon
Slice the trimmed salmon fillet into 3-mm-thick slices. Take 4 squares of buttered aluminium foil (approx. 15 cm x 15 cm in size), divide the salmon into slices and roll into roses. Place each rose on a square of buttered foil.
Line the base of a steaming kettle with the oak sawdust and place over a high heat. When it starts to smoke, place the salmon roses on a perforated tray and place this in the kettle. Smoke the salmon in high heat for 15 seconds and remove from kettle.
Place on a baking tray and finish the cooking in the oven at 200°C for 1–2 minutes. Remove and season with salt and pepper.

PRESENTATION
Place a spoon of herbed sour cream in the centre of a plate. Remove the salmon from the foil with a spatula and place on the sour cream.
Place the jelly into a piping bag with a 1-cm-diameter nozzle, pipe around the outside of the sour cream.
Garnish with quenelles of caviar, tomato cubes and chopped chervil to serve.

GRATINATED PASSIONFRUIT PARFAIT WITH EXOTIC FRUITS (Pg 110, bottom left)

Serves 4

80 g	Passionfruit juice
60 g	Butter, melted
3	Egg yolks
120 g	Sugar
9 g/3	Gelatine powder/leaves, soaked in cold water
70 g	Whipped cream
40 g	Icing sugar

Mixed fruit for decoration

PREPARATION
Boil the passionfruit juice and add the melted butter.
Whisk the egg yolks and sugar together and pour into the passionfruit mixture. Place into a stainless steel bowl over a pan of boiling water, and whisk for 5 minutes.
Add gelatine to the mixture, stir well and pass through a sieve. Place over ice and continue whisking until cool, then fold in the whipped cream. Pour into the moulds and freeze overnight.
Remove from the freezer and place on a grill pan. Dust with icing sugar, then place under a hot grill for a few seconds to caramelise the sugar. Remove the mould immediately or the parfait will melt. Transfer to a plate and garnish with fresh fruit.

PAN-FRIED ESCALOPE OF GOOSE LIVER WITH GRAPE SAUCE (above)

Serves 2

Grape Sauce

15 g	Butter
30 g	Shallots, peeled and finely cubed
500 ml	Port wine
100 ml	Red wine
1 tbsp	Xeres vinegar
1 tbsp	Honey
100 ml	Red wine sauce
Salt and freshly ground white pepper to season	
70–80 g	Grapes, skinless, seeded and cut in half lengthways

Goose Liver

4	Escalopes of fresh goose liver, (approx. 50–60 g each), sliced 1-cm thick
30 ml	Vegetable oil for frying

PREPARATION

Grape Sauce
Melt the butter in a heavy-based saucepan, and gently fry the shallots until all moisture has evaporated. Add the port wine, red wine, Xeres vinegar and honey and bring to the boil. Reduce the liquid over a medium heat until almost dry, then add the red wine sauce and simmer gently for 5–6 minutes. Adjust the seasoning with salt and freshly ground white pepper, then strain the sauce through a fine-mesh sieve. Cover with a lid and keep warm.

Goose Liver
Season the goose liver escalopes with salt and pepper and fry them with a small amount of oil in a non-stick frying pan until nicely browned on both sides, but still quite pink at the centre. Remove from the pan and keep warm on paper towels.

PRESENTATION
Reheat the sauce, add the grapes and boil briefly; adjust seasoning if necessary. The sauce should be saltish and sour with a hint of sweetness and have a nice peppery flavour.
Arrange two of the goose liver escalopes on each pre-warmed plate. Pour the grape sauce over them and serve immediately.

CAPPUCCINO OF GOOSE LIVER
WITH WHITE AND BLACK TRUFFLES (above)

Serves 7–8

300 g	Goose liver
150 g	Butter
150 g	Shallots, chopped
10 g	Black peppercorns, cracked
400 g	Red port wine
10 g	Madeira wine
650 ml	Chicken stock (see recipe on the right)
350 ml	Cream
Salt and pepper to season	
1 tbsp	Alba truffle oil
21–24	Paper-thin slices of black Perigord truffles

PREPARATION
Blend the goose liver and 100 g of the butter until smooth. Remove from the bowl and refrigerate.
Sauté the shallots in the remaining 50 g of butter until translucent, then add the peppercorns, red port wine and Madeira wine, and bring to the boil. Simmer until the liquid reduces by half. Add the chicken stock and cream and continue to simmer until the shallots are very soft and mushy.
Add the goose liver, return to the boil and transfer immediately to a blender. Blend for 1 minute, then season with salt, ground white pepper and the truffle oil. Whisk the soup with a hand-held blender or a food processor to get foam on the surface, then ladle portions into pre-warmed soup plates. Garnish each portion with 3 slices of black truffles and serve immediately.

CHICKEN STOCK

Makes 800 ml

1	Onion, unpeeled, cut in half and charred on a hot plate
150 g	Celery stalks, cut into cubes
150 g	Carrots, peeled and cut into cubes
100 g	Leek, cut into cubes
3	Big tomatoes, cut into quarters
20	Parsley sprigs
5	Garlic cloves, flattened
1	Bay leaf
2	Whole cloves
½ tsp	Crushed white peppercorns
50 ml	Vegetable oil
1.5 kg	Chicken bones and wing
2 litres	Water

PREPARATION
Wash the chicken bones under running water for 10 minutes. Place all the vegetables, herbs, spices and oil in a stock pot and fry very gently for 5 minutes.
Add the chicken bones and cook for another 5 minutes. Now add the water and bring to the boil, then reduce heat and simmer slowly for about 2 hours.
Skim off any surface foam that accumulates during cooking. Remove from the heat, leave to rest for 10 minutes, then strain the stock through a fine-mesh sieve.
Allow to cool completely and then store in the refrigerator. Chicken stock will keep well in the refrigerator for a few days. It can also be stored frozen.

CRISP FRIED SEABASS ON RATATOUILLE NIÇOISE WITH BASIL INFUSION (opposite)

Serves 4

Sauce

250 ml	Riesling
50 ml	Noilly Prat
150 g	Unsalted butter, cold
	Salt to taste
	A squirt of lemon juice
50 g	Basil leaves, julienned

Ratatouille Balls

120 g	Eggplants, cut into cubes
50 g	Shallots, chopped
120 g	Zucchini, cut into cubes
3	Garlic cloves, finely chopped
120 g	Bell peppers, various colours, cut into cubes
	Salt and freshly ground pepper to season
4	Thyme sprigs
4	Bay leaves
1 tbsp	Tomato paste
20 g	Semolina
2	Eggs, beaten
	Flour for dusting

Seabass

4	Seabass fillets (approx. 140 g each)
	Salt and freshly ground pepper to season
	Olive oil and butter for pan-frying

Garnish

1	Green zucchini, medium-sized
1	Yellow zucchini, medium-sized
	Salt and freshly ground pepper to season
	Butter for frying
16–20	Parisienne potatoes, boiled and sautéed in butter
	A few threads of saffron
4	Basil leaves, julienned and deep-fried

PREPARATION

Sauce
In a small saucepan, reduce the Riesling and the Noilly Prat by two-thirds over a medium heat. Whisk in the butter cubes, one at a time, then season with salt and lemon juice. Remove from the heat and add the basil leaves. Set aside for 1 hour to infuse. Strain the sauce and add the basil leaves just before serving.

Ratatouille Balls
Remove the skin of the eggplant, cut the flesh into cubes and finely dice the skin.
Sauté the shallots, zucchini and garlic in a frying pan until soft. Add the bell peppers and eggplant flesh.
Season with salt, pepper, thyme, bay leaves and tomato paste for colour. Simmer slowly for approx. 5 minutes and set aside.
Cook a small amount of the ratatouille with semolina to thicken the mixture, then leave aside to cool.
Roll the ratatouille into small balls and coat with flour, egg and cubed eggplant skin.
Deep-fry for 1 minute until the skin is crisp.

Seabass
Season the fish fillets and score the skin with a sharp knife. Pan-fry in olive oil until the skin is golden brown and crispy. Add some butter, then turn the fish over and finish cooking.

Garnish
Cut the green-and-yellow zucchini into 1-mm-thick slices. Blanch in boiling salted water for 1 minute, then plunge into cold water. Dry with paper towels, then season and sauté with butter for 1 minute. Boil potatoes in water with saffron. Remove when cooked.

PRESENTATION
Place a 10-cm-diameter ring in the centre of a serving plate and arrange the fried zucchini slices outside of the ring, alternating the two colours.
Fill the inside of the ring with the ratatouille. Remove the ring. Place the seabass on top. Spoon the sauce around the outside of the ratatouille. Garnish with deep-fried basil leaves, deep-fried ratatouille balls and Parisienne potatoes.

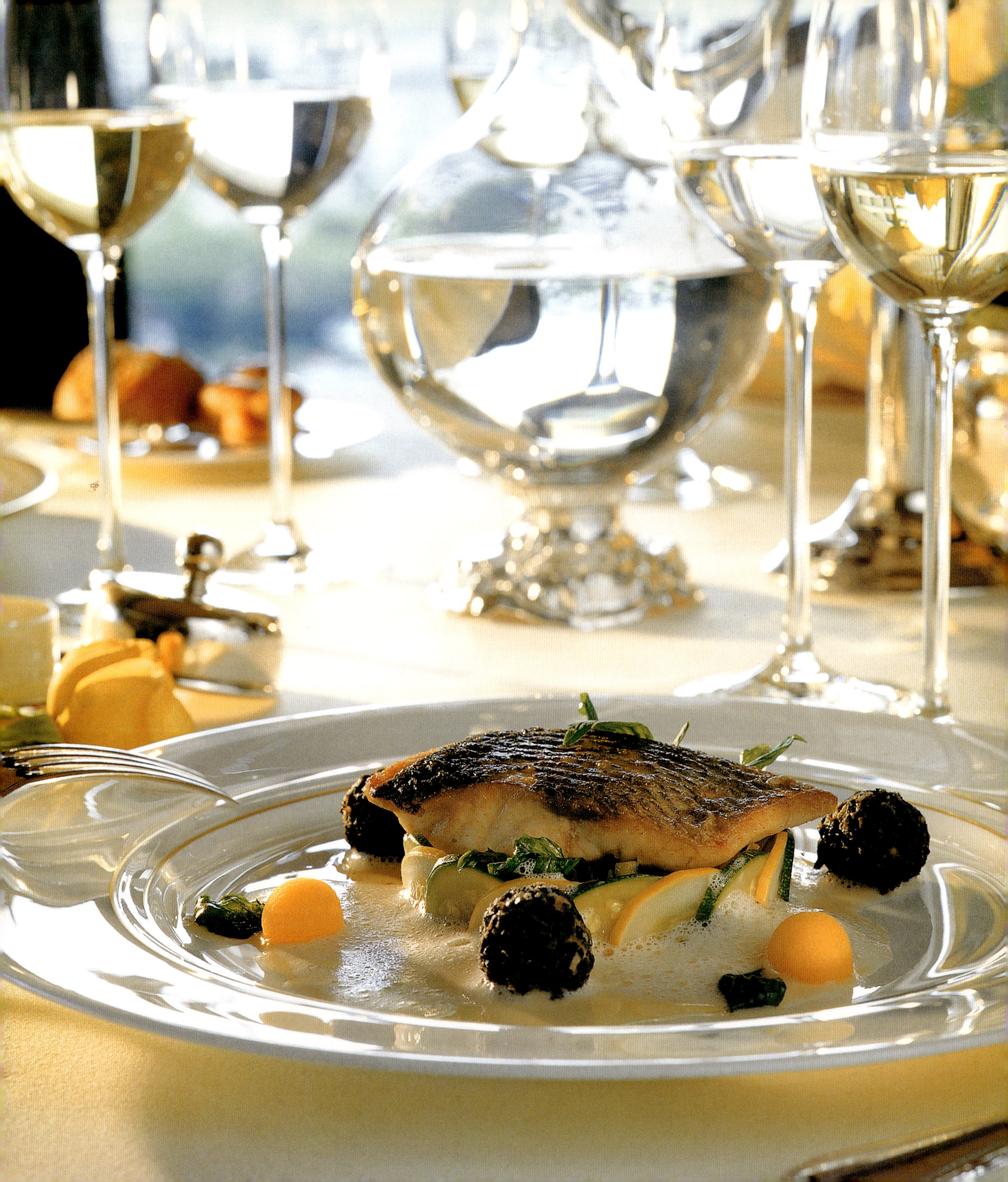

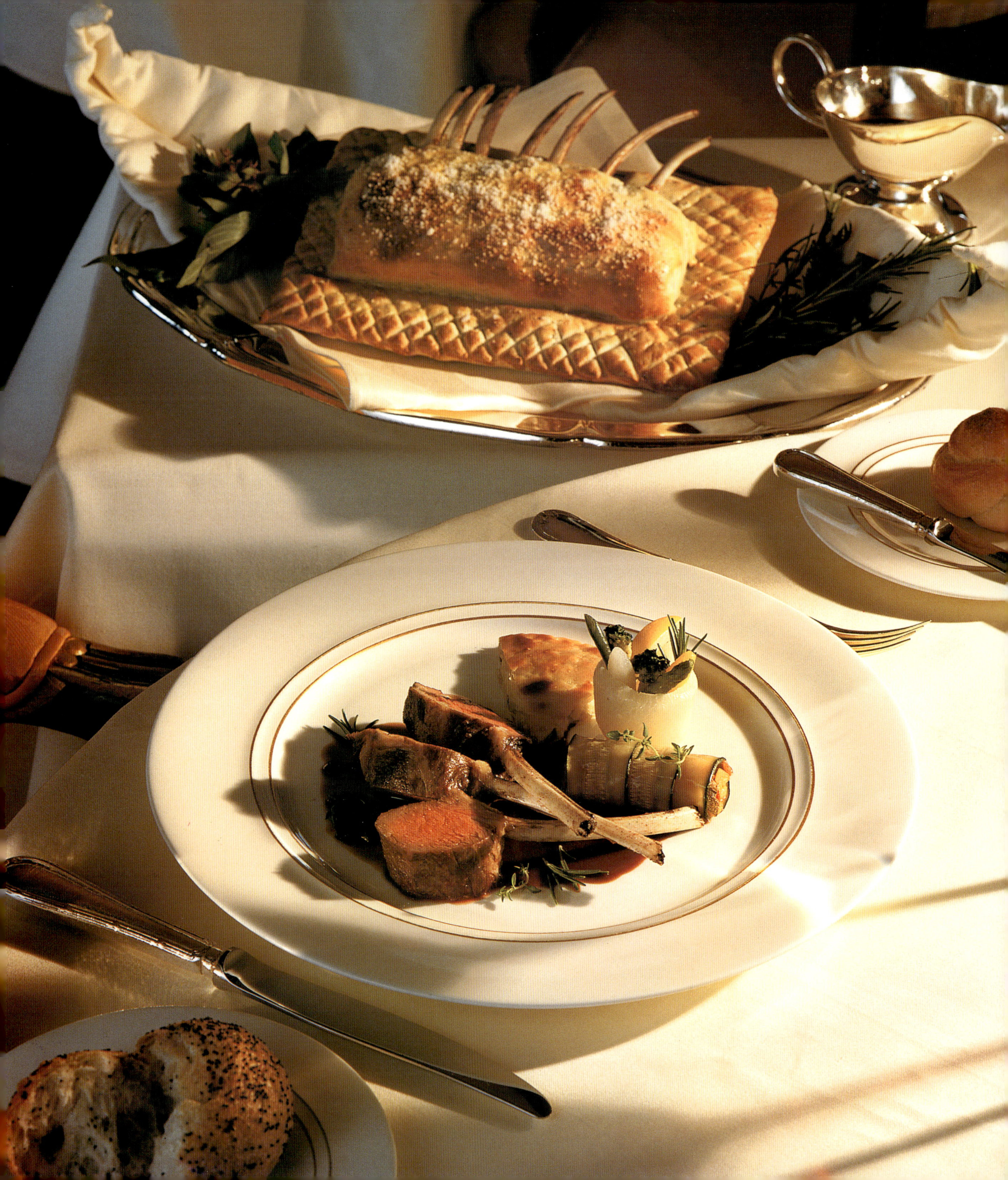

LAMB LOIN BAKED IN SALT CRUST WITH BLACK OLIVE SAUCE (opposite)

Serves 4

200 g	Assorted vegetables (carrots, zucchini, green asparagus) for garnish
Butter for frying	

Salt Dough

500 g	Salt
500 g	Flour
2	Eggs
170 g	Water
30 g	Rosemary, finely chopped
30 g	Thyme, finely chopped
2	Egg yolks

Lamb Loin

120 g	Pork fat
2 pcs	Lamb loin, trimmed (approx. 450–500 g each)
Salt and pepper to season	
10 g	Rosemary, chopped
10 g	Thyme, chopped
6 cloves	Garlic, peeled, blanched and sliced
1	Egg yolk, beaten
Olive oil and butter	

Black Olive Sauce

120 ml	Lamb jus (see recipe below)
40 g	Black olives, chopped
20 g	Parsley, chopped

PREPARATION

Salt Dough
Mix all the ingredients together in a bowl to form a smooth dough. Roll on a floured surface until 8-mm thick. Cut into four 20 x 25-cm rectangles.

Lamb Loin
Slice the pork fat into 1-mm-thick rectangles (smaller than the salt dough) and lay, each side overlapping, on baking paper. Season the lamb loins with salt and pepper and pan-fry quickly on each side. Cool in the refrigerator.
Once cool, place each loin on a piece of pork fat and sprinkle with chopped herbs and garlic. Roll them up in the pork fat and place in the centre of a piece of salt dough. Brush the edges of the dough with egg yolk and cover with another piece of dough. Press the edges together and brush with egg yolk. Bake in a pre-heated oven at 220°C for 11 minutes. Remove and rest for 5 minutes. Cut the dough open, remove the wrapped lamb to a carving board and remove the pork fat. Carve into 6 slices.

Black Olive Sauce
Heat the lamb jus. Add the chopped black olives and parsley. Add seasoning as required.

PRESENTATION
Sauté the vegetables with some butter and season with salt and pepper. Pour the black olive sauce on a dinner plate. Arrange the lamb on the sauce and place the vegetables around it.

LAMB JUS

Makes 1 litre

150 ml	Vegetable oil
1 kg	Lamb bones, chopped into 2-cm pieces
150 g	White onion, peeled and cut into 1-cm cubes
120 g	Carrots, peeled and cut into 1-cm cubes
45 g	Celery stalks, cut into 1-cm lengths
50 g	Leek, cut into 1-cm lengths
5-6	Garlic cloves, flattened
50 g	Tomato paste
1	*Bouquet garni* (parsley, bay leaves and thyme)
200 g	Very fresh and ripe tomatoes, cut into 1-cm cubes
10	Cracked black peppercorns
2 pinches of coarse sea salt	
3 litres water	

PREPARATION
Pre-heat oven at 200°C. Heat 100 ml of oil in a heavy-based roasting tray, add the bones and roast for about 30 minutes until they turn a very dark golden brown colour. Add the prepared vegetables and garlic, and roast for another 15–20 minutes until they caramelise. Turn the bones and vegetables over occasionally with a wooden spoon. When the mixture is caramelised, remove everything from the tray and place them in a large saucepan. Drain and discard the fat from the roasting tray, return to a medium heat and deglaze the pan with 200 ml of cold water. Bring to the boil, scraping the bottom of the tray with a metal spoon for the roasting juice and pour this into the pan with the bones. While roasting the bones, fry the tomato paste with the remaining oil for about 30 minutes until the paste turns dark brown and loses most of its acidity. Add this roasted tomato paste, *bouquet garni*, tomatoes, cracked peppercorns and a good pinch of coarse sea salt to the pan. Cover with about 3 litres of cold water and bring to the boil. Reduce the heat and allow to simmer for about 4 hours. Skim the jus regularly to remove any foam that forms on the surface. After 4 hours, remove from the heat and leave to rest for 50–60 minutes to allow all the fat to accumulate on the surface. Skim this off, and strain the jus through a fine-mesh sieve. Allow to cool completely, then refrigerate.

ROAST PIGEON IN POTATO COAT WITH MUSTARD SAUCE (opposite)

Serves 4

4	Potatoes (15 x 10 cm), peeled, cut into pear shape
2	Pigeon (approx. 450 g each)
300–350 g	Assorted vegetables (baby carrots, asparagus, etc), cooked in salted water for garnish

Mousse

80 g	Chicken breast, trimmed and cut into cubes
40 g	Pigeon thigh meat, trimmed and cubed
1	Egg
1	Egg white
	Salt and freshly ground pepper to season
120 g	Whipping cream
	Unsalted butter for frying
20 g	Soaked trumpet mushrooms, chopped
20 g	Soaked morels, chopped
10 g	Parsley, chopped

Mustard Grain and Brown Sauces

30 g	Mustard seeds, washed and drained
60 g	Shallots, finely chopped
10 g	Butter
500 ml	White wine
250 ml	Apple juice
2 tbsp	Xeres vinegar
500 ml	Chicken stock (see recipe on Pg 101)
	Salt and sugar to season

Brown Sauce

2 tbsp	White wine
400 g	Pigeon jus (see recipe below)
160 g	Butter
40 g	Chives, chopped

PREPARATION

Mousse
Mix the chicken and pigeon meat with the egg yolk and white. Season with salt and pepper, place into a blender and add the cream. Blend until smooth. Sauté the mushrooms with some butter. Place the chicken mixture in a bowl and add the mushrooms and chopped parsley. Make sure the mushrooms and mousse are the same temperature. Refrigerate.

Potato Coat
Slice off the base of the potato so it will sit flat. Remove the inside of the potatoes with a Parisienne scoop, leaving a 1-cm-thick wall. Blanch in boiling salted water for 2 minutes and then plunge into iced water and leave aside.
Remove the skin and breast from the pigeon. Season with salt and pepper. Drain the potatoes and dry with a towel.
Spoon a 1-cm-thick layer of chicken mousse in the potato, top with pigeon breast, and top with chicken mousse. Turn the potato over onto buttered aluminum foil and place on a baking tray. Cook in a pre-heated oven at 190°C for 8 minutes. Remove and leave to rest for 5 minutes.

Mustard Grain and Brown Sauces
Wash the mustard seeds. Sauté the shallots with the butter, deglaze with white wine, apple juice and Xeres vinegar, and add the chicken stock. Boil gently for 1½ hours, reducing the liquid to one-third. Strain through a sieve. Reduce the white wine and pigeon jus to one-quarter, add butter and boil for 1 minute. Just before serving, add freshly chopped chives.

PRESENTATION
Place the sauces in the centre of the plate. Cut the potato in half, and arrange on the sauces. Garnish with the assorted vegetables to serve.

PIGEON JUS

Makes 800 ml

600–700 g	Pigeon bones, cut into 2–3-cm pieces
100 ml	Vegetable oil
600 g	White onion, peeled and cut into 1-cm cubes
40 g	Shallots, peeled and cut into 1-cm cubes
100 g	Carrots, peeled and cut into 1-cm cubes
50 g	Celery stalks, cut into 1-cm cubes
50 g	Leek, cut into 1-cm cubes
3–4	Garlic cloves, peeled and crushed
250 ml	White wine
2 litres	Cold water
200 g	Very ripe tomatoes, cut into 1-cm cubes
1	*Bouquet garni* (parsley, bay leaves, thyme, sage)
	Cracked black peppercorns and coarse sea salt to taste

PREPARATION
Sauté the pigeon bones over high heat to a golden brown colour, add the vegetables and fry for 5–10 minutes. Drain off all the fat and deglaze the pan with the white wine. Let evaporate until dry, then add water. Bring to the boil, then reduce the heat and allow to boil gently. Remove any foam on the surface. Add the tomatoes, *bouquet garni*, pepper and salt. Remove the foam and fat regularly and leave to cook gently for 2½ hours. Then remove from the heat and leave to rest for 20 minutes. Strain the resulting jus through a very fine-mesh sieve and press the bones strongly with a ladle to extract all the jus. Leave to cool, then skim off the fat from the surface with a small ladle. Store refrigerated.

Le Normandie

PAN-FRIED TURBOT ON ASPARAGUS-PUMPKIN RAGOUT WITH POTATO-CHIVES BROTH (below)

Serves 4

Turbot
2 tbsp	Olive oil
4 pcs	Turbot escalopes (approx. 125 g each)

Salt and pepper to season

Asparagus Pumpkin Ragout
80 g	Asparagus, peeled and cut into small cubes
80 g	Pumpkin, peeled and cut into small cubes
200 g	Fresh cream
40 g	Butter

Salt, pepper and nutmeg to season

Potato Broth
20 g	Butter
80 g	Onion, chopped
170 g	Potatoes, sliced
1	Garlic clove, chopped
1 litre	Chicken stock (see recipe on Pg 101)
60 g	Unsalted butter, chilled
30 g	Chives, chopped

PREPARATION
Potato Broth
Melt the butter in a medium-sized saucepan, add the onions, potatoes and garlic, and gently sauté until the onions are pale and translucent. Add the chicken stock, salt and pepper to taste and allow the soup to boil gently for 45–50 minutes until the potatoes have disintegrated. Blend until smooth, then pass through a fine-mesh sieve. Return the soup to the pan, cover and keep warm.

Asparagus Pumpkin Ragout
Quickly blanch the asparagus and pumpkin in salted boiling water until tender but firm. Drain and put aside in ice water. Place the cream and 30 g of butter in a small saucepan, bring to the boil and allow to reduce until the mixture has thickened slightly. Add the well-drained asparagus and pumpkin cubes and season with salt, pepper and nutmeg.
Remove from the heat, cover with a lid and keep warm.

Turbot
Heat the olive oil in a frying pan, season the turbot escalopes with salt and pepper and fry until nicely brown. Just before the turbot escalopes are done, discard the olive oil from the frying pan and add the remaining butter.
Turn the turbot escalopes once or twice in order to coat each side with foaming butter. Remove from the heat and keep warm.

PRESENTATION
Re-heat the potato broth and blend in the chilled butter cubes one by one, whisking vigorously with a wire whisk. Add chives. Spoon some of the asparagus-pumpkin ragout into the centre of 4 warmed serving plates, and top with turbot. Pour the broth around to serve.

CHOCOLATE AND CHERRY DOME WITH ALMOND CRISP (below)

Serves 4

Chocolate Dome

100 g	Griotte cherries, (bottled, 50 g cherries, 50 ml juice)
5 g	Cornflour
300 g	Whipping cream
35 g	Cherry brandy
165 g	Dark couverture chocolate

Brandy Snap

180 g	Icing sugar
110 g	Butter
90 ml	Maple syrup
90 g	Cake flour
4 tbsp	Grated milk chocolate

PREPARATION
Chocolate Dome
Bring the cherries to the boil in a small saucepan.
Just before boiling, blend the cornflour with a little cold water, then mix with the boiling cherries, stirring constantly. Allow the cornflour to cook for 1 minute, then remove and cool in a bowl. Whisk the cream with cherry brandy until it forms soft peaks. Warm the chocolate in a stainless steel bowl over a saucepan of hot water until it is warm and melted. Pour the chocolate into the cream and quickly whisk to make a chocolate mousse.
Fill 4 dome-shaped moulds with the chocolate mousse. Set in the refrigerator for half an hour. Remove and scoop out the centre of the chocolate mousse, leaving a layer of mousse approximately 1-cm thick to line the mould.
Spoon 3 griotte cherries and some syrup into the centre of each chocolate mousse 'dome'.
Over a saucepan of hot water, stir the chocolate mousse until it is soft again and pour into each dome mould so as to cover the cherries. Smooth it flat with a spatula. Return to the chiller and leave to set for 2–3 hours.

Brandy Snaps
Mix the icing sugar and butter together until well creamed. Add the syrup and flour and mix well. Spread a layer of the mixture about 1-mm thick onto a piece of non-stick baking paper.
Place the paper on a baking tray and bake at 200°C, until the mixture is golden brown. Remove from the oven and leave to rest for a couple of minutes. Then use a sharp knife to cut into desired shapes while still warm.
If the mixture becomes too hard to cut, return it to the oven until it softens, and then cut again.
Store the pieces in an airtight container until ready for use.

PRESENTATION
To serve, remove the mousse from the mould onto a serving plate. Garnish with couple of brandy snaps and some grated milk chocolate.

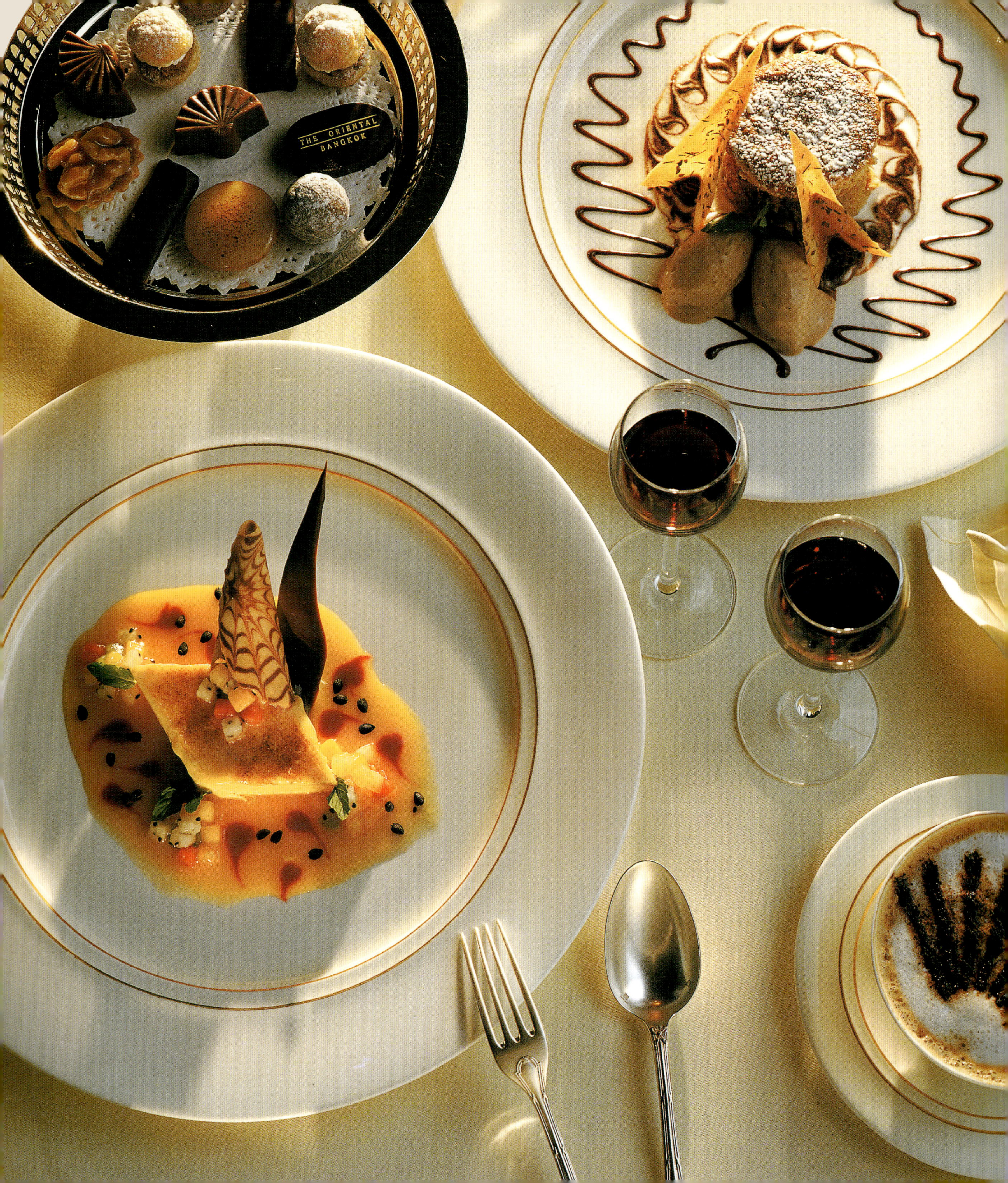
THE ORIENTAL
BANGKOK

WARM UPSIDE-DOWN SPICED PUDDING WITH PRALINE ICE CREAM (opposite, top right)

Serves 4

Praline Ice Cream

40 g	Dark couverture chocolate
40 g	Nougat
200 ml	Milk
200 ml	Cream
20 g	Sugar
2	Egg yolks
1	Egg
Grated rind from ½ orange	
15 ml	Grand Marnier liqueur
10 ml	Amaretto
15 ml	Cognac

Rum Sauce

120 g	Whipping cream
120 g	Heavy cream
25 g	Icing sugar
25 ml	Rum

Pudding

35 g	Ground almonds
15 g	Biscuit crumbs
1 tsp	Cinnamon
1 g	Ground cloves
20 ml	Rum
Grated rind and juice from 1 orange	
25 g	Icing sugar
45 g	Soft butter
3	Egg yolks
45 g	Grated chocolate
3	Egg whites
25 g	Sugar

PREPARATION

Praline Ice Cream

Melt the chocolate and the nougat separately over warm water.
Boil the milk, cream and half the sugar.
Beat the egg yolks, egg and remaining half of the sugar over simmering water until light and frothy.
Pour the boiled milk-cream mixture onto the beaten eggs, beating continuously until this becomes foamy.
Fold in the couverture, nougat and orange rind, until well combined. Leave to cool completely. Add the liqueurs, then pour the ice cream mixture into the ice cream machine, and freeze according to the manufacturer's instructions.

Rum Sauce

Beat the two creams together until lightly stiff. Fold in the icing sugar and rum.

Pudding

Pre-heat the oven to 190°C.
Lightly butter four individual soufflé moulds and dust with sugar.
Combine the almonds, biscuit crumbs, cinnamon, cloves, rum, orange rind and juice, and leave to rest for 30 minutes.
Cream the icing sugar and butter separately for 5 minutes until the sugar has dissolved and the mixture is pale in colour.
Add the egg yolks gradually, beating after each addition, then fold in the spiced almond mixture and grated chocolate.
In another bowl, beat the egg whites and the sugar until the whites form stiff peaks.
Gently fold the beaten egg whites into the soufflé mixture.
Carefully pour the soufflé mixture into the prepared moulds, place in a baking dish with hot water (3-cm high).
Bake for 25 minutes.

PRESENTATION

Remove the soufflé from its mould onto a serving plate. Drizzle the rum sauce around the soufflé immediately. Form 2 ice cream quenelles with a tablespoon, and set onto the sauce.

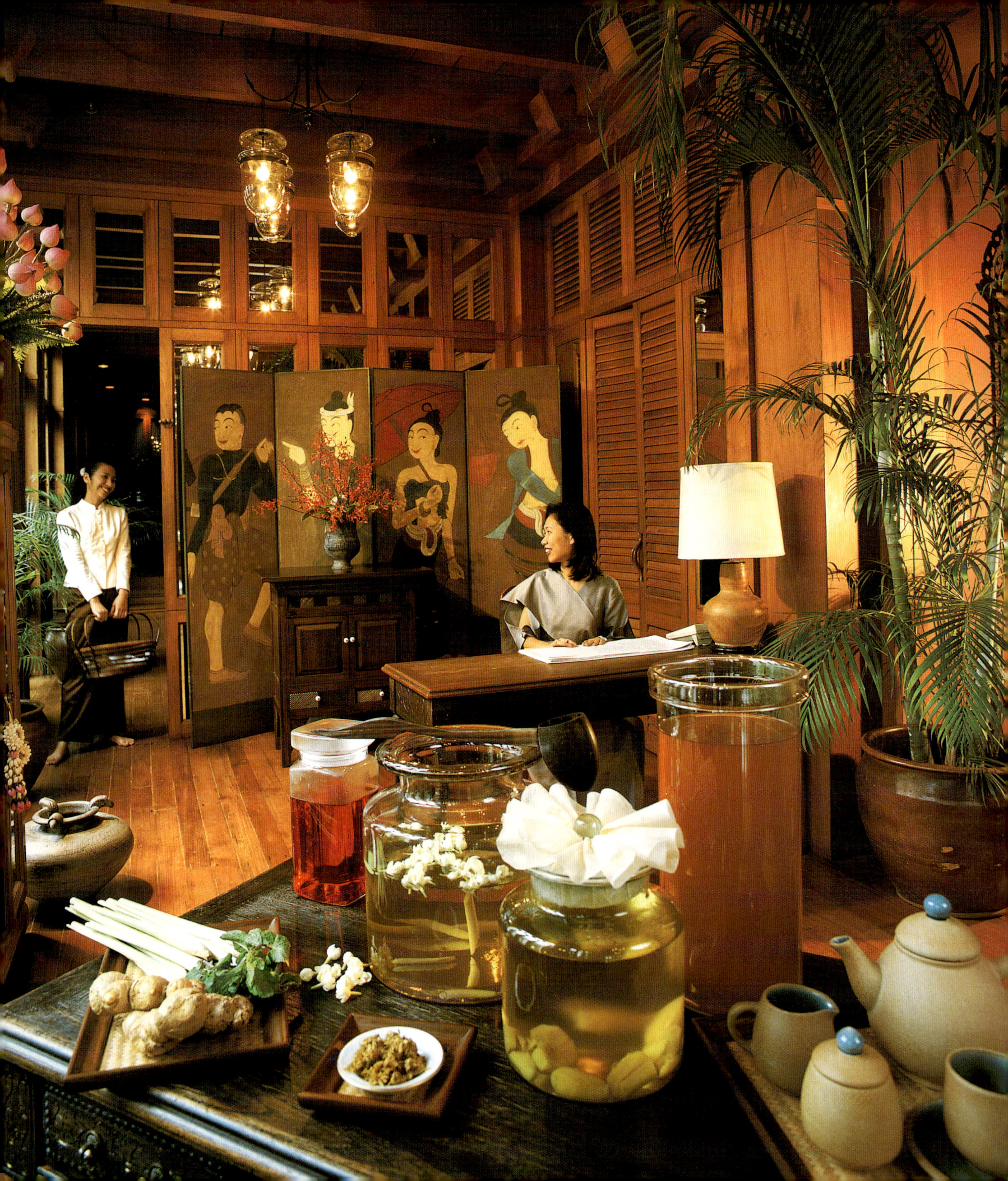

THE ORIENTAL SPA

"Thai food is naturally healthy," says Executive Chef Norbert Kostner. "The secret lies in the way most of it is cooked, quickly stir-fried or steamed, and in the ingredients used." In devising menus to complement the treatment programmes at The Oriental Spa, the chefs thus had a traditional basis from which to create a selection of dishes, each uniquely delicious but low in calories, fat points and cholesterol. Only the freshest seafood from the Gulf of Thailand and organically grown vegetables from the Royal Project in Chiang Mai are used, and each dish is artistically presented for maximum visual appeal as well as taste.

A typical day's menu of Spa cuisine might start with Grilled Herbed Crabmeat and Minced Chicken served with Lemongrass Sauce (76 calories and 1 fat point), and go on to a Herbed Soup of Vegetables and Fish (119 calories, 1 fat point), a Red Curry of Chicken and Garden Vegetables (193 calories, 7 fat points), Steamed Jasmine Rice (52 calories, and 1 fat point), a selection of carved tropical fruits (29 calories, 1 fat point), and herbal tea or mineral water – a grand total of 412 calories and 6 fat points.

The general menu offers a wider range of equally tempting choices, all designed to fit well within the recommended daily consumption of 1400–1700 calories and 30–40 fat points. Among these are Lettuce, Fresh Herb and Seabass Salad, River Prawn and Straw Mushroom Soup, Red Chicken Curry, and Vegetable Fried Rice; plus invigorating health drinks concocted with papaya and pomelo, mango and tangerine, low-fat yoghurt, cucumber and dill, or carrot and jicama, as well as assorted herbal teas.

Obviously, undergoing a health treatment at The Oriental Spa doesn't involve giving up the pleasures of superbly prepared food.

The complex task of balancing great taste and a beautiful presentation with maximum health benefits and minimum calories, fat and cholesterol, is undertaken by chefs of The Oriental Spa

LETTUCE, FRESH HERB AND SEABASS SALAD (below)

Serves 1

120–150 g	White seabass fillet, skin removed
	Salt and freshly ground white pepper to season
3 tbsp	Extra virgin olive oil
3–4	Garlic cloves, peeled and lightly crushed
1–2	Fresh rosemary sprigs
60 g	Mixed lettuce leaves and herbs (e.g. parsley, chives, fennel fronds, chervil, tarragon), washed and chilled
2–3	Red radishes, finely sliced
	Freshly squeezed juice of 1–2 limes

PREPARATION

Season the fish fillet with a little salt and pepper.
Heat $1/2$ tbsp olive oil in a medium-sized frying pan, add the fish, garlic and rosemary sprigs and fry the fish for about 2 minutes on each side until brown. As soon as the fish is cooked, remove it and the garlic cloves from the frying pan, drain and keep warm on absorbent kitchen paper.
Place the lettuce leaves, herbs and red radish disks in a large bowl, add the remaining olive oil and lime juice, and season with salt and pepper. Mix lightly to coat the lettuce leaves with the dressing. Adjust the seasoning if necessary.
Arrange the lettuce leaves on a chilled serving plate and place the warm fish fillet on top.
Top the fish fillet with the garlic cloves and serve immediately.

Chef's note: You should minimise the use of salt in Spa recipes. This salad was once prepared for Kurt Wachtveitl, General Manager of The Oriental, the day after he had a heavy dinner, and it has been served to him at least once a week ever since.

MUNG BEAN NOODLE SALAD WITH SHRIMPS AND CHICKEN (below, bottom)

Serves 1

60–70 g	Mung bean noodles
20–30 g	Fresh wood-ear mushrooms
20–30 g	Shrimps, cooked, peeled, de-veined and cut in half lengthwise
20–30 g	Chicken breast, steamed and cut into fine ribbons
20–25 g	Shallots, peeled and sliced
10–15 g	Spring onion, finely sliced
2–2½ tbsp	Freshly squeezed lime juice
2½ tbsp	Low-sodium light soy sauce
1	Large red chilli, cored, seeded and cut into fine strips for garnish

A few coriander leaves for garnish

PREPARATION

Blanch the wood-ear mushrooms in boiling water for 30 seconds, drain and rinse under cold running water, then put aside. Soak the glass noodles in warm water for 5–6 minutes, then drain and cut them into 15-cm lengths. Place them in a kitchen sieve and plunge the sieve containing the noodles into boiling water for 8–10 seconds only. Stir the noodles to prevent them from sticking together.

Remove the boiled noodles from the boiling water and rinse them under running cold water. Shake off any excess water – the noodles should only be moist.

Combine the noodles, wood-ear mushrooms, shrimp, chicken, shallots, spring onion, lime juice and soy sauce in a medium-sized bowl. Mix gently but thoroughly until all ingredients are well coated.

Transfer the salad to a serving plate, garnish with chilli strips and coriander leaves to serve.

HERBED FRUIT SALAD
Yaam Polamai (opposite, bottom)

Serves 4

2	Medium-sized pineapples
70–80 g	White grapes, cut in half and seeds removed
70–80 g	Red grapes, cut in half and seeds removed
70–80 g	Chinese oranges, peeled and cut into ½-cm cubes
70–80 g	Green apple, cut into ½-cm cubes
70–80 g	Red apple, cut into ½-cm cubes
70–80 g	Yam, peeled and cut into ½-cm cubes
8 g	Dry-fried sundried sliced garlic
8 g	Dry-fried sundried sliced shallots
100 g	Boiled shrimp, cut into ½-cm cubes

A pinch of sugar or artificial sweetener
A pinch of salt to season

70 ml	Lime juice

Coriander leaves and red chillies slices for garnish

PREPARATION

Cut the two pineapples in half lengthways and scoop out the flesh to create 4 serving bowls. Cover with a moist kitchen cloth and keep refrigerated.

Place the prepared fruit, yam, garlic, shallots and shrimp in a mixing bowl, and season with sugar or artificial sweetener, salt and lime juice. Mix gently but well, and marinate for 5 minutes. Stir once more and adjust the seasoning if necessary.

Arrange the salad in the 4 scooped-out pineapples and garnish with the coriander leaves and red chillies.

VEGETABLE FRIED RICE

Serves 2

½ tbsp	Vegetable oil
15–20 g	White onion, peeled and cut into a small dice
80 g	Fragrant jasmine rice, steamed
15–20 g	Sweet green peas, cooked
10–15 g	Black raisins, rinsed in cold water and well drained

A small pinch each of salt and freshly ground white pepper
Low-sodium light soy sauce to season

20–30 g	Ripe, firm tomatoes, seeded and cut into 1-cm cubes

PREPARATION

Heat the oil in a wok or heavy-based frying pan and sauté the diced onions and cook until all moisture has evaporated and the onions are pale and translucent.

Add the rice, green peas and the black raisins, and stir until all ingredients are hot and fairly dry. Season with a little salt, pepper and a few dashes of the soy sauce.

Stir in the tomato cubes until they are heated through, and serve immediately.

RED CHICKEN CURRY
Gaeng Ped Gai (opposite, left)

Serves 4

20 g	Corn oil
3 tbsp	Spa red curry paste
200 g	Sliced chicken breast, skinned
450 ml	Water
80 g	Eggplants, cut into 2-cm cubes
200 g	Plain unsweetened low-fat yoghurt

A pinch of sugar or artificial sweetener

70–80 ml	Fish sauce (*nam pla*)
10–12	Kaffir lime leaves, finely sliced
40 g	Wax peppers, cored and finely sliced
4	Mild red chillies, sliced
40 g	Fresh green peppercorns
3 tbsp	Cornflour, mixed with 120 ml of water
30	Thai basil leaves

Spa Red Curry Paste

15	Dry large red chillies, cut lengthways, seeds and core removed
14 slices	Greater galangal root, peeled and sliced
80–100 g	Shallots, peeled and sliced
8–10	Garlic cloves, peeled
4 tbsp	Lemongrass, finely sliced
1 tsp	Kaffir lime rind, finely chopped
1 tsp	Dry-roasted shrimp paste

PREPARATION

To prepare the red curry paste, soak the chillies in cold water until tender. Remove from the water and pat dry with paper towels. Now place all ingredients in a stone mortar and pound until very fine and well emulsified.

Heat up the oil in a saucepan, add the curry paste and stir-fry on a medium heat until fragrant and translucent.

Add the sliced chicken, stir for a few seconds until the chicken pieces are well coated with fried curry paste.

Add the water and the eggplants.

Bring to the boil, then simmer gently for 4–5 minutes.

Take care not to overcook the chicken.

Add the yoghurt and mix well.

Season with sugar or artificial sweetener and fish sauce.

Add the kaffir lime leaves, wax peppers, red chillies and green peppercorns. Bring to a gentle boil and add the cornflour little by little. Allow to boil, then immediately remove from heat.

Add the fresh Thai basil leaves just before serving.

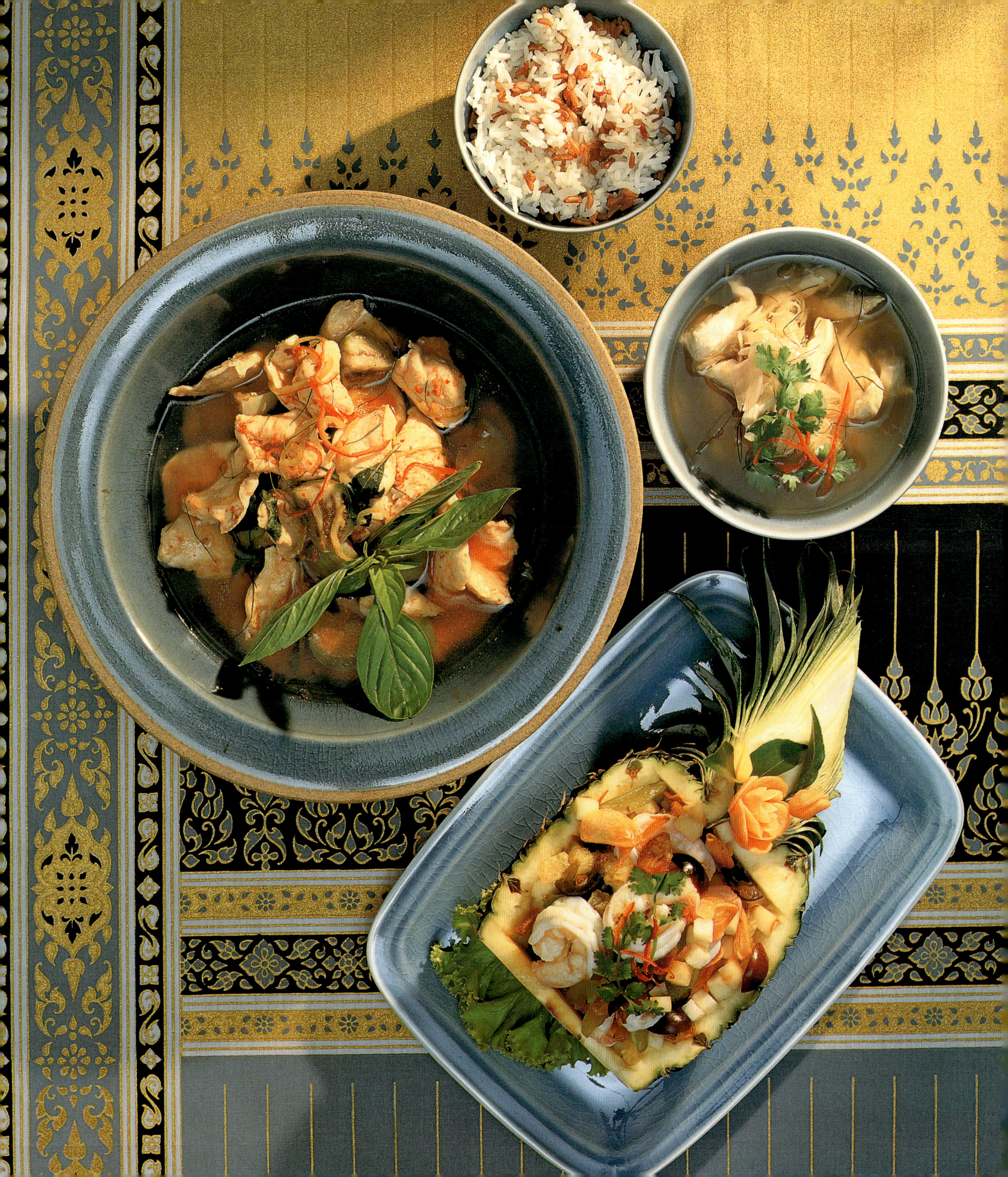

STEAMED FILLET OF WHITE SEABASS WITH LIME AND LEMONGRASS

Serves 1

60–80 g	White seabass fillet, with skin and bones removed
2	Garlic cloves, peeled and finely sliced
2–3	Bird's eye chillies (*prik kee noo*), crushed
1 tbsp	Greater galangal, peeled and finely sliced
1 tbsp	Lemongrass, finely sliced
1 tbsp	Fish sauce (*nam pla*)
1 tbsp	Freshly squeezed lime juice
2 tbsp	Water
2–3	Kaffir lime leaves, torn into small pieces
3 tbsp	Chinese celery, cut into 4-cm pieces

PREPARATION

Arrange the fillet of seabass on a serving plate. Sprinkle the garlic, chillies, galangal and lemongrass evenly over.
Combine the fish sauce, lime juice and water, and pour over the fish, then cover the serving plate tightly with kitchen film.
Place the fish in a pre-heated steamer and cook over a high heat for 6–7 minutes. (The fish should be slightly undercooked when removed from the steamer.)
When the fish is ready, remove the plastic film, sprinkle with the Chinese celery and serve with a small helping of steamed rice.

CLEAR CHICKEN SOUP
Tom Gai Prung (Pg 117, right)

Serves 4

600 ml	Water
10 g	Lemongrass, finely sliced
10 g	Kaffir lime leaves, finely sliced
10 g	Greater galangal, finely sliced
12 g	Ginger, sliced in julienne
90 g	Shallots, sliced
120 g	Sliced chicken breast, skinned
3 tbsp	Fish sauce (*nam pla*)
3 tbsp	Lime juice

Red chillies, cored and finely sliced for garnish
Kaffir lime leaves, finely sliced for garnish

PREPARATION

Bring the water to the boil in a soup pot. As soon as it boils, add the lemongrass, kaffir lime leaves, greater galangal, ginger, shallots and chicken. Allow to simmer for 3–4 minutes. Season with fish sauce and lime juice. Return to the boil, then serve at once. Garnish the soup with the sliced red chillies and kaffir lime leaves.

Chef's note: This soup must be served immediately or it will turn bitter from the lime juice and kaffir lime leaves.

RIVER PRAWN AND STRAW MUSHROOM SOUP

Serves 1

300 ml	Water
1 pc	Greater galangal (approx. 2–3-cm), finely sliced
2–3	Kaffir lime leaves, shredded
½	Lemongrass stalk, finely sliced
15–20 g	Straw mushrooms, cleaned and cut into quarters
80–100 g	Blue river prawns, peeled and de-veined
1–1½ tbsp	Freshly squeezed lime juice
2–3	Bird's eye chillies (*prik kee noo*), crushed
1–1½ tbsp	Fish sauce (*nam pla*)

A few fresh coriander leaves
A few strips of large red chilli, cored and seeded

PREPARATION

Bring the water to the boil, add the galangal, kaffir lime leaves and lemongrass, and simmer for 7–10 minutes to infuse.
Add the mushrooms, increase the heat a little and cook gently for 2 minutes, then add the prawns, and simmer, without stirring, for 2–3 more minutes. Finally, add the lime juice and crushed chillies, and season with fish sauce.
Transfer to a pre-warmed serving bowl and garnish with the coriander leaves and chilli slices. Serve very hot with a small helping of steamed fragrant jasmine rice.

WINGED BEAN SALAD WITH PRAWNS

Serves 1

90–100 g	Young winged beans, finely sliced
¼ tbsp	Roasted chilli jam
1–1½ tbsp	Freshly squeezed lime juice
1 tbsp	Low-sodium light soy sauce
15 g	Shallots, peeled and sliced
20–25 g	Poached prawns, peeled, de-veined and cut in half lengthwise

A few fresh coriander leaves for garnish
A few strips of large red chilli, cored and seeded for garnish

PREPARATION

Cook the sliced winged beans in boiling water until tender but still crunchy, then strain, rinse under cold running water and pat dry with a clean kitchen cloth.
Combine the chilli jam, lime juice and soy sauce in a medium-sized bowl, then add the sliced shallots, prawns and winged beans and mix gently, just until all ingredients are coated with the sauce.
Adjust the seasoning if necessary, then transfer to a serving plate and garnish with the coriander leaves and chilli strips.

THE ORIENTAL SPA DRINKS

PAPAYA-POMELO DRINK

Makes 600 ml

250 g	Ripe papaya, peeled, seeded and cut into 2-cm cubes
250 g	Pomelo segments, peeled, pith and seeds removed
100 ml	Mineral water
1 tsp	Freshly squeezed lime juice

PREPARATION
Put papaya into the jug of a blender, liquidise the pomelo with a juicer, then add the resulting juice, mineral water and lime juice to the papaya in the jug. Blend mixture until smooth and serve in chilled glasses.

MELON AND WATERMELON JUICE

Makes 600 ml

150 g	Melon (honeydew or canteloupe), peeled and seeded
450 g	Watermelon, peeled and seeds removed

PREPARATION
Process both melons in a blender until smooth. If the resulting juice is too thick, just dilute with some mineral water. Serve in chilled glasses.

TOMATO, CELERY AND PARSLEY JUICE

Makes 400 ml

450 g	Ripe tomatoes, cut into quarters
50 g	Celery stalks, with the green leaves
30 g	Fresh parsley with the stems
A pinch of salt	

PREPARATION
Wash the vegetables, pat them as dry as possible with kitchen tissue. Feed the vegetables through a juicer. Season juice with a pinch of salt and stir well. Serve in chilled glasses.

MANGO AND TANGERINE JUICE

Makes 550 ml

300 g	Ripe mango, peeled and cut into 2-cm cubes
1 litre	Freshly squeezed tangerine juice
1.5 litres	Sparkling mineral water

PREPARATION
Process all ingredients in a blender until smooth and serve in chilled glasses.

LOW-FAT YOGHURT, CUCUMBER AND DILL DRINK

Makes 500 ml

150 g	Cucumbers, peeled, cored and cubed
10 g	Dill with the stems, washed and patted dry
350 g	Unsweetened yoghurt (see recipe below)
A pinch of salt	

PREPARATION
Feed the cucumbers and dill through a juicer. Transfer resulting juice, the yoghurt and salt to a blender and process briefly. Pour into chilled glasses to serve.

CARROT AND JICAMA JUICE

Makes 450 ml

300 g	Carrots, peeled and cut into quarters lengthwise
250 g	Jicama, peeled and cut in wedges
A small pinch of ground cinnamon	

PREPARATION
Feed the carrot and jicama through a juicer, then pour the resulting juice into chilled glasses and sprinkle with ground cinnamon to serve.

HOME-MADE UNSWEETENED YOGHURT

Makes 2.1 litres

2 litres	High-quality full fat, pasteurised milk
80-100 g	Plain unsweetened yoghurt (to ferment)

PREPARATION
Pour the milk into a stainless steel cooking pot and bring to a light boil. When it starts to boil, reduce heat and simmer for 2–3 minutes. Remove and cool to 36–37°C. Whisk in the yoghurt, then strain mixture through a fine-mesh sieve. Transfer to warm (36–37°C) clay pots or glasses, place these on a tray and wrap well with a clean towel. Store in room temperature for 6–8 hours to set. Do not move or shake the tray or the yogurt will not set. When set, store in the refrigerator. It will keep well for 4–5 days.

Chef's note: Pay close attention to hygiene and sanitation when preparing home-made yoghurt.

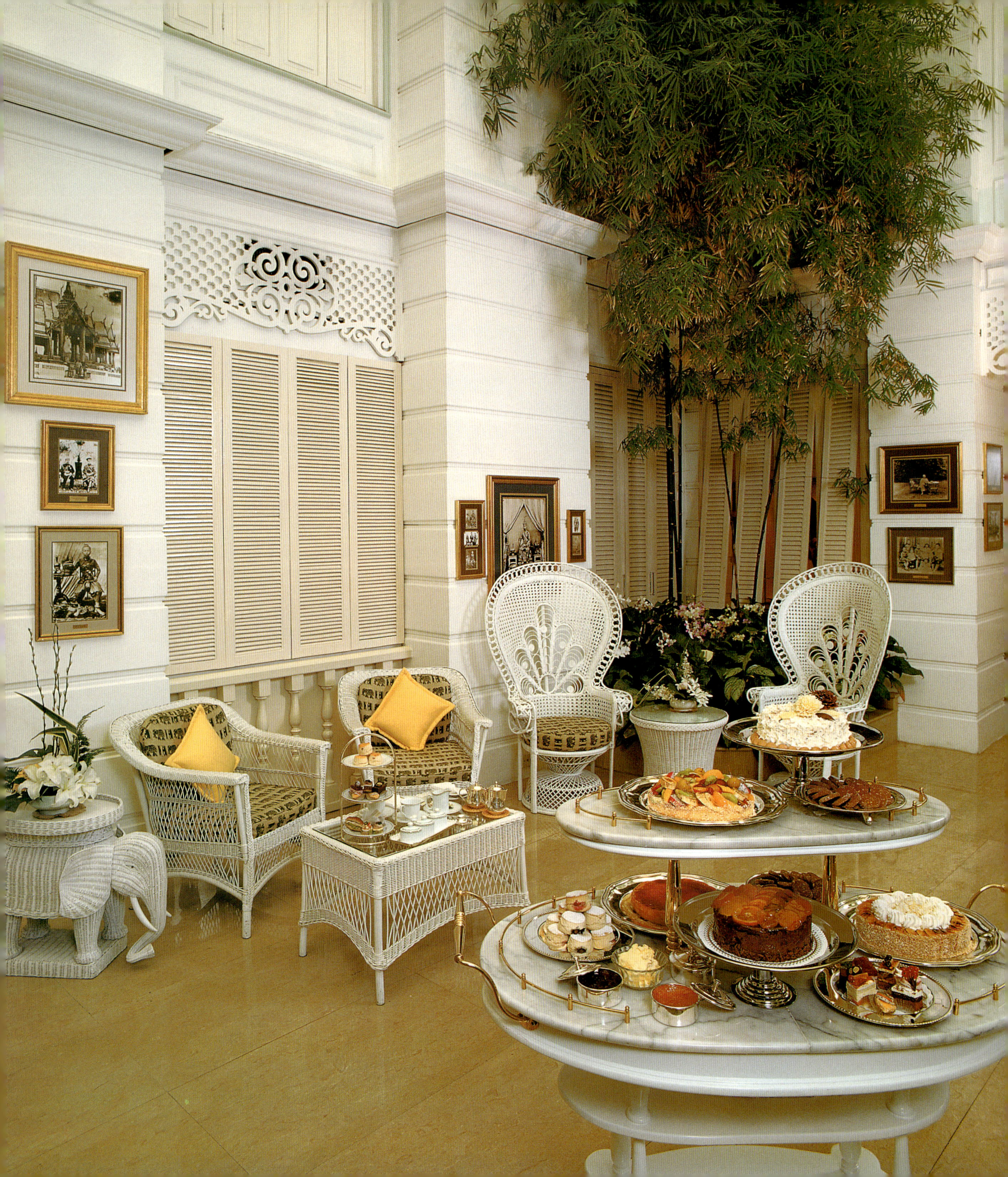

MORE TASTES OF THE ORIENTAL

For a potent sense of nostalgia, few Bangkok experiences can rival that of tea in the Authors' Lounge, with its cool green-and-white décor, feathery stands of bamboo, old sepia photographs of past Thai royalty, and the graceful double stairway leading up to some of the hotel's most sumptuous suites, named after famous writers who stayed in them. The menu offers no fewer than fifteen varieties of tea, from Earl Grey and Lapsong Souchong to ginseng and lemongrass, as well as home-made scones with Devonshire clotted cream, tea sandwiches, and a tempting assortment of pastries, cakes and cookies. Lingering over such a repast, in such an atmosphere, the enchantment of bygone days is palpable.

A different sort of experience awaits in the Bamboo Bar. Ever since it opened in the immediate post-war years, this has been a popular gathering place for both guests and locals. The lethal 'Andersen's Special' invented by The Oriental's very first bartender is happily no longer being offered, but an amazing variety of other concoctions are, bearing names like Bamboo Sunset, Bird of Paradise, and Cool Banana. All the more familiar drinks, alcoholic and otherwise, are there as well, and a jazz singer enlivens the intimate room at night.

The Oriental opened its first bakery in 1887 and soon established a reputation for turning out the best breads and pastries in Bangkok. The tradition continues today. Bakery products as well as a large selection of home-made pastas, jams, pickles, herbal teas, chocolates and delicatessen items are available not only at the hotel but through The Oriental Shops in three different outside locations. A Salon de l'Oriental on the ground floor of the upmarket Emporium Shopping Centre also offers an extensive menu of Oriental-style cooking, from breakfast pastries to traditional high tea.

From the Authors' Lounge and Bamboo Bar, to the Bakery and Salon de l'Oriental, The Oriental Hotel hosts a wide range of outlets with ambrosial treats to pamper the tastebuds

AUTHORS' LOUNGE

AUTHORS' LOUNGE CHOCOLATE CAKE (opposite)

Serves 10

Chocolate Cake

40 g	Butter, unsalted
120 g	Marzipan
4	Egg yolks
100 g	Dark chocolate, melted
120 g	Egg whites
100 g	Sugar
60 g	Cake flour
65 g	Almonds flakes
Grated rind of 1 lemon	
1 tsp	Baking powder
1 tsp	Vegetable oil
1 tbsp	Amaretto liqueur

Buttercream

250 g	Butter
250 g	Icing sugar
1 tbsp	Evaporated milk
100 g	White chocolate
50 g	Dark chocolate, chopped coarsely
50 g	Roasted flaked almonds

PREPARATION

Chocolate Cake
Butter and flour a 20-cm cake tin.
Place the butter and marzipan into the bowl of a mixer and beat for 5 minutes at medium speed, until light and fluffy.
Add the egg yolks, one at a time, mixing well after each addition.
Slowly add the melted chocolate and mix in well.
Whisk the egg whites until stiff, then gradually add the sugar, 1 tbsp at a time, and continue whisking until the mixture reaches a meringue-like consistency.
Add the flour, almonds, grated lemon rind and baking powder to the butter mixture. Then fold in the meringue. When all the ingredients are well mixed, fold in the oil and Amaretto liqueur.
Carefully spoon the mixture into the cake tin and cook for approximately 35 minutes in a pre-heated oven at 180°C until firm to the touch.
Remove from oven and turn out onto a cooling rack.
Leave to cool and prepare the buttercream.

Buttercream
Place the butter and icing sugar into a bowl and place in a mixer. Blend together for 5 minutes on high speed until light and fluffy. Then add the evaporated milk and mix in.
Add the melted white chocolate, mix, then remove from the mixer. Finally add the chopped dark chocolate.
Cut the cooked chocolate cake in half horizontally through the centre. Spread the bottom layer with half of the butter cream and cover with the top of the cake.
Add the flaked almonds to the rest of the butter cream and coat the top and sides of the cake with it. Gently dust with cocoa powder. Place on a plate and serve.

Chef's note: If you would like the cake to have a little more punch, sprinkle both layers of cake with Amaretto liqueur.

ICED BANANA PARFAIT WITH COCONUT CRUST

Serves 8–10

Coconut Crust

150 g	Butter
200 g	Digestive biscuits
100 g	Coconut powder (dessicated coconut)

Banana Parfait

Juice of 1 lemon	
375 g	Ripened banana flesh
100 ml	Banana liqueur
2	Egg whites
80 g	Sugar
150 ml	Whipped cream

Whipped cream and milk chocolate shavings for decoration

PREPARATION

Coconut Crust
Lightly brush a 20-cm cake tin with removable base with butter. Line the base and sides with non-stick baking paper.
Place the digestive biscuits into a plastic bag and crush with a rolling-pin until they have the texture of fine breadcrumbs. Place into a bowl and add the coconut powder. Melt the butter in a saucepan and stir into the biscuits, mixing well.
Place the mixture in the cake tin and press firmly onto the base using the back of a spoon. Set aside in a cool place.

Banana Parfait
Place the lemon juice and banana into a bowl and work the bananas into a pulp with a fork. Add the banana liqueur.
Whisk the egg whites to soft peaks and add the sugar gradually, 1 tbsp at a time, until a stiff meringue is achieved.
Gently fold the whipped cream into the banana mixture, then fold in the meringue.
Place the mixture in the cake tin on top of the biscuit crust and smooth flat with a spatula. Freeze overnight.

PRESENTATION
To serve, remove from the tin. Peel the paper off the sides and base, and place on a serving plate. Decorate with whipped cream and chocolate shavings.

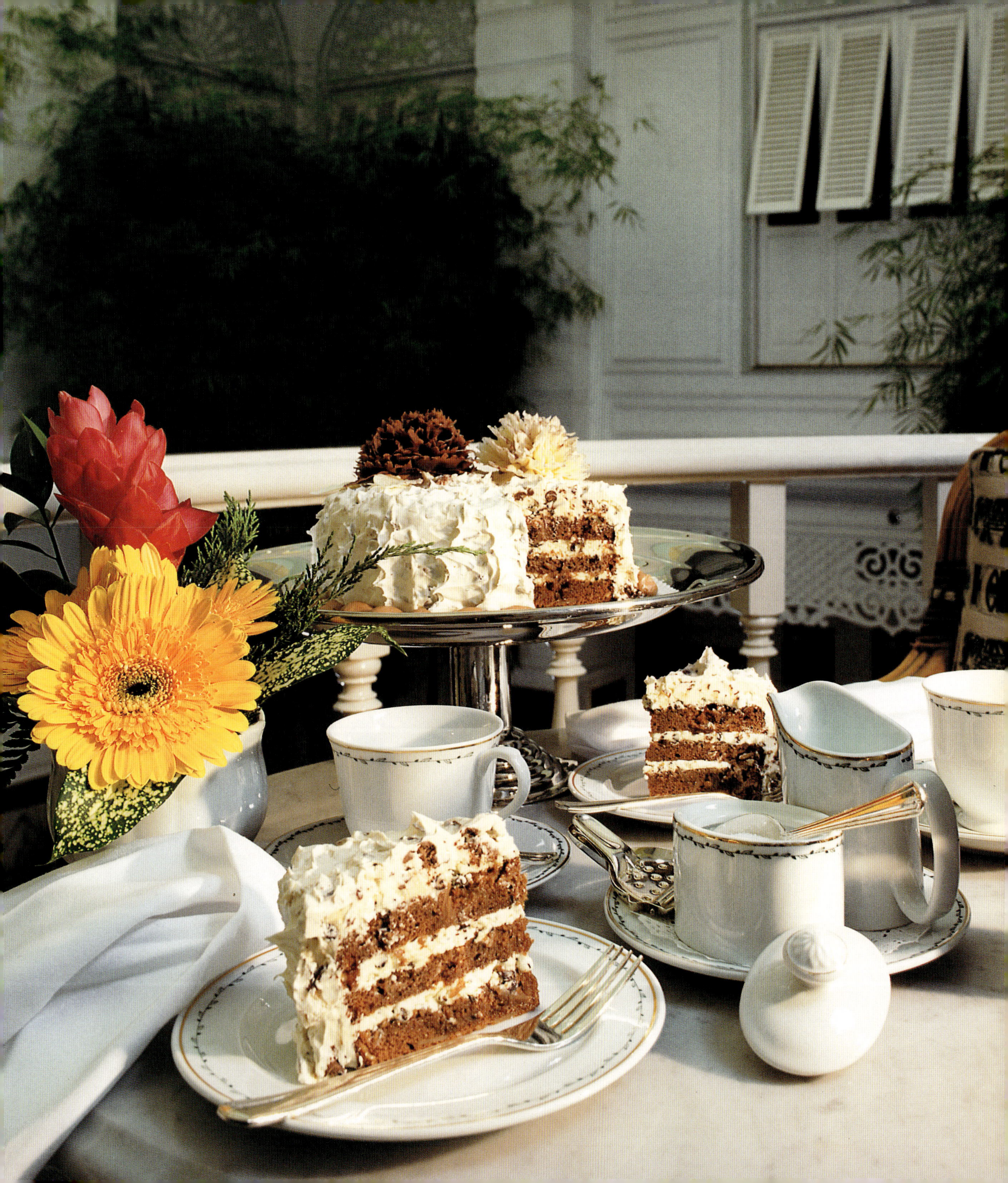

AUTHORS' LOUNGE

FRESH FRUIT TART (above)

Serves 10

300 g	Sweet pastry

Filling

200 g	Butter (at room temperature)
500 g	Almond paste
4	Eggs
45 ml	Rum

Topping

800 g	Assorted fresh fruit (strawberries, mango, kiwi fruit, peach, apricots, etc.), peeled and sliced
200 ml	Vanilla cream
50 g	Apricot jam to glaze

PREPARATION

Place a tart ring, measuring 23 cm in diameter and 2.5 cm in depth, on a baking tray, lined with baking paper.

Roll out the sweet pastry evenly until it becomes a circle measuring about 30 cm in diameter.

Line the tart ring with the pastry, pressing it into the base of the ring neatly and evenly.

Prick the base of the pastry with a fork and trim off the edges. Set aside in a cool place.

Place the butter in a mixing bowl, and process it with a mixer set on medium speed.

Gradually add the almond paste in small pieces, allowing it to mix well after each addition.

After all the almond has been added, repeat the procedure with the eggs. Finally, add the rum.

Transfer the mixture into the lined tart ring and bake in a pre-heat oven at 180°C for 45 minutes until the mixture is golden brown and firm when touched.

Remove and place on a cooling rack.

When cool, spread the tart with a little vanilla cream and garnish with the fruit, arranging them neatly on the tart.

Glaze with warmed apricot jam and place the tart on a serving plate. Refrigerate before serving.

CHOCOLATE AND PISTACHIO NUT COOKIES

Serves 10

600 g	Unsalted butter
375 g	Icing sugar
25 g	Sugar
¼ tsp	Salt
900 g	All-purpose flour
100 g	Cocoa powder
1	Egg
100 g	Almond flakes
100 g	Pistachio nuts
1	Egg white

Extra sugar for rolling

PREPARATION

Place the butter, icing sugar and sugar into a mixer. Process until the ingredients are well mixed but not overworked. Sieve the salt, flour and cocoa powder onto a piece of baking paper.
Add the egg to the butter mixture and mix in. Add the flour mixture and allow just to mix in.
Once done, remove from the mixer.
Knead the mixture gently by hand into a dough. Incorporate the almond flakes and pistachio nuts. Divide into 2 parts and roll into 4-cm diameter sausage shapes. Refrigerate overnight or freeze for a couple of hours.
Remove from the refrigerator or freezer and brush the sausages with the egg white. Roll in the sugar until the sides are coated if the dough is too hard, leave at room temperature for a while so that it softens a little. Place onto a chopping board and slice into disks approx. ½-cm thick. Lay the cookie disks on a baking tray lined with baking paper, leaving space between each cookie.
Bake the cookies in a pre-heated oven at 180°C for 20–25 minutes. Remove and leave to cool on the baking tray.
Store in an air-tight container to preserve freshness.

WHITE SESAME ICE CREAM

Serves 20

400 g	White sesame seeds
1.3 litres	Milk
600 g	Fresh cream
80 g	Powdered milk
16	Egg yolks
350 g	Granulated sugar

PREPARATION

Place the sesame seeds in a large heavy-based frying pan and dry-toast them over medium heat until uniformly golden brown. Remove from the heat and spread on a large tray to cool. When cool, grind them as finely as possible in a kitchen spice grinder. Place 400 ml of the milk in a saucepan with the ground sesame seeds and bring to a very light boil. As soon as it starts to boil, lower the heat, cover with a lid and allow to simmer without boiling for 8–10 minutes.
Pour the remaining milk, cream and milk powder into a heavy-based stainless steel saucepan and bring to the boil. Add the milk-sesame mixture and bring it back to the boil. Let boil for just 10–20 seconds, then cover with a lid and remove from the heat for half an hour to let the flavours intensify.
Place the egg yolks and the sugar in a fairly large stainless steel bowl and whisk until well-incorporated.
Return the milk to simmering point, then slowly pour it onto the egg-sugar mixture, whisking continuously and vigorously until all the milk has been added.
Return the mixture to the same saucepan, warm over a medium heat and stir continuously with a wire whisk until the mixture has thickened and will coat the back of a wooden spoon.
Remove from the heat and continue to whisk slowly but continuously for 6–7 minutes more, then strain into a bowl through a very fine-mesh sieve. Place this bowl over a larger second bowl containing ice water and leave to cool, stirring occasionally.
When the mixture is completely cold, churn it in an ice cream machine according to the manufacturer's instructions.
Remove from the machine when the mixture starts to become stiff and creamy. Store in the freezer until required.

AUTHORS' LOUNGE

CITRUS FRUIT TART (opposite, top left)

Serves 10

335 g	Sweet pastry
25 ml	Lime juice
25 ml	Lemon juice
50 ml	Kumquat juice
40 ml	Grapefruit or pomelo juice
Zest of 1 orange	
335 g	Sugar
10	Saffron strands
6	Eggs
30 g	Melted butter

PREPARATION

Work the sweet pastry a little and roll out into a disk 2-mm thick and 30 cm in diameter.
Grease a 22-cm-diameter tart ring or mould and place it on a sheet of baking paper on a baking tray. Line the ring carefully with the pastry and try to avoid making any cracks. Leave to rest in the refrigerator for 30 minutes. Once rested, line the pastry shell with a disk of baking paper and fill it with beans or rice. Blind-bake the pastry shell in a pre-heated oven at 180°C for about 15 minutes.
Remove the baking paper and beans.
Pour the citrus juices and orange zest into a saucepan with sugar and saffron and stir over medium heat to dissolve the sugar. Whisk the eggs together in a bowl, and when the juice mixture is almost boiling, beat this into the eggs.
Stir in the melted butter and strain the mixture into another bowl, removing the saffron strands. Pour the final mixture into the pastry shell until nearly full.
Carefully place the tart into the oven and cook for 35–40 minutes, until the mixture is set and firm when touched. Remove from the oven and leave to cool.
Before serving, you may want to sprinkle the tart with a little sugar and place under a hot grill to caramelise the sugar.

MANGO CHEESECAKE WITH PISTACHIO SPONGE BASE (opposite, bottom)

Serves 10

5	Eggs
200 g	Icing sugar
100 g	Breadcrumbs
100 g	Ground pistachios
100 g	Ground almonds
5 g	Cake flour
A pinch each of nutmeg and salt	
5 g	Baking powder
100 g	Melted butter
9 g/3	Gelatine powder/leaves
350 g	Cream cheese
125 g	Sugar
125 g	Mango purée, tinned
½ tbsp	Lemon juice
140 g	Whipped cream
100 g	Diced mango, tinned
2	Mangoes, peeled and sliced for garnish

PREPARATION

Lightly grease 2 cake tins, measuring 22 cm in diameter, and dust them with flour.
Pre-heat the oven to 180°C.
Place the eggs and icing sugar into a bowl and whisk together for 5 minutes until the mixture turns a creamy pale colour.
Combine the breadcrumbs, pistachio nuts, almonds, flour, salt, nutmeg and baking powder in a bowl and mix well. Gently fold the dry mixture into the egg mixture with a spatula. Add the melted butter and fold in well. Divide the mixture between the two cake tins and smooth flat with a spatula.
Bake for 35–40 minutes, or until the sponge springs back when touched. Remove the tins from the oven, turn the cakes out onto a cooling rack and leave to cool.
Carefully trim off the crust from the top and sides of one of the sponges and place it into a 22-cm stainless steel cake ring on a tray. Freeze the other sponge base for use later.
Soak the gelatine leaves in cold water to soften.
Blend the cream cheese and sugar together in a mixing bowl for about 5 minutes or until well creamed.
Slowly add the mango purée and lemon juice and mix in well. Then gently fold in the whipped cream.
Remove the gelatine from the water and squeeze it dry. Place into a saucepan and melt over a low heat.
Take a little of the cheesecake mixture and mix with the gelatine, then quickly return this to the rest of the cheesecake mixture and mix well. Finally, fold in the diced mango.
Pour the cheesecake mixture into the ring, on top of the pistachio sponge, and spread it out evenly. Leave the cheesecake to set for at least 4 hours or overnight in a refrigerator.
Just before serving, remove the cake ring by running a warm knife around the inside of the ring and lifting it off.
Decorate the top of the cheesecake with freshly sliced mango. Glaze and serve.

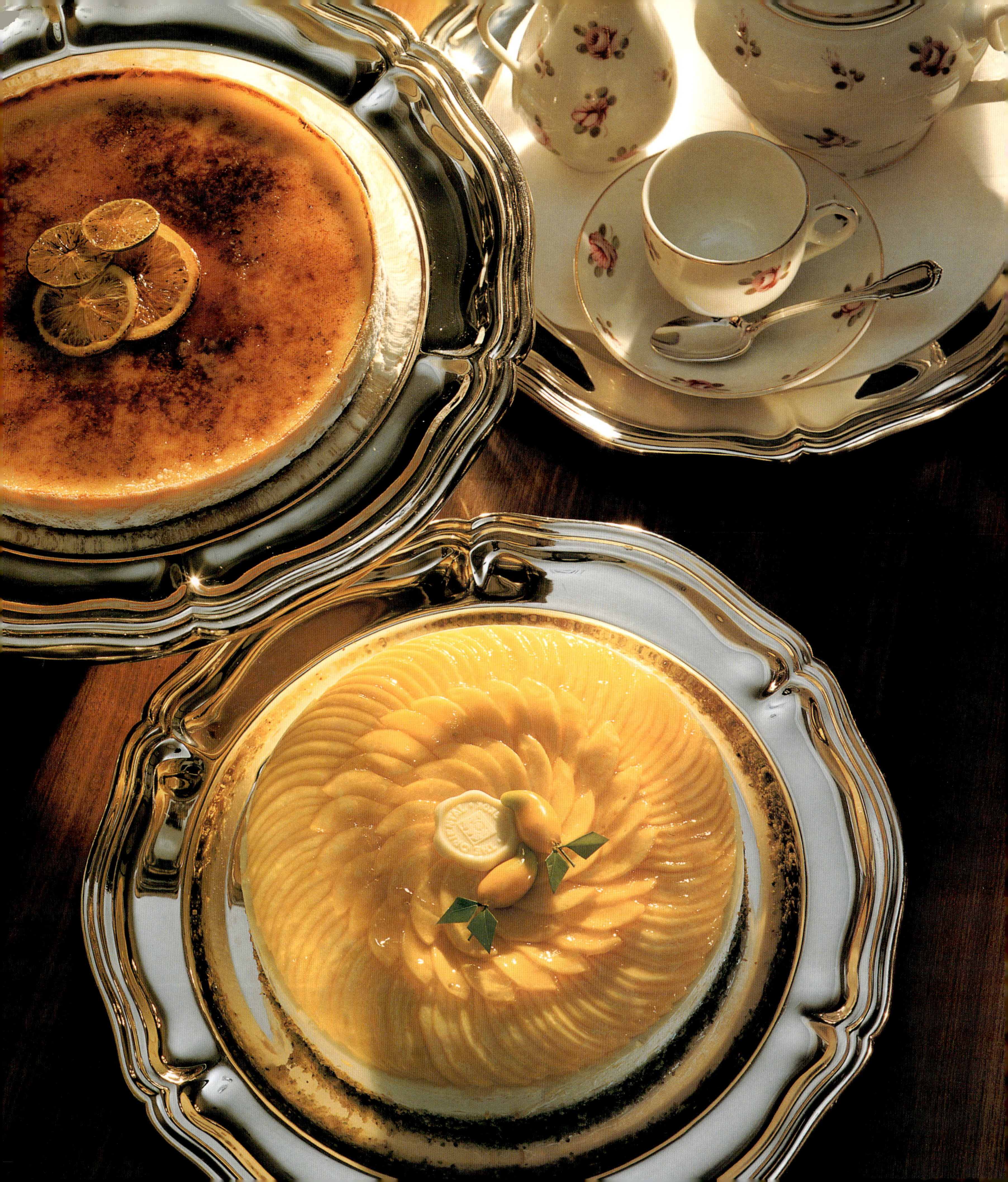

SALON DE L'ORIENTAL

SPICY TUNA AND VEGETABLE SALAD WITH LEMON-OIL DRESSING (opposite, top right)

Serves 4

500 g	Yellowfin tuna fillet
2	Medium-sized potatoes
80 g	Small French beans
80 g	Small green Thai asparagus
80 g	Red onion, sliced
80 g	Tomatoes, peeled and seeded
50 g	Iceberg lettuce
50 g	Tatsoi leaves
50 g	Cos lettuce
50 g	Raddicchio leaves
40 g	Black olives
Salt and pepper to season	

Lemon-Oil Dressing

100 ml	Extra virgin olive oil
50 ml	Lemon juice
30 ml	Water
Salt and cracked black pepper	

PREPARATION
Season the fresh yellowfin tuna with salt and freshly ground black pepper. Heat some olive oil in a frying pan and sear the tuna on each side for about 30 seconds, then set aside. Boil the potatoes in lightly salted water until soft. When the potatoes are still a bit warm, peel and cut into 1-cm-thick slices. Blanch the French beans and the green asparagus until crisp and cool in some ice water, so that they keep their colour.

Lemon-Oil Dressing
Pour the lemon juice into a bowl and stir in the extra virgin olive oil. Add the water and season as required.

PRESENTATION
Mix the beans, asparagus, red onion and sliced tomatoes with two-thirds of the dressing. Season with some salt and crushed black pepper. Toss this with the salad leaves carefully and arrange the mixture in the centre of a serving plate.
Set four potato slices around the salad. Slice the tuna fillet into 1-cm-thick slices and place on top of the potatoes.
Chop the black olives and mix with the remaining lemon-olive oil dressing. Drizzle the dressing around the tuna slices and sprinkle some cracked black pepper on the rim of the plate.

BLACKENED BEEF SANDWICH (opposite, top left)

Serves 1

150 g	Onion, cut into 1-cm-thick rings
Oil for frying	
5 g	Sugar
Salt and pepper to taste	
1	Roast onion sesame baguette, cut in half lengthwise
140 g	Lean beef striploin
4 g	Blackened seasoning
35 g	Iceberg lettuce
60 g	Tomato slices
75 g	Pickled vegetables

PREPARATION
Sauté the onion rings in a frying pan over low heat until golden brown. Add some sugar and let it caramelise, then season with salt and pepper to taste.
Spread some butter on the baguette and grill until crisp.
Coat the striploin with the blackened seasoning and grill to desired doneness

PRESENTATION
Place one half of the baguette on a serving plate and top with the iceberg lettuce and tomato slices. Add the caramelised onion, then cut the striploin into smaller pieces and arrange it on top of the onion. Top the striploin with pickled vegetables and cover with the second slice of baguette. Serve with a crunchy salad or Cajun-spiced potato skins.

GRILLED VEGETABLES AND GUACAMOLE ON SUNFLOWER BREAD (above, bottom right)

Serves 4

40 ml	Lime juice
40 g	Onion, chopped
60 g	Tomatoes, peeled, with seeds removed, chopped
10 g	Red chillies, finely chopped
200 g	Ripe avocados, peeled and with seeds removed
20 g	Coriander, chopped
Salt and black pepper to season	
80 g	Yellow capsicum
80 g	Red capsicum
80 g	Green zucchini
80 g	Red onion
80 g	Fennel
80 g	Baby corn
40 ml	Extra virgin olive oil
15 ml	Tabasco sauce
30 g	Garlic, crushed
10 g	Fresh rosemary
10 g	Fresh basil leaves
8 slices	Sunflower bread
4 tbsp	Butter
60 g	Iceberg lettuce
60 g	Tomato slices

PREPARATION

To prepare the guacamole, combine the lime juice, onion, tomatoes and chillies, add the avocado and crush with a fork into small chunks. Add the coriander leaves and mix well. Season with salt and pepper. If not used immediately, seal with plastic wrap and refrigerate.

Deep-fry the yellow and red capsicum for about 1 minute. Remove and drain until cold. Peel and remove the seeds.

Cut the zucchini, red onion and fennel into $1/2$-cm slices, blanch with the baby corn for 30 seconds, then plunge into cold water to keep them crisp. Combine the extra virgin olive oil with the tabasco sauce, crushed garlic cloves, rosemary and basil leaves. Toss the vegetables in this and marinate for 30 minutes. Remove the vegetables from the marinade and grill them on a hot grill. Season with salt and freshly ground black pepper.

PRESENTATION

Spread the bread slices with some butter and grill them so that they are crisp and have a nice grill pattern. Take one slice and place the iceberg lettuce and the tomato slices on it, then top this with the grilled vegetables. Put 1 tbsp guacamole on top of the vegetables. Cover with a slice of grilled bread.

Serve with a crunchy salad or Cajun spiced potato wedges.

BAMBOO BAR

THE ORIENTAL'S MAI TAI

Serves 1

45 ml	Gold Rum
10 ml	Grand Marnier
60 ml	Orange juice
60 ml	Pineapple juice
30 ml	Lemon juice
15 ml	Grenadine syrup

A dash of egg white

PREPARATION
Shake all ingredients with ice. Garnish with a slice of lemon, pineapple, a cherry and an orchid.

Chef's Note: Bar Supervisor K. Sompong Pooonsri created this cocktail for the hotel's 110th anniversary celebrations.

CASABLANCA

Serves 1

45 ml	Light rum
90 ml	Pineapple juice
60 ml	Coconut cream
10 ml	Grenadine syrup

A dash of egg white

PREPARATION
Blend all ingredients, pour into a glass and garnish with an orange slice, a cherry and an orchid.

BIRD OF PARADISE

Serves 1

25 ml	Vodka
25 ml	Blue Curacao
90 ml	Lychee juice
25 ml	Lemon juice
10 ml	Sugar syrup

PREPARATION
Shake all ingredients with ice and garnish with a lemon slice and an orchid.

CHAO PHRAYA DREAM

Serves 1

15 ml	Dry gin
15 ml	Sweet Vermouth
15 ml	Cherry Heering
45 ml	Orange juice
30 ml	Lemon juice
15 ml	Grapefruit juice
15 ml	Grenadine syrup
15 ml	Sugar syrup

A dash of egg white

PREPARATION
Shake all ingredients with ice. Pour into a pilsner glass. Garnish with a slice of lemon, pineapple, a cherry and an orchid.

Chef's note: Chao Phraya Dream, created by K. Sompong, was the winning drink of Thailand's Bartender Contest over ten years ago.

COCONUT COOLER

Serves 1

30 ml	Light rum
15 ml	Cointreau
30 ml	Lemon juice
90 ml	Pineapple juice
10 ml	Sugar syrup
3 drops	Coconut flavour

A dash of egg white

PREPARATION

Shake all ingredients with ice.
Pour into a pilsner glass.
Garnish with a slice of lemon, pineapple, a cherry and an orchid.

THE ORIENTAL HOTEL

Serves 1

30 ml	Martini Red
25 ml	Bacardi rum
10 ml	Benedictine
10 ml	Lemon juice
10 ml	Syrup

PREPARATION

Stir all ingredients with ice. Garnish with a cherry.

CARIBBEAN SUNSET

Serves 1

30 ml	Gin
15 ml	Crème de banane
15 ml	Blue Caraçao
30 ml	Cream

A dash of lemon juice
A dash of grenadine

PREPARATION

Shake all ingredients but the grenadine. Strain into a tulip glass. Add the grenadine. Garnish with a slice of fresh lemon and an orchid.

ORIENTAL SLING

Serves 1

30 ml	Mekong whisky
15 ml	Crème de menthe
10 ml	Kahlua
30 ml	Lemon juice
45 ml	Orange juice
45 ml	Pineapple juice
15 ml	Sugar syrup

A dash of egg white

PREPARATION

Shake all ingredients with ice.
Pour into a pilsner glass.
Garnish with a slice of lemon, pineapple, a cherry and an orchid.

ORIENTAL SOUR

Serves 1

30 ml	Amaretto liqeuer
30 ml	Fresh lemon juice
10 ml	Sugar syrup
1–2 dashes	Angostura Bitter

A slice of orange
8 mint leaves

PREPARATION

Stir all ingredients with crushed ice, and serve in an old-fashioned glass.

SUNRISE

Serves 1

15 ml	Tequila
10 ml	Galliano
10 ml	Crème de banane
10 ml	Cream
10 ml	Grenadine syrup

PREPARATION

Shake all ingredients with ice.
Strain into a cocktail glass.

LONDON CALLING

Serves 1

15 ml	Vodka
15 ml	Tequila
15 ml	Brandy
30 ml	Lemon juice
15 ml	Grenadine syrup

A splash of sparkling wine

PREPARATION

Shake all ingredients except the sparkling wine and strain into an ice-filled highball glass, then add a splash of sparkling wine to serve.

JAMS AND CHUTNEYS

BLACKCURRANT AND RUM CURD

Makes 2 kg

150 g	Blackcurrants
260 ml	Dark rum
700 g	Granulated sugar
350 g	Unsalted butter, cut into small cubes
60 ml	Lemon juice
30 g	Lemon rind, thinly peeled off in large pieces
8	Eggs
2	Egg yolks

PREPARATION

Soak the blackcurrants in warm water for 10 minutes, strain and dry with a kitchen towel. They must be free of water.
Soak the currants in 60 ml of the dark rum and leave to macerate for 2 hours. The rum should be completely absorbed.
Place all other ingredients in a stainless steel bowl and place this on top of a saucepan of simmering water (this water should not boil). Cook, stirring continuously but gently with a wooden spoon, until the butter has melted and the sugar has dissolved. Remove and discard the lemon rind. Continue to cook, stirring continuously and ensuring that the curd does not stick to the sides of the bowl.
It will take about 30–40 minutes until the curd is thick and creamy. This should have the consistency of good honey. Remove the bowl from the heat and continue stirring until the curd is just warm, then fold in the soaked currants. Pour into sterilised glass jars, filling up to the rim, and seal.
The curd will keep for about 2 months if refrigerated.

EXOTIC SPARKLING LIME AND GINGER CURD

Makes 1.7 kg

700 g	Sugar, granulated
370 g	Butter, unsalted, cut in small cubes
220 g	Sparkling lime juice
50–60 g	Sparkling lime rind, peeled off thinly and in large pieces
70–80 g	Ginger, peeled and cut in very fine petals
7	Eggs
3	Egg yolks
20 ml	Gin

PREPARATION

Place all ingredients in a 30–35-cm stainless steel mixing bowl and stir with a wire whisk until the sugar is dissolved.
Place the bowl on top of a saucepan with simmering water (this water should not boil). Start cooking the curd, stirring continuously but gently with a wooden spoon until the butter has melted and the curd is emulsified.
Continue cooking for about 30–40 minutes, making sure that the curd does not stick to the sides of the bowl.
When you see that the curd is thick and creamy, remove the bowl from the heat and pass it through a fine-mesh stainless steel sieve into a second bowl to cool. Continue stirring slowly until the curd is lukewarm.
Pour into sterilised glass jars up to the rim and seal.
The curd will keep for about 2 months if refrigerated.

APPLE AND PASSIONFRUIT PRESERVE

Makes 3.7 kg

55 g	Pectin
1.1 kg	Castor sugar
1 kg	Ripe passionfruit, washed
2 kg	Golden Delicious apples, washed
400 ml	Tangerine juice
250 ml	Water

PREPARATION

Mix the pectin with 100 g castor sugar and keep aside.
Cut the passionfruit in half, scoop out all of the flesh and force it through a mesh sieve to obtain the passionfruit juice. You should obtain about 600 ml of juice. Retain 200 g of the passionfruit seed and pulp after straining. Peel and core the apples, and cut into 1-cm cubes. As you do this, place the cut cubes into the passionfruit juice to prevent the apples from oxidising (they will turn brown).
Place all the ingredients except the pectin-sugar mixture into a heavy-based saucepan, bring to the boil, then lower the heat and allow to simmer for 45–50 minutes, stirring occasionally to prevent the preserve from sticking to the bottom of the pan. By now the preserve should be shiny with a nice golden colour. Add the pectin-sugar mixture and stir with a wire whisk until the added pectin-sugar mixture has dissolved. Continue to gently boil the mixture for another 10–12 minutes, stirring frequently. Remove from the heat, give it a few more stirs and then remove any foam from the surface.
Pour into sterilised jam jars and seal. Cool and store refrigerated or in a cool, dark place.

TELEGRAPH CUCUMBER AND ONION RELISH

Makes 2.3 kg

500 ml	Distilled white vinegar
400 ml	Water
20 g	Salt
350 g	White onion, peeled, cut into ½-cm cubes
350 g	Green bell peppers, cored, cut into ½-cm cubes
1	Large green chilli, with seeds removed, chopped
750 g	Telegraph cucumbers, cored, cut into ½-cm cubes
200 g	Brown sugar
¼ tsp	Allspice powder
¼ tsp	Clove powder
20 g	Mustard seeds
10 g	Dill seeds
50 g	English mustard powder
10 g	Turmeric powder
45 g	Cornstarch

PREPARATION

Combine the vinegar, water and salt, bring to the boil and simmer for about 10 minutes.

Add the onion, green bell peppers and chilli and cook for 10–12 minutes, then add the cucumbers and simmer for 5 minutes. Stir in the sugar and boil for 5 minutes. Combine all the spices and cornstarch, mix well, and slowly add cold water, stirring with a wire whisk to obtain a runny paste. Add this paste to the chutney and stir well with a wooden spoon.

Reduce the heat and simmer very gently for about 15 minutes, stirring frequently to prevent the chutney from sticking to the bottom of the pan. Adjust the seasoning with salt if necessary. Remove from the heat, stir a few more times, and skim any foam from the surface. Pour into sterilised pickling jars, seal and leave to cool. Store refrigerated, or in a cool dark place.

SPICY TOMATO-CHILLI CHUTNEY

Makes 2.2 kg

1 kg	Large red chillies
200 ml	Malt vinegar
300 ml	Water
30 g	Salt
120 g	Brown sugar
250 g	White onion, peeled and coarsely chopped
500 g	Tomatoes, peeled, seeded and coarsely chopped
100 g	Tomato paste
25 g	Cornstarch
1 tsp	Allspice powder
1 tsp	Ground coriander seeds

PREPARATION

Grill the chillies over a naked flame until they are charred and the skin blisters. Scrape off the burned and blistered skin as much as possible with a small knife. Then cut the chillies in half lengthways and remove all the seeds and the stem. Chop the chillies and put them aside.

Place the vinegar, water, salt and ½ of the sugar in a heavy-based stainless steel saucepan and bring to the boil. Simmer for 5–7 minutes, then add the onion, tomatoes and tomato paste. Stir with a wooden spoon and continue simmering for 30 minutes, stirring occasionally to prevent the chutney from sticking to the bottom of the pan. Add the remaining sugar and cook for 5 minutes more. Combine the cornstarch, allspice and ground coriander seeds with cold water to obtain a runny paste. Add this paste to the boiling chutney, stir well and continue to cook for another 8–10 minutes. Adjust the seasoning with salt if necessary. Remove from the heat, and skim any foam from the surface with a tablespoon. Pour into sterilised pickling jars, seal and leave to cool.

Store refrigerated or in a cool dark place. Allow to mature for about two weeks before using to concentrate the flavours.

JAMS AND CHUTNEYS

THE ORIENTAL MUSTARD PICKLE

Makes 1.3 kg

250 g	Small pickling cucumbers, cut into 3-cm pieces
250 g	Small cauliflower rosettes
250 g	Young runner beans or snap beans, cut into 3-cm
250 g	Baby carrots, peeled and cut in half lengthways, then into 3-cm lengths
250 g	Capsicums, of various colours, with seeds removed and cut into 2-cm squares
250 g	Very small shallots, peeled
350 g	Coarse sea salt

Pickling Brine

200 ml	Dry white wine
900 ml	White wine vinegar
200 ml	Cider vinegar
400 ml	Water
300 g	Granulated sugar
2 tbsp	Mustard seeds
4–5	Bay leaves
30–40 g	Fresh horseradish, peeled and cut finely into disks
1 tbsp	Dill seeds
100 g	Mustard powder
20 g	Turmeric powder
70 g	Cornflour

PREPARATION

Place all the prepared vegetables and shallots in a bowl, sprinkle with the sea salt and mix well. Leave to rest in a cool place for at least 12 hours. Drain and rinse the vegetables under cool running water for about 10 minutes. Drain again and pat dry in a paper towels.

To prepare the pickling brine, pour the wine, vinegars, water and sugar into a heavy-based saucepan, bring to the boil and allow to simmer for 10 minutes. Remove from the heat, add the mustard seeds, bay leaves, horseradish and dill seeds, cover tightly with a lid and leave to infuse for 30 minutes. Return saucepan to the heat and bring to the boil.

Add the vegetables and boil gently for 4–5 minutes.

Mix together the mustard powder, turmeric powder and cornflour, adding sufficient vinegar to make a thick paste; and stir this mixture into the boiling vegetables. Allow to cook slowly for 5–7 minutes, stirring frequently to prevent the pickles sticking to the bottom of the pan. Adjust seasoning with salt and sugar. Remove from the heat. Pour into clean glass jars, seal, and leave to cool. Keep refrigerated for 12 days before consuming.

SAVOURY CHINESE SNOW PEAR AND ONION CHUTNEY

Makes 2.9 kg

700 ml	Distilled white vinegar
300 ml	Water
1.2 kg	White onions peeled and cut into 1/2-cm cubes
600 g	Chinese snow pears, peeled and cut into 1/2-cm cubes
30 g	Cornflour
20 g	English mustard powder
10 g	Turmeric powder
1/8 tsp	Powdered allspice
1/8 tsp	Powdered green cardamom
500 g	Granulated sugar
Salt to season	

PREPARATION

Place the vinegar and water in a heavy-based saucepan, bring to the boil, then cook very gently for 7–10 minutes. Add the onion cubes and cook until the onions are soft, for 10–12 minutes. Add the pears and continue cooking for about 15–20 minutes or until the pears are soft.

Combine the cornflour, mustard, turmeric, allspice and green cardamom in a bowl and mix well. Slowly add cold water, stirring with a wire whisk to obtain a runny paste. Add this to the boiling pear-onion chutney, stirring well with a wooden spoon. Reduce the heat and simmer for about 15 minutes, stirring frequently to prevent the chutney from sticking to the bottom of the pan. Season with salt if necessary.

Remove from the heat, stir again and skim to remove any foam that may have accumulated on the surface.

Pour into sterilised pickling jars, seal and leave to cool.

Store refrigerated or in a cool, dark place.

PINEAPPLE AND GINGER JAM

Makes 2.6 kg

10 g	Pectin
1.05 kg	Granulated sugar
2 kg	Ripe sweet pineapples, peeled
80 g	Young ginger, peeled and cut into very fine threads

PREPARATION

Mix the pectin with 50 g of granulated sugar.
Cut the pineapple into small cubes (try to collect all the juice). Place the pineapple cubes, the collected juice and ginger threads in a heavy-based saucepan, bring to the boil, then reduce heat and cook slowly for 20–25 minutes. Stir occasionally to prevent the mixture sticking to the bottom of the pan.
Then add the sugar, stir well until dissolved, and continue cooking for another 25–30 minutes.
By now the jam should be shiny and clear. Add the sugar-pectin mixture, stirring well, and continue to cook for a further 10 minutes.
Remove from the heat, stir once more, and skim to remove any foam from the surface.
Pour into sterilised jam jars, seal and leave to cool.
Store refrigerated or in a cool dark place.

EXTRA-BITTER LEMON MARMALADE

Makes 4.75 kg

15 g	Pectin
1.6 kg	Granulated white sugar
2 kg	Ripe un-treated yellow lemons, with no bruises or black spots
1 litre	Orange juice, freshly squeezed
1 kg	Demerara crystal sugar
250 ml	Water

PREPARATION

Mix the pectin with 200 g of granulated sugar.
Wash and scrub the lemons in warm water.
Place them in a heavy-based saucepan and cover with cold water. Bring to the boil, then immediately lower the heat and allow to simmer, covered with a lid, for about 1 hour. Make sure that the water does not boil.
Remove the lemons from the pan and place them in cold water to cool off a little. When the lemons are cool enough to handle, remove them from the water and place them in a colander.
Cut the lemons in half and scoop out all the flesh and pips, and force this pulp through a not-too-fine mesh sieve before putting aside. Cut the lemon cups into quarters, removing any white pith by scraping with a spoon.
Cut the peel into strips about 3-mm thick.
Place these strips in a saucepan filled with enough cold water to submerge the peel. Bring to the boil and leave to simmer for half an hour before straining through a mesh sieve.
Place the pulp, lemon peel, the remaining white sugar and half of the orange juice in a heavy-based saucepan. Bring to the boil, then reduce the heat and simmer for about 30–35 minutes, stirring frequently until the mixture is shiny and caramelised.
Now add the remaining orange juice and the demerara sugar and allow to boil for at least 45 minutes, stirring frequently. By now the marmalade should be shiny and a nice dark brown colour. Add the pectin-sugar mixture, stirring well, and continue to cook and stir for another 10 minutes.
Remove from the heat, stir a few more times, then skim the surface to remove any foam that may have accumulated. Pour into sterilised jars and seal. Leave to cool and store refrigerated or in a cool dark place.

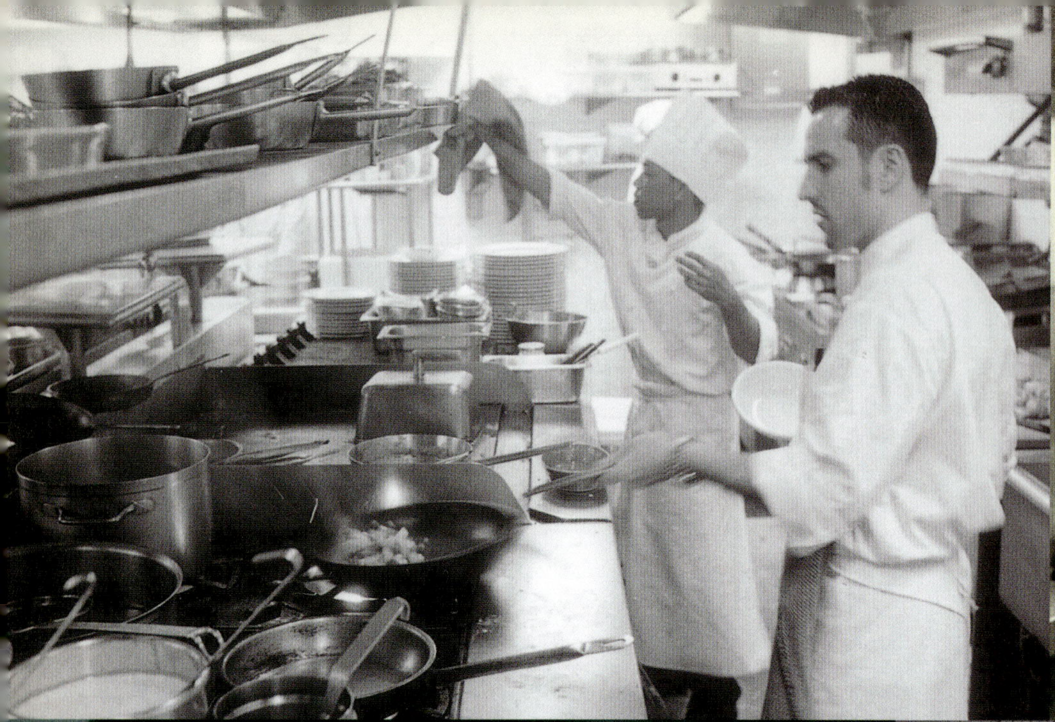
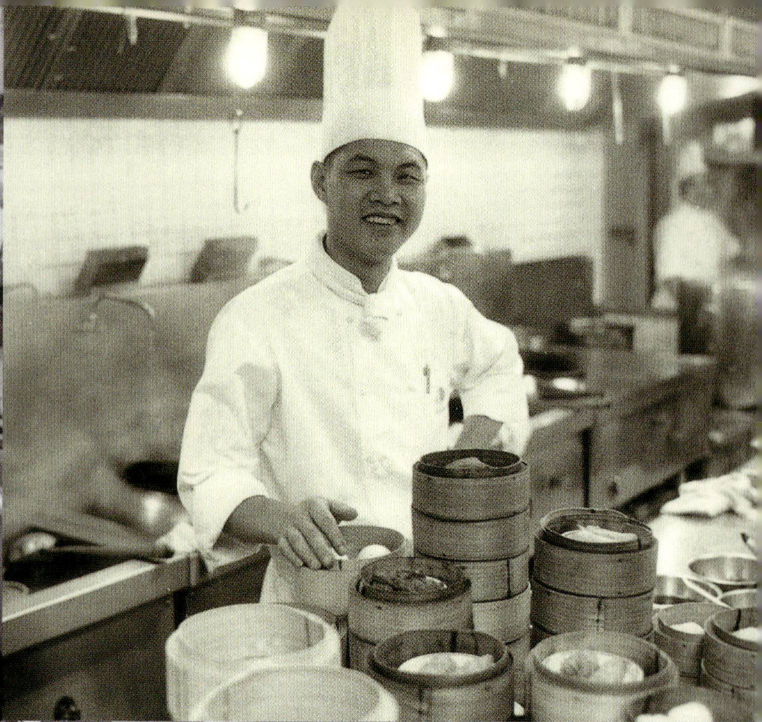
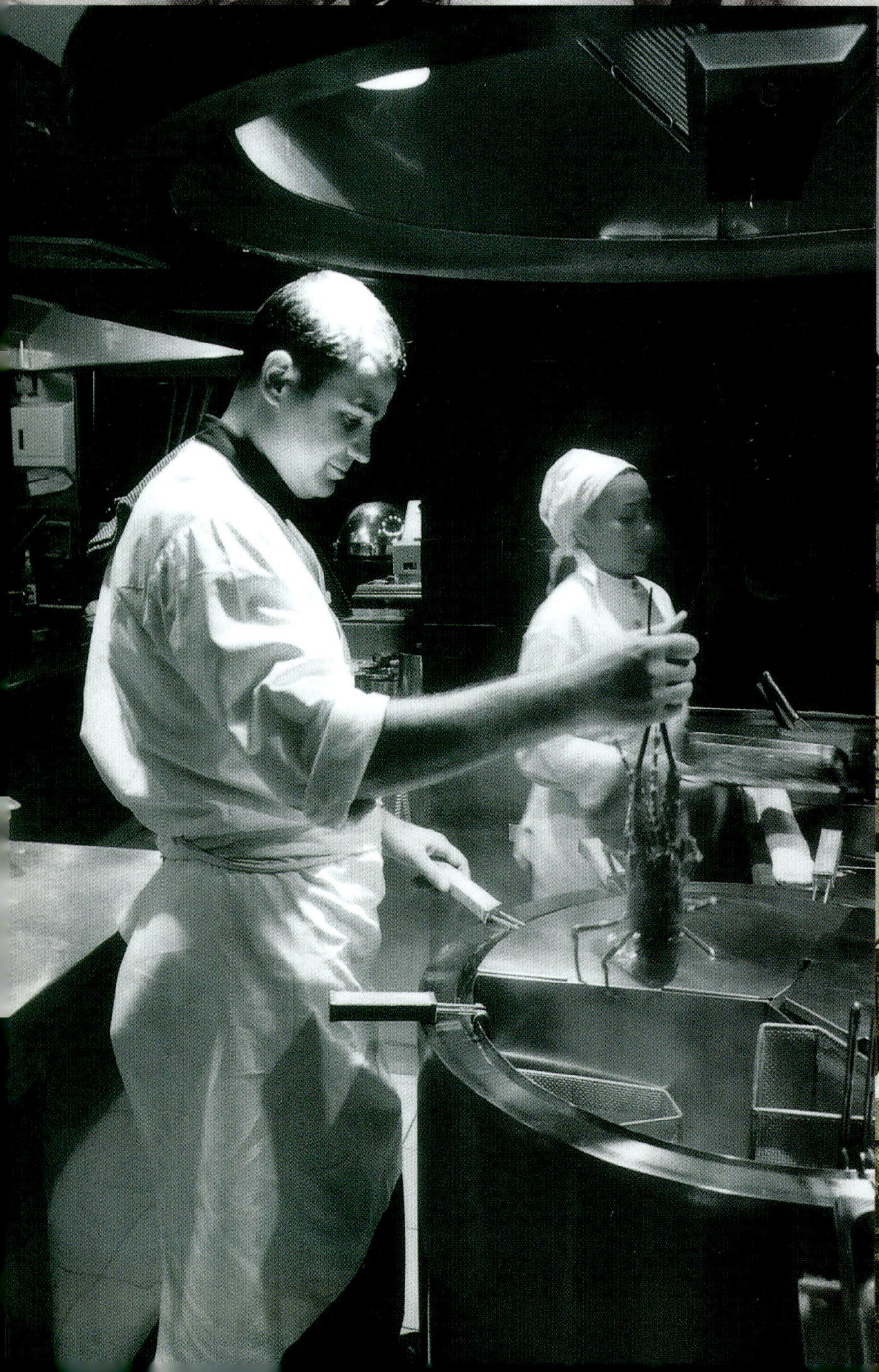
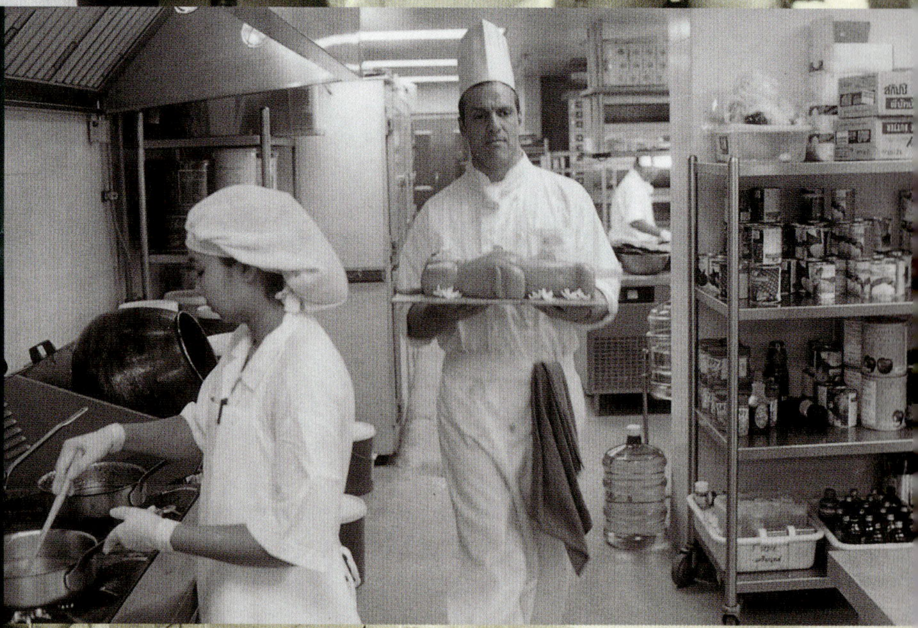
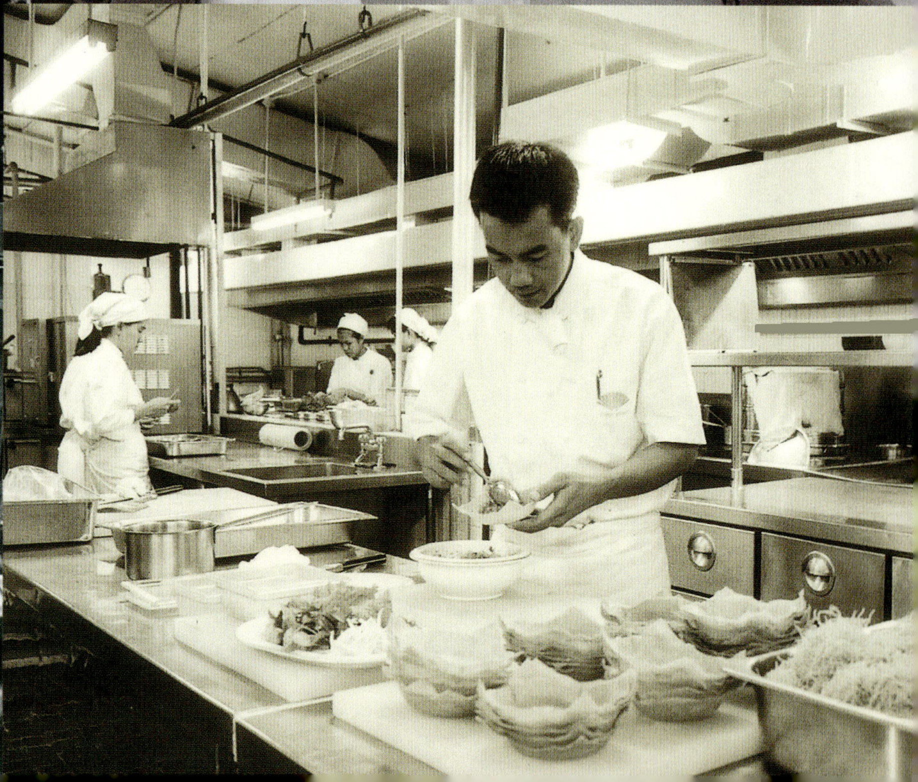

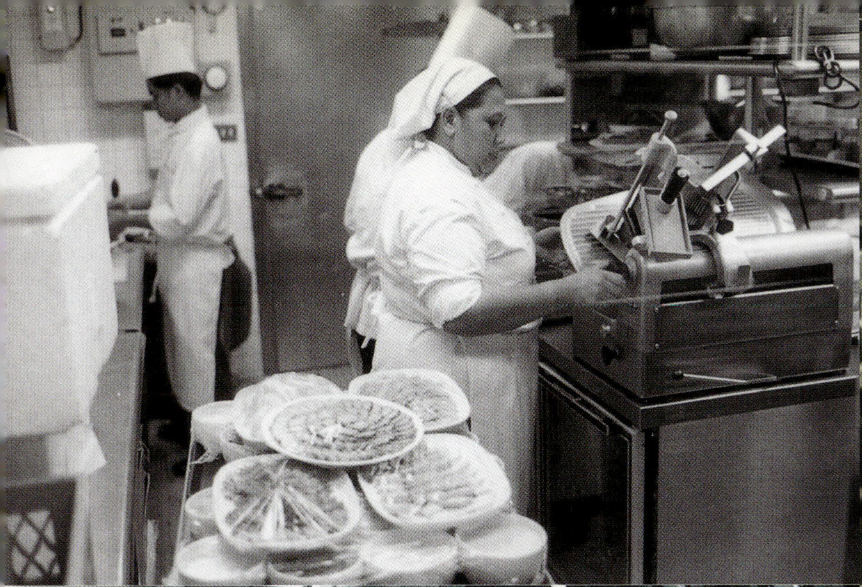
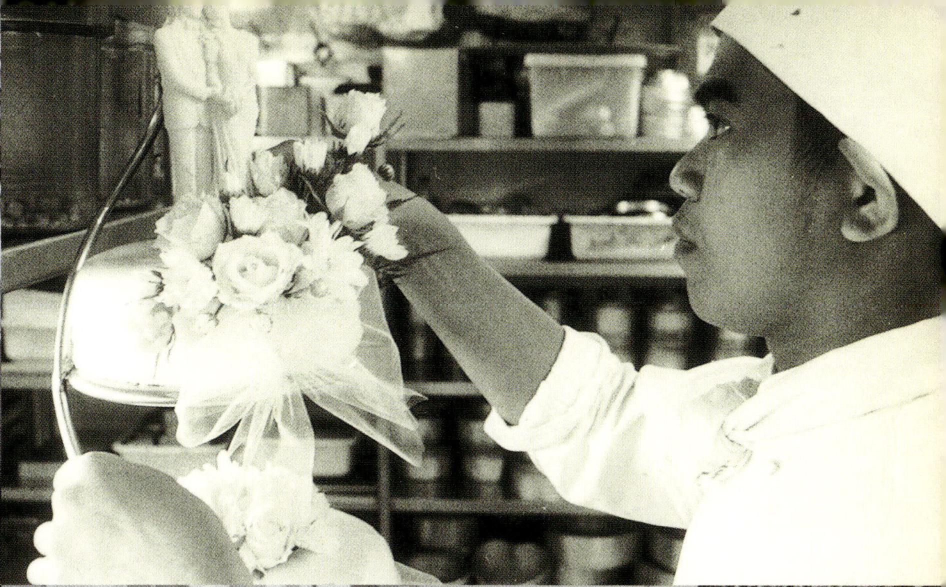
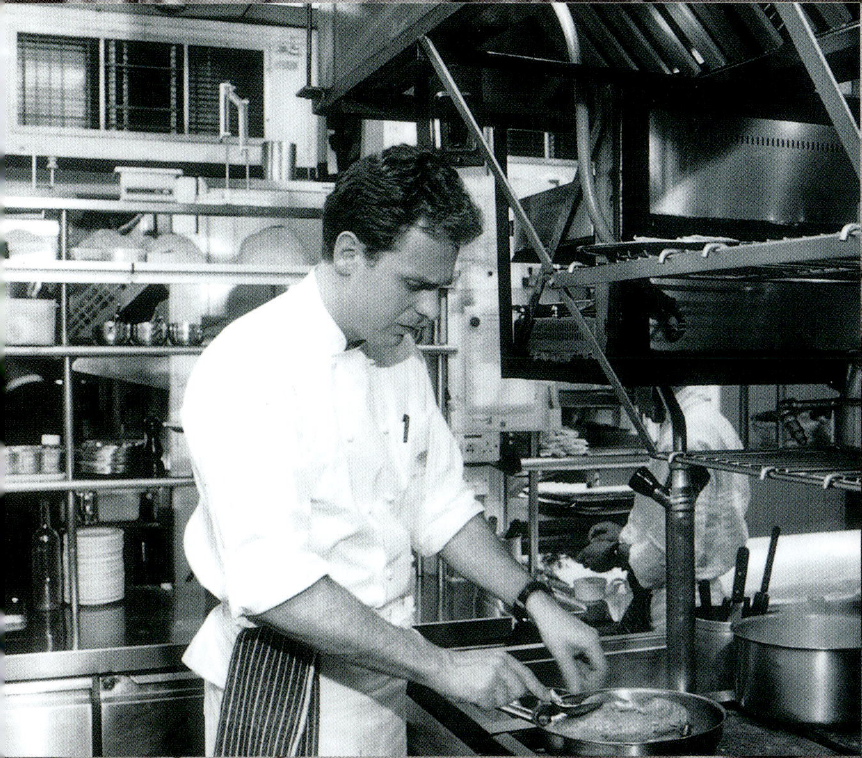
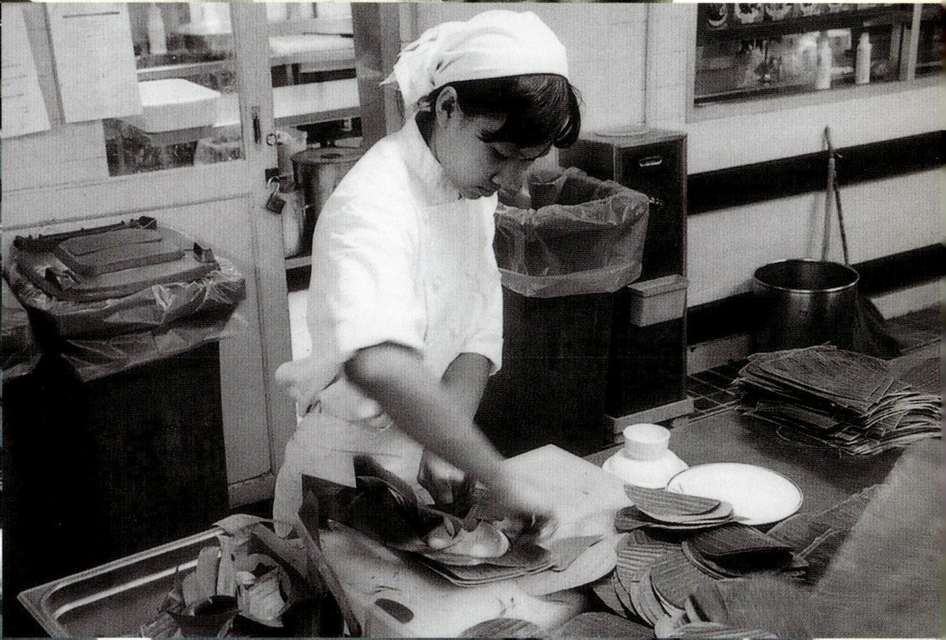
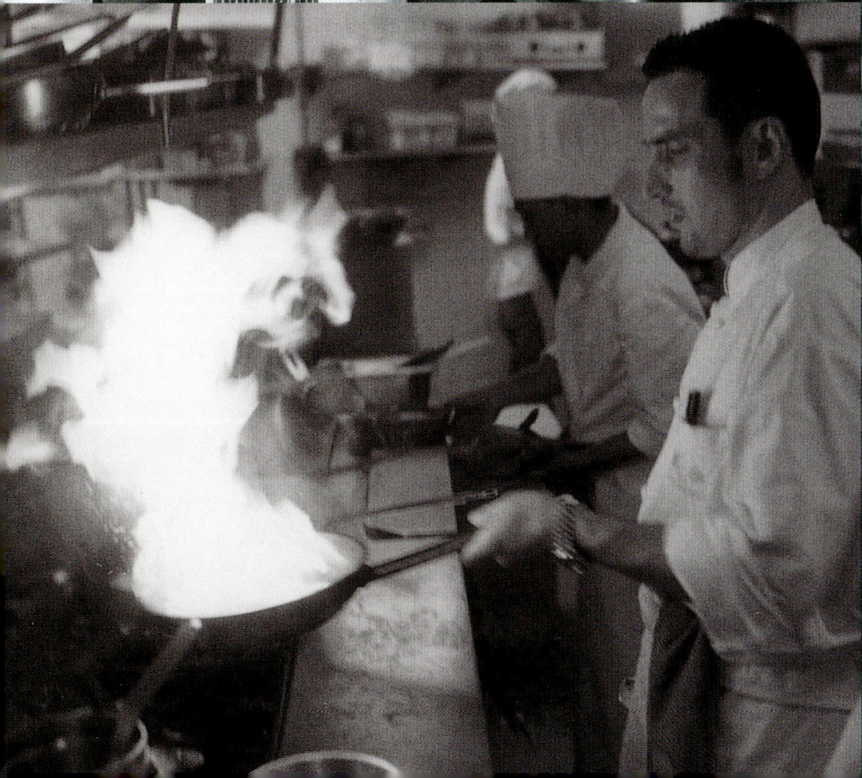
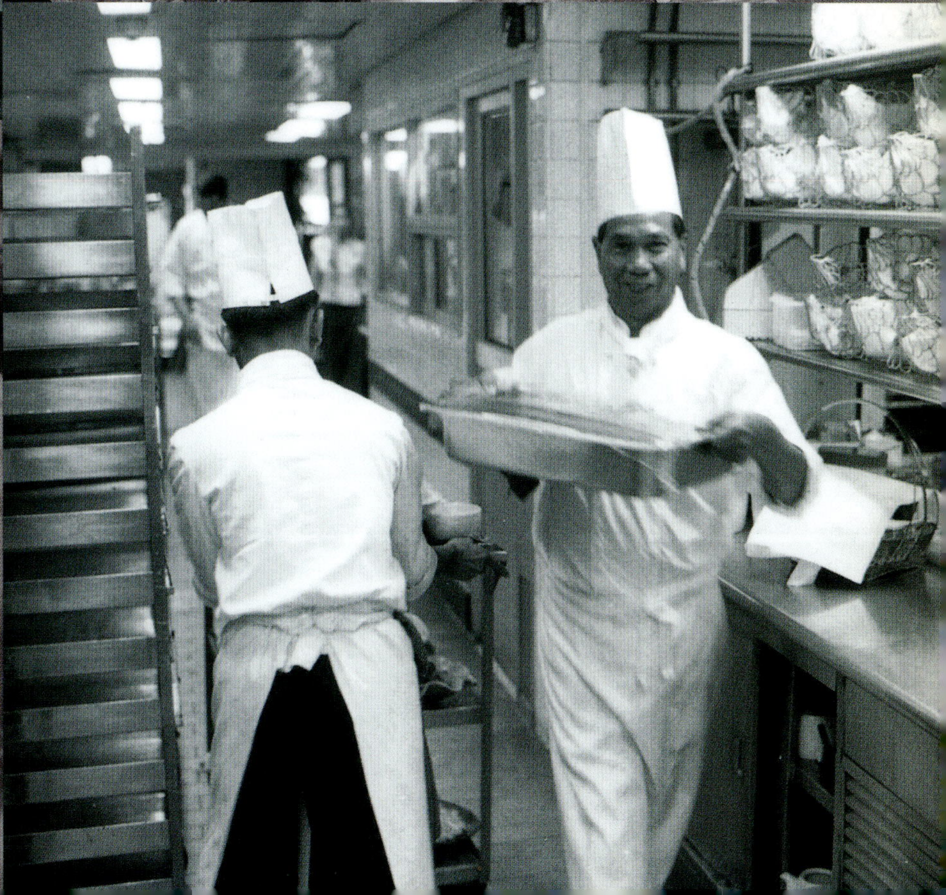

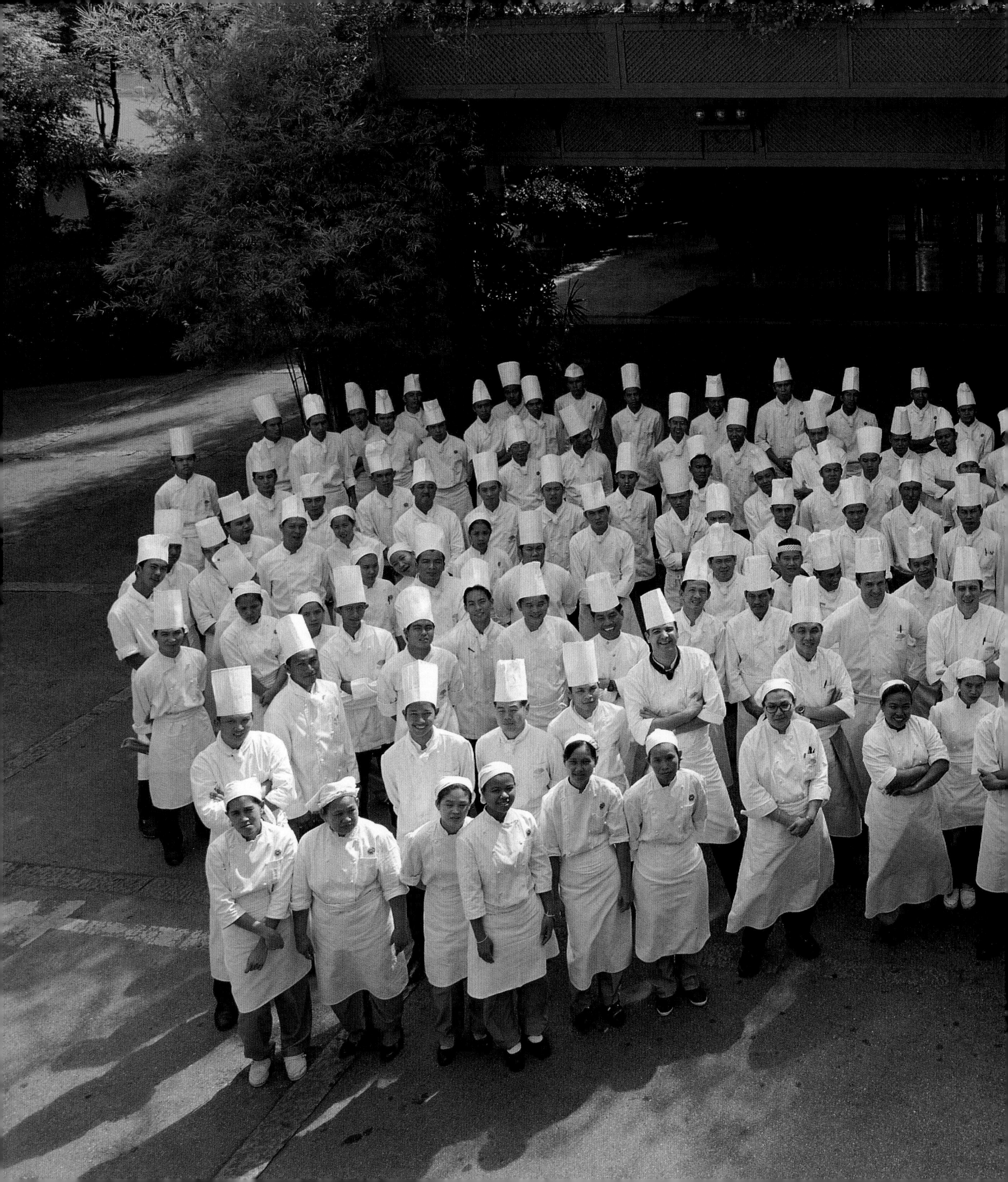

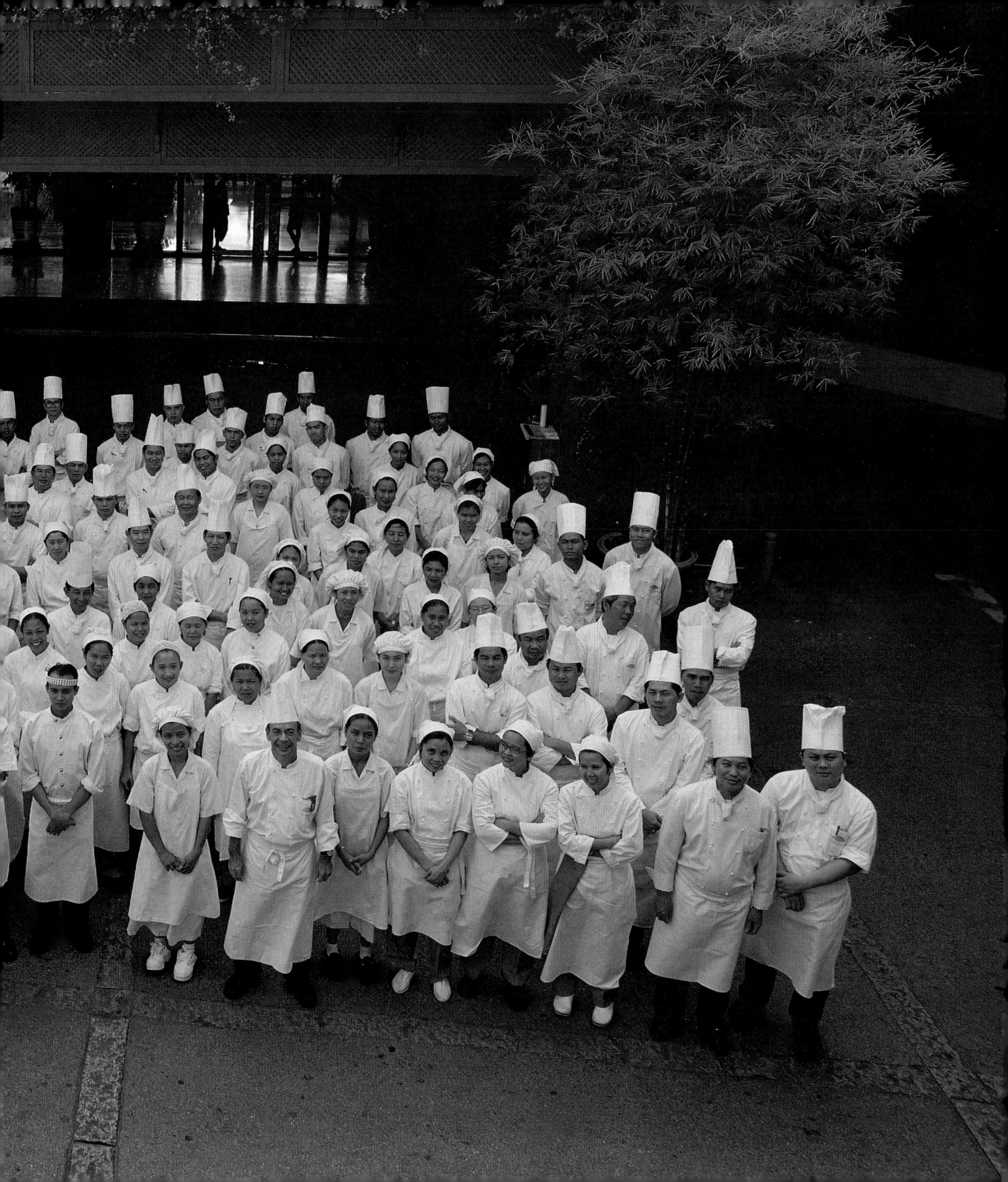

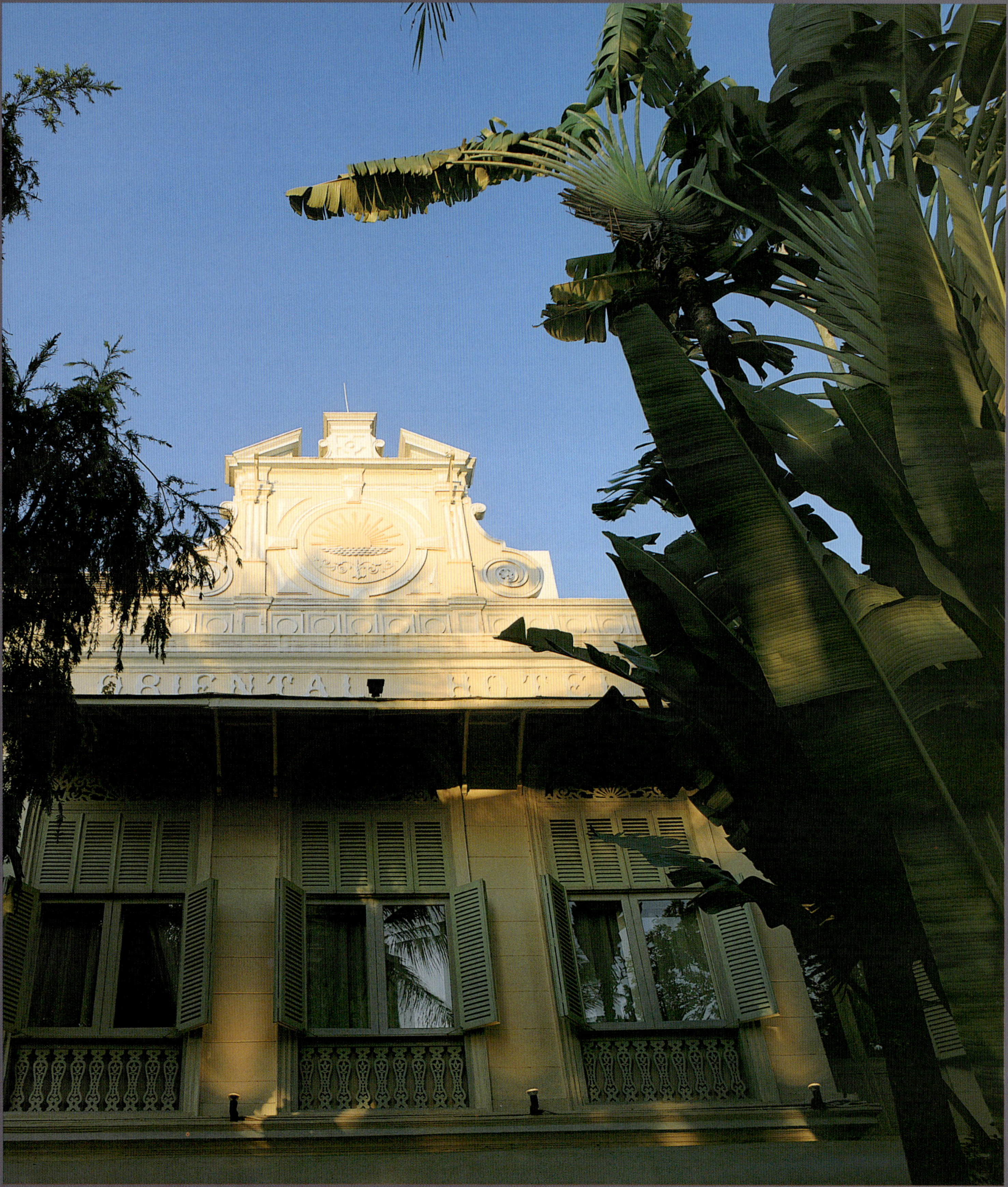
ORIENTAL

[THE MAKING OF A LEGEND]

In 1976, as part of the ceremonies to mark the opening of its lofty new River Wing, The Oriental announced that it was celebrating its 100th birthday. Actually, the date was somewhat arbitrary; Bangkok's oldest and most celebrated hotel could have claimed an earlier one, at least for an establishment bearing the name in more or less the same location. It could perhaps, for instance, have gone back to before 1865, when the Protestant missionary Dr Dan Beach Bradley recorded a great fire that consumed numerous wooden buildings, including an otherwise undescribed Oriental Hotel. Certainly there was one in the early 1870s, catering to the seamen who were then just beginning to come to Bangkok in sizeable numbers.

When Dr Bradley first arrived in 1835, however, there was nothing that could be remotely described as a hotel and few visitors were in search of one. Bangkok was still a traditional Thai city, built along the lines of the old capital of Ayudhaya, little known to the outside world. Some 90 per cent of its people lived in floating houses, moored sometimes in three or four rows on both banks of the Chao Phraya River; there were no proper roads except in the vicinity of the King's palace and all communication was by water, either on the broad river or along the network of canals, or *klongs*, that threaded through the city. Foreign trade was largely conducted by Chinese junks, arriving in late January with the northeast monsoon and remaining anchored in the river for several months before setting sail again in June.

All that began to change after 1855, the year in which King Rama IV signed a historic treaty with Sir John Bowring of Great Britain and opened the kingdom to active commerce with Europe. One had already been signed between Siam and the United States in 1833, with little evident result, but the effect of the Bowring Treaty was dramatic. Two years later, two hundred foreign ships called at Bangkok. Foreign

Opposite: The Authors' Wing, crowned by the pediment of the original hotel
Left: Baggage sticker from the 1930s

Above: The winding Chao Phraya River dominated the life of Bangkok for its first century and a half

legations and trading companies followed, and soon the city had a sizeable population of Westerners, most of whom worked on or near the Chao Phraya.

This influx brought several changes to the city. One was the first real street, New Road, which ran parallel to the river for much of its length and was soon lined with shophouses. Another was a demand for accommodation, especially from foreign seamen who were spending more time in Bangkok and understandably wanted to do so on dry land after their long voyages from distant Europe.

The earliest hotels were small wooden guesthouses on or near the river bank, which tended to cater to specific nationalities – Germans or Danes, for instance – who traded with Thailand. They were fairly rough places, often run by other seamen, the scenes of frequent brawls and other disturbances. Dr Bradley describes one eventful evening that involved the black proprietor of a place called Cottage Home, a neighbouring bar owner named George Howard, an "Englishwoman of questionable character" named Miss Howard, and four British sailors from a ship in port, all of whom got into a drunken melée. "*Delerium tremens* seems to rival smallpox as the most common disease among Westerns," noted the missionary sadly.

As trade grew and a somewhat better class of visitors began to arrive, there was clearly a need for a different kind of place to stay. One of these, founded in the early 1870s, was definitely called The Oriental. It was located across the street from the present one, on the site later occupied by the East Asiatic Company building, and it was operated by two Danish seamen, H. Jarck and C. Salje. By 1878, it was sufficiently well-established to advertise in the first issue of the *Siam Directory*, offering "Family accommodations, American Bar, Billiard Saloon, baths, newspaper kept, boats for hire, table d'hote, breakfast at 9 a.m., tiffin 1 p.m., dinner 7 p.m.", as well as "Appropriate rooms for private parties".

The hotel was convenient to both the French Legation and the Concordia, a social club for steamer captains and businessmen, and just a short walk along what became known as Oriental Avenue from bustling New Road. It apparently became a popular centre for eating and drinking, and while there are reports of occasional brawls in the American Bar, the owners were able to add a new wing in 1880 and also to start advertising a "Manufactory of Mineral Water". Perhaps they over-extended themselves, or perhaps they merely got homesick; in any event, soon after going into the water business, they sold The Oriental to two other sea captains named Moller and Meisner, and vanished from Bangkok.

It was around this time that a new figure appeared on the scene, one who would have a momentous effect not just on The Oriental but on Thailand as a whole.

Born in 1852, H.N. Andersen was a Danish sailor who came to Bangkok for the first time in 1873. He returned a year or so later, this time to join Siam's royal fleet of sailing ships. With the coming of steamships, he realised, a new era in trading had arrived, one requiring fast schedules as most ships remained in port only to unload and load. This he demonstrated in 1883 when he made a thousand per cent profit on a load of teakwood (then an unusual commodity of trade) which he delivered to Liverpool, returning quickly with a full load of coal. In 1884, he formed a partnership with a Thai nobleman to establish the firm of H.N. Andersen and Company, forerunner of the great East Asiatic Company.

Andersen lived at The Oriental while getting his new business underway and eventually took it over from Moller and Meisner, also acquiring the area from the river up to New Road. The time was ripe, he decided, for Bangkok to have a proper world-class hotel; indeed, several others were already being planned. The kingdom was flourishing under the rule of King Chulalongkorn (Rama V, who ruled from 1868 until 1910) and more and more visitors were arriving by steamship from Singapore and Hong Kong; something special was needed if it was to compete with the neighbouring countries.

In 1886, with a loan of 40,000 silver dollars, Andersen filled in the swampy land next to the hotel and developed a street leading to New Road. The recently-established Italian architecture firm of Cardu and Rossi was hired to design the new structure, which was ready by the following year. The *Bangkok Times* (then only five months old) announced the much-anticipated event as follows on May 14, 1887:

"The new Oriental Hotel will be opened to the public on Thursday the 19th. The first-class hotel is situated next to the [Concordia] Club and the Oriental Avenue, having entrances from both thoroughfares. It has forty commodious and well furnished rooms. We have been asked to say that no invitations have been sent out for the opening …but the proprietors Messrs Andersen & Co. wish all to know they will be welcome on that occasion from 4 p.m. onwards when the fountains of magnanimity will be turned on and rain hospitality all around."

Practically the entire foreign community, as well as many aristocratic Thais, took up the invitation, most arriving by boat at the riverside landing. Strolling across the lawn that led down to the water, they must have been impressed by the hotel's imposing façade, crowned by a pediment that displayed a golden rising sun. Iron

Above: Danish sailor H.N. Andersen built Bangkok's first world-class hotel to give the city a competitive edge over its neighbours
Bottom left: Ruins of the ancient capital of Ayudhaya which Bangkok resembled in its early years

staircases led to turrets atop the two wings, from which guests were offered views of the river and surrounding city, then rare except from a few of the loftier Buddhist pagodas.

The interior was even more impressive: rich carpets from Brussels, mahogany furniture in the bedrooms, a spacious lobby decorated with divans upholstered in peacock-blue velvet. At dusk the oil lamps were lit, and a lavish champagne banquet for 180 more distinguished guests was served on the lawn by Chef Georges Troisoeufs, formerly of the French Legation. Those who wanted further refreshment were kept supplied by a skilled bartender known only as Spider. Two orchestras played in the background and dancing – quadrilles, waltzes, and polkas – went on until the early hours, when the last guests tottered down to their boats to conclude the first of what were to be countless festive evenings at The Oriental.

A few days before the grand event, officials from the Grand Palace had come down the river to inspect the premises. They were given samples of all 18 dishes to be served at the banquet, each wrapped in a white cloth and sealed, to be presented to His Majesty the King. This, too, marked a first: over the years, The Oriental would often be called on to prepare the food for feasts at the royal palace.

That same month the new Oriental sealed its reputation as Bangkok's social centre with a banquet held in honour of Queen Victoria's Golden Jubilee, an event also duly noted by the *Bangkok Times*:

"The interior of the Hotel had been tastefully decorated for the occasion and numerous guests met with an enthusiastic welcome from the committee. Among those present was His Royal Highness Prince Svasti Sobhon, Lord Mayor of Bangkok. During dinner, several bands played splendidly and it was past ten o'clock before dancing could commence. A fireworks display took place at 11 p.m. concluding with a Royal Salute of 101 guns. A congratulatory telegram was sent to Her Majesty informing her that the Jubilee Victoria Ward had been established in her honour. Prince Svasti remained till past midnight, highly gratified with the reception he had been met with. The Oriental Hotel looked beautifully

Below: The Authors' Wing, the oldest part of the present hotel, houses suites named after the famous writers
Top right: The Oriental in its early years; guests entered from the river

luminous and everyone went home delighted when at about 4 a.m. the admirable musicians struck up *Rule Britannia*."

The Oriental's very earliest guest books have been lost, not surprising in view of the rollercoaster fortunes that the hotel has survived over the years. There is, however, record of the arrival of Mr. N. Lazarus, optician by trade, in January 1888; he was installed in Room 5, where it was announced he planned to stay "a short time only, when all suffering from imperfect vision will again have the opportunity of spectacles and *pince-nez* properly adjusted." Other guests included a decorator whose speciality was the art of restoring billiard tables, a dealer in precious stones, and a barrister who offered his services to "litigants, gamblers, speculators, etc."

By the following year, the guest list was displaying a cosmopolitan quality that reflected the growing popularity of Bangkok among world travellers. Resident during February, for instance, were visitors from such far-flung places as New York, London, Rome, Geneva and Hamburg.

Another visitor, this one in 1890, who never spent a night but who established a much-treasured precedent, was none other than His Majesty King Chulalongkorn. He arrived by river in the early evening of 17 December, without fanfare as he preferred, and spent an hour or so looking over the much-discussed facility with Captain Andersen and the manager before going to inspect the nearby Customs House, then the hub of the kingdom's maritime trade. He thus became the first of countless royal figures and heads of state to enjoy The Oriental's hospitality.

Left: *King Chulalongkorn, who became the first royal visitor to The Oriental in the year of its opening*

The Oriental was fast acquiring a reputation as a social centre not just for visitors but also for both Thai and foreign residents of Bangkok. On 22 September 1888, for example, H.H. Prince Prisdang, Director-General of the Post and Telegraph Department, gave a banquet at the hotel for some of his officials. It started with a creation called Hot Potch Italienne, and then went on to a fish course, meat (five kinds, including beef and lamb), and six choices of pudding.

Next year, on the occasion of a dinner given for the diplomatic and consular body by the Belgian Consul from Singapore, the *Bangkok Times* reported: "The cuisine at The Oriental is noted in Bangkok for its excellence and on this occasion it was fully equal to – if not above – its special standard."

In 1888, a bandstand was built on the lawn beside the river; the Thai Navy Band, led by an Italian, gave regular performances of Western

Right: Running parallel to the Chao Phraya, New Road was the city's first real street

music every Monday evening. Two large fountains were added to the garden the following year, and according to the *Bangkok Times*, succeeded in "considerably cooling the atmosphere and refreshing the star-gazers in the neighbourhood for nothing." The bar of the hotel, cooled by a *punkah* – a sheet of canvas hung from the ceiling and pulled back and forth by hand to create a breeze – was also crowded nightly, its speciality a lethal-sounding concoction known as 'Andersen's Special', composed of Dutch gin, Angostura bitters, eggyolk, sugar and nutmeg, stirred with a bamboo stick. (The Andersen thus honoured, incidentally, was not the owner but an unrelated partner named P. Andersen, who served for a time as manager.)

Many years later, leafing through the old pages of the *Bangkok Times*, the French author Romain Gary found a few distinctly exotic former guests. There was, for instance, a certain Count Zalata from the Ukraine who, according to Gary, had to flee his country on a charge of having raped 72 peasant girls; Chekov's comment on reading reports in the Russian papers was supposedly, "The man was obviously in training for something, but for what?" And there was Madame Stelin, in whose arms Félix Faure, sixth President of the French Republic had died; she fled to Bangkok to escape the scandal, stayed two months, and then, said Gary, "went back to Paris and on to even better things."

Bangkok itself was changing, too. New Western-style buildings were going up everywhere and in 1889, a horse-drawn tramway some six kilometres long, using 300 ponies, began operating on New Road. Electricity, first introduced at the Grand Palace several years earlier, became more widespread and was installed throughout The Oriental in 1891.

The hotel was thus illuminated for one of the most colourful events of its until-then short history. This was the arrival in April 1891 of the Crown Prince of Russia, the future Nicholas II, and his considerable entourage. The Prince was taken off to the Grand Palace (where he and King Chulalongkorn quickly formed a close friendship that was to prove useful when the King made his first trip abroad) but The Oriental offered free hospitality to his officers. They arrived in impressive uniforms, including helmets surmounted by silver and silver double eagles, and proceeded to consume every drop of alcohol on the premises within a day.

※

The year 1893 was a bad one for Thailand. The French, eager to expand their empire in Indo-China, had for some time been trying to force the kingdom to cede to them large parts of what is today Laos and Cambodia. In September 1893 they took direct action. Two French gunboats breached the defenses at the mouth of the Chao Phraya, sailed defiantly up the river, and anchored in front of the French Legation, next to The Oriental. Their Minister, Auguste Pavie, presented an ultimatum demanding the disputed territories and threatened a blockade of trade in the Gulf; unsaid but certainly implied was the possibility of firing on the Grand Palace, which lay not far upstream.

"The excitement in Bangkok during the last few days," wrote the *Bangkok Times*, "without being prodigious, has been considerable. A most animated scene took place at The Oriental Hotel towards the dinner hour on Saturday evening, when quite a crowd gathered at the water's edge in anticipation of some hostile movement on the part of the French gunboats. Disappointed, however, these gentlemen were obliged to go and dine in peace."

The spectators might have witnessed another kind of hostile movement from the Thais themselves. The gunboat crews, perhaps suffering from the unaccustomed tropical heat, had taken to bathing nude in the river, in full view of shocked locals. This so incensed one elderly member of the royal family that he devised a plot to sink the ships and might well have done so had word not reached the King in time to put a stop to the idea.

King Chulalongkorn was in a difficult position. Determined not to provoke further hostilities – and aided by the British, who were equally determined to keep Siam as a buffer state between French territories and theirs – he gave in to the demands. The incident was never forgotten, however; coupled with a further loss of territory to the French a few years later, it was to create an undercurrent of bitterness and lead to more conflict early in World War II.

Things did not run quite as smoothly at The Oriental after Captain Andersen sold it to a new

LOUIS T. LEONOWENS

Among the local businessmen who used the hotel as a kind of private club was Louis T. Leonowens. He had first come to Bangkok as a young boy with his mother, who later achieved fame as the heroine of *Anna and the King of Siam*, and *The King and I*. Anna's published accounts of her life as teacher in the court of King Rama IV were not well received in royal circles, but apparently no such disapproval attached itself to Louis. Returning in 1882, he was appointed a cavalry officer by King Chulalongkorn and went on to a prosperous career in the teak industry of the north. On visits to Bangkok, he always stayed at The Oriental and gave lavish entertainments there for his Thai and European friends.

In 1893, his wife died and he sent his two children off to live with his mother and sister in Canada, leaving his grand house in Bangkok deserted and said by the servants to be haunted. At least partly out of grief, he formed a syndicate to buy The Oriental from Captain Andersen. He never intended to play a day-to-day role in running the hotel; a drinking companion named Franklin (Bill) Hurst was put in charge as manager, while Leonowens tried to reconstruct his life.

The bungalow that housed Louis T. Leonowens and Company, one of several that stood on Oriental Avenue

ORIENTAL HOTEL
Bangkok, 20th April, 1894.
— TIFFIN —

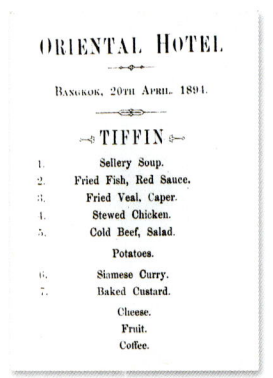

1. Sellery Soup.
2. Fried Fish, Red Sauce.
3. Fried Veal, Caper.
4. Stewed Chicken.
5. Cold Beef, Salad.
   Potatoes.
6. Siamese Curry.
7. Baked Custard.
   Cheese.
   Fruit.
   Coffee.

Above: A menu from a period in which the hotel's famous food seems to have suffered a decline
Bottom right: The Oriental was the place 'to see and be seen', and as such, played host to many big social events

syndicate as he wanted to devote more time to his growing company. Perhaps it was the lax management style, or perhaps the new proprietor Louis Leonowens spent too much time consuming those Andersen's Specials with his manager Franklin Hurst. There may have been competition from other hotels that had recently appeared, like The Bangkok and The Alhambra, both of which advertised prominently in the *1894 Directory for Bangkok and Siam*, published by the *Bangkok Times*. Or possibly a combination of these factors.

Guests certainly continued to arrive and to be properly impressed. Professor Maxwell Sommerville of Pennsylvania, travelling with his wife, came in 1897: "We were impressed with the courtesy of the Siamese from the moment we stepped on shore, which was on a beautiful terrace, shaded by a grove of luxuriant trees, through which sanded paths led to The Oriental Hotel…Through archways we passed into the principal hall, about seventy feet broad by thirty feet deep, serving at the same time as reception room, library, office, general thoroughfare. billiard room, and buffet. This buffet is a long piece of furniture known in many countries as a bar. It is attended by several Siamese, under the supervision of two *moonshees*, who are of Chinese descent…From this buffet is dispensed all imaginable cooling and heating draughts to the thirsty people of this torrid country, and throughout their working hours."

Big social events were still held at The Oriental, too. On 8 July 1893, for example, British residents gathered to celebrate the wedding of the Duke of York (the future George V) and Princess Mary of Teck, while on 4 April 1894, the German community toasted Prince Bismark's 80th birthday.

But all was not as before. A suggestion that the cuisine may have fallen off is provided by a menu from 1894, which listed such unimaginative fare as Sellery Soup, Fried Fish with Red Sauce, Fried Veal with Capers, Stewed Chicken, Cold Beef, Salad, Potatoes and Siamese Curry, followed by Baked Custard, Fruit and Coffee. There is also a story, possibly apocryphal, that Leonowens became so enraged at discovering irregularities in Hurst's account books that he rode on horseback up the outside stairs of the hotel to fire him.

Another hint of declining standards may be gleaned from a diary kept (and later published) by Mr and Mrs Emile Jottrand of Belgium. Appointed as a legal advisor to the Royal Thai Government, Mr Jottrand arrived with his wife in 1898, and they were put up at The Oriental while a house was prepared. The first entry, dated 23 October, reads, "Finally, a Sunday afternoon – equally dreary in any part of the world – leaves us with nothing to do for some hours. It's the first bit of free time since our arrival four days ago. I take

The Making Of A Legend

Left: Painting of the old Oriental with the river in the foreground

the opportunity to write, even if we are camped here in the most primitive manner in a third-class hotel, the first and only one in Bangkok, where one finds with great pains a clean and convenient corner for correspondence."

Whatever the reason, the syndicate sold its interests in 1899, and several new owners and managers followed. W.S. Robertson, who took over in 1903, lasted less than a year before he fled town with numerous creditors hot in pursuit. He returned to face trial, with the result that in August of 1904, the *Bangkok Times* carried an announcement that must have saddened the hotel's loyal customers: "The Oriental is to let unfurnished, with or without the annexed houses on the ground floor of the new wing."

The hotel was acquired this time by an American, Carl G. Edwards. He engaged a Frenchwoman, Madame M.O. Bujault, as manager, and she brought not only previous experience but determination to the job of nursing The Oriental back to health. She revived the musical dinners that had been so popular, with a Viennese orchestra playing in the background, and, perhaps more importantly, brought in a new chef from France.

In February 1904, when The Oriental was still suffering under the larcenous hand of Robinson, a group of Thais and Europeans had met at the hotel to lay the foundations for the Siam Society, for "the investigation and encouragement of the Arts and Sciences in relation to Siam and neighbouring countries," and this was to grow into one of the leading research associations in the region. In

Top left: The former headquarters of the East Asiatic Company, on a site formerly occupied by the earliest Oriental built in the early 1870s
Top right and above: Nearly all visitors arrived by ship in the early days, the larger vessels anchoring at the mouth of the river

1905, a future president of that organisation, who as Phya Anuman Rajadhon became a leading scholar, came to work at The Oriental.

Fresh out of nearby Assumption College, he was 17 years old and his main qualification for employment was a facility in English. He was assigned the primary task of writing "neatly in English the daily menus for lunch and dinner. I did not have to write the breakfast menu as it was the same every day." Towards the end of his long life, when he composed his memoirs, Phya Anuman had become hazy about several details. For instance, he thought the hotel had been founded by Louis T. Leonowens and that Carl Edwards was German, due to the fact that he spoke that language to some of the hotel guests.

But he clearly remembered how some of the guests were acquired: "One or two days a week, a medium-sized ocean liner would bring in no more than 15 first class passengers from Singapore. Of these, five or six would be guests at the hotel…When the hotel learned from the post office shipping guide, which it subscribed to, that such and such a ship would come in through [the town of] Paknam [literally, 'the river mouth'] at such and such a time, two hours before the ship was due at the harbour, if it was a passenger liner, the hotel would dispatch someone to meet it. The man sent was generally an Indian wearing the hotel uniform and a stiff military cap with a silk band bearing the name of the hotel in big letters around it. The man would ask whether the passengers would like to stay at the hotel. If the answer was positive, he would carry the luggage to a small launch…If he was lucky he would find two or three passengers and invite them to the hotel."

He also recalled seeing "Misser Lui", as Louis T. Leonowens was generally known in Thailand, at the hotel with his second wife, and being greatly impressed by his command of spoken Thai. Leonowens was by then 50 years old and nearing the end of his time in the kingdom that had so enchanted him as a child. He had founded a company bearing his name the same year Phya Anuman came to work at The Oriental; within a year he would be off to England, where he died in the influenza epidemic of 1919.

Besides music, Madame Bujault saw to it that

The Oriental got talked about in the local press for other reasons. In March 1909, it was "a 'Dinner de Luxe' in which Australian meats will figure as evidence of the excellence of the cold storage importation schemes." And in July the *Bangkok Times* reported that "the veranda of the dining room…was transformed into a richly decorated reserved dining room where a party of friends gave a farewell reception to Mr. Rigotti (the architect who designed the Throne Hall) who is returning to Italy after two years of residence in Bangkok. The grand clou of the evening was of course the dinner which was prepared and served to satisfy the taste of the most refined gourmet, the cordon bleu of Madame Bujault having this time rivalled the cleverest confrères of 'Chez Paillard' and 'Café Riche' in Paris."

The Anantasamakhom Throne Hall on which Annibale Rigotti had worked, along with several other Italian architects, was the centrepiece of an extensive 'New City' that King Chulalongkorn was building in the Dusit district. On his two state tours of Europe he had been impressed by the broad tree-lined boulevards and parks in the cities he visited and had resolved to transform his own capital along similar lines. Though Bangkok as a whole stubbornly insisted on growing in its own haphazard manner, much of his vision can still be seen today in Dusit. The Throne Hall itself, however, was still only partially completed when he suddenly died in October 1910, after 42 eventful years as ruler of Thailand.

Madame Bujault left The Oriental and Thailand in May of that same year and was replaced by Maria Maire, who would remain for more than two decades. Before her departure, though, proof of how far she had taken the hotel from its period of bankrupt shame could be found in the pages of a massive volume called *Twentieth Century Impressions of Siam*, a British production that came out at the end of 1908:

"The leading hotel in Bangkok, and the one at which visitors invariably stay is The Oriental. It enjoys an excellent situation in the centre of the city, on the east bank of the Menam, possesses good accommodation, and is comfortably furnished throughout. It is unquestionably the largest and best hotel in Siam and contains forty bedrooms, several private suites, a large dining room, and a concert-hall capable of holding 400 persons. Many of the European papers and periodicals are to be found in the lounge at the entrance to the hotel, while opening out from the dining room is a spacious verandah commanding an excellent view of the river."

Madame Maire quickly demonstrated her culinary credentials after taking command, offering a dinner on 25 June 1910 that began with Potage Saint Germain, and went on to Poisson Frit à la Marinade, Oie à la Chipolata, Filet de Boeuf Bouquetière, Porc de Lait Rôti, and Glace au Kirsch.

There was an inevitable pause in festivities during the year-long period of mourning that

Left: One of the former shuttle boats that took guests for short distances on the Chao Phraya River

152

followed King Chulalongkorn's death, but the next year saw a brisk revival with the coronation of King Vajiravudh. The new King actually had two coronations – one, following ancient custom and ceremony, shortly after his father's death, and a second, more European-style affair at the end of 1911. For the first time in Thai history, invitations were sent to foreign capitals, most of which the King had visited as Crown Prince, resulting in a flood of eminent visitors. Some 25 foreign representatives arrived in Bangkok, including ten members of royal families, among them Prince Alexander of Teck from Great Britain, Grand Duke Boris from Russia, Prince Waldeman from Denmark, and the Crown Prince of Japan.

"Siam is feeling very proud and a little anxious," the *Bangkok Times* wrote in an editorial. "Never before have there gathered in this capital so many princes of foreign reigning families. Such a gathering of royalties and the guests of the Sovereign is comparatively a rare thing in a European capital, and is without precedent outside Europe."

While the royalties themselves were put up in various palaces, some in their large entourages as well as members of the press stayed at The Oriental; and Madame Maire made sure they were given a proper reception with newly refurbished rooms and lavish floral displays. One of the guests was the celebrated jeweller Fabergé, whose creations were especially coveted in the Russian court.

The Oriental continued to thrive in the years after this great event. There was, for instance, a festive party for the departing Italian Minister in 1912 and, the following year, a performance in the hotel's concert hall of Molière's *Le Médecin Malgré Lui* to mark the inauguration of the Alliance Française. In 1916, the great dancer Vaslav Nijinsky gave a performance of Western ballet, the first ever seen in Bangkok. As these suggested, The Oriental was determined to maintain its reputation as a centre of Bangkok's social and cultural life, even as World War I raged in distant Europe.

❦

Despite all the efforts, the period following World War I was a difficult one for the hotel. A worldwide economic slump cut into the number of visitors and affected local entertaining as well. The facilities, too, were beginning to show the effects of age, despite the refurbishing in 1911.

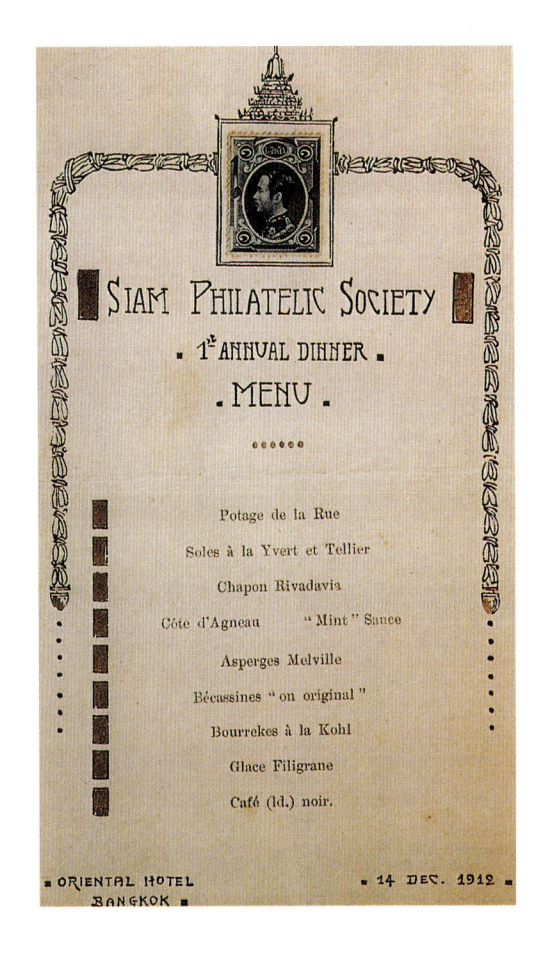

Left: Menu card dated 1912; under Madam Maire, the food notably improved
Opposite: Various views of The Oriental, from a 1908 book entitled Twentieth Century Impressions of Siam; from top, the entrance of the hotel; the dining room; and the lobby lounge

Right: By 1908, there were over 300 cars in the city and life in Bangkok began to move away from the river. Opposite: Air travel, which began in the early 1930s, led to a dramatic influx of tourists

Henri Cucherousset, a journalist based in French Indo-China, caused a stir in 1920 when he described it as "a small place with forty bad, comfortless rooms in an old building on the bank of the river". It had, he admitted, an impressive entrance hall and a good dining room, but that did not compensate for a lack of "proper bathing facilities" and a generally run-down appearance. "It must be ten years," he wrote, "since the place had a coat of paint".

The *Bangkok Times* came to The Oriental's support, insisting that it was "one of the best in the East" and demanding an apology from the impertinent journalist. Madame Maire, however, realized that there was more than a little truth in the comments. The hotel *did* need a good deal of work to bring it back up to its old standards, and it would cost a sizeable sum to get it done. In 1924, therefore, The Oriental Hotel Company Ltd. was formed, new funds were raised, and an ambitious renovation programme was started.

The next decade or so saw many changes to Thailand and, inevitably, to The Oriental as well. Transportation was one of the most visible. Road-building had increased at a dramatic pace, the New Road trams had been electrified as early at 1893 (some ten years before such a service was available in Copenhagen), and railway travel had arrived, first with a line to Pak Nam at the mouth of the river, and eventually with a northern line extending all the way to Chiang Mai and a southern one that linked up with the Malayan system to Singapore. In 1901 one of the King's sons drove the first automobile along a Bangkok street; by 1908 there were over 300 cars in the city, and by 1930 they were commonplace. With this development came another, subtle change, not fully appreciated at the time. New roads and automobiles made the city increasingly less dependent on water for transportation; slowly but inevitably, Bangkok began to spread over swampy plains to the east, away from the river and The Oriental.

Air travel, too, arrived early. In 1911, only eight years after William and Orville Wright had made their first flight in a "heavier-than-air craft" on a lonely beach in North Carolina, a Belgian pilot gave a demonstration of the new wonder by taking off from the race track of the Royal Bangkok Sports Club in a biplane and making a lazy loop over the neighbourhood, then mostly open fields. In the early 1920s a Thai-operated air-mail service was started to the north-eastern provinces; by 1931, now called the Aerial Transport of Siam Company, it was carrying passengers and mail to the region and advertising that those "taking breakfast in Korat will be able to have tiffin in Nakorn Phanom".

The first foreign company on the scene was KLM Royal Dutch Airline, which in 1929 offered a regular passenger service between Amsterdam and Batavia (now Jakarta); at the time, and indeed until 1940, it was the longest scheduled air service in the world, taking 12 days (89 flying hours) and stopping at 18 airfields en route, including Bangkok's Don Muang. Britain's Imperial Airways was next in 1933, operating four-engined flying boats on a route that ended in Singapore.

An old-time British resident of Bangkok, many years later, remembered coming to the city on one of these planes. It landed on the Chao Phraya River, about halfway to Don Muang; there, it was met by a launch from The Oriental, which ferried passengers downriver to the hotel's landing. He also remembered the hotel's method of dealing with the voracious mosquitoes that attacked the ankles of guests during dinner. This consisted of tying thick black sacks around the lower legs, effective unless the guest forgot and suddenly tried to walk from the table.

In deference to the increasing number of clients arriving by road rather than by water, The Oriental moved its main entrance to the road on the side of the building, not as impressive, perhaps, but a good deal more convenient.

The year 1932 was a momentous one. It saw the departure of Madame Maire, who married an English businessman she had met in Bangkok. Local newspapers noted the event, some with nostalgia for a time now past. "When Madame Maire took over," said one correspondent, "the only method for ordinary folk to reach Bangkok was by water. There were no trains to Chiang Mai or restaurant cars to Phrae and life was a good deal simpler and, be it added, a good deal pleasanter than now."

In April 1932, Bangkok celebrated its first century and a half with gala festivities that included a Royal Barge procession and the opening of the first bridge across the Chao Phraya. Just two months later, the absolute monarchy came to an end when a small group of

Telegrams:
ORIENHOTEL, BANGKOK

Oriental Hotel

Bangkok

Oldest and most Popular Hotel in all of Siam. Situated on river front, fine gardens, French Chef. Cuisine and all appointments first class—rates moderate. Our Steam Launch meets all Steamers, also Auto Car at disposal of guests. *Now being remodeled. Modern Toilet Fittings, Etc.*
ALL LANGUAGES SPOKEN

Proprietor: A. Maire

civil servants and military officers staged a bloodless coup and King Prajadhipok (Rama VII) agreed to grant a constitution.

Despite these events, life went on for The Oriental. Madame Maire's place was taken by Lt Col. and Mrs Sylow, then in 1935 by Mr J.O. Hossig. The famous continued to come, despite competition from other hotels that included, for a brief period, a splendid former royal palace where guests were treated to performances of Thai classical dance in a miniature Greek temple.

Noel Coward came on one of his numerous visits and, while relaxing with a drink on the terrace, was inspired to add a few lines to his immortal Mad Dogs and Englishmen: "In Bangkok/at twelve o'clock/They foam at the mouth and run." Douglas Fairbanks, the 'King of Silent Films', came and announced that he planned to meet the King of Siam. Barbara Hutton, the Woolworth heiress, came during the hottest season and, since the hotel offered no swimming pool at that time, took advantage of an invitation to have a dip at the Royal Bangkok Sports Club.

J. O. Hossig, in an effort to liven things up, gave a grand party for 200, with a dance floor on the lawn and the best local orchestra. He varied the predominantly French menu by offering something else; an advertisement suggested: "Surprise your guests at home with a rich hors d'œuvre, a full assortment of Danish sandwiches or a nice ice-bomb from The Oriental."

But time was running out for carefree world travellers. War came to Europe in 1939 and its shadows spread ominously to the Far East. On 3 December 1941, though some already feared that disaster was imminent, a hopeful advertisement appeared in Bangkok newspapers: "Reserve your table now at The Oriental Hotel for the special Christmas dinner on Thursday, 25th December. It will be in good old Yuletide fashion. Gramophone concert. Dancing on request."

On 30 December, another advertisement appeared: "Open as usual. The Oriental Hotel. Special discount for Japanese Army and Navy officers and government officials."

By then, no one had to ask why the special discount was being offered.

❦

Thailand (as the country was officially now known) had already signed a treaty of friendship with Japan. The treaty paid off when, following a brief skirmish along the Indo-Chinese border, a Japanese-brokered agreement returned most of the territories lost the previous century (which in turn had to be later returned to French hands). In 1942, under pressure from its new ally, the Thai

Left: Jim Thompson, one of the original group who wanted to restore The Oriental after World War II; instead, he revived the famous Thai silk industry Opposite: Views of The Oriental in the 1920s; the one below is taken from Oriental Avenue

Above: The Authors' Lounge, with a double staircase leading up to suites above

government formally declared war on Great Britain and the United States, though its ambassador refused to deliver the declaration to the latter and thus paved the way for a faster resumption of relations when the fighting ended. For the time being, however, the Japanese were in control; British and American residents, some of them old-timers, went into internment camps, and for the next four years, The Oriental was operated by Tokyo's Imperial Hotel.

A few bombs were dropped on Bangkok by Allied planes in the last year of the war – some of them on buildings near The Oriental, like the British Borneo Company headquarters – but the city was spared the widespread destruction suffered by so many others. Nevertheless, August 1945 found it shabby and exhausted, with almost everything in short supply. The Oriental, under the temporary management of an Englishwoman named Maria Robins, was requisitioned first as a home for prisoners liberated from camps in Thailand, then for women and children freed in Java, finally for the American military. Largely stripped of its furnishings, including china, linen, and accessories, its plumbing and electric wiring in sad disrepair, the hotel had only its basic structure and its prime riverside location to recommend it to any future buyer.

Two characters appeared as the soldiers were about to move out. One was an American named Jim Thompson, an acting colonel in the Office of Strategic Services (OSS), who was looking for an enterprise that would keep him in Thailand; the other was Germaine Krull, war correspondent for a French news agency, who was doing the same. Together, they decided to organise a company to restore The Oriental, with Krull providing the management and Thompson, an architect by training, drawing up plans for improvements to the building.

The arrangement did not materialise, at least as far as Thompson was concerned. He dropped out and transferred his attentions to the Thai silk industry, which he would go on to make world-famous. (He lived at the hotel for a year or so while getting his company started, however, and sold some of his first silks by simply standing around the lobby with lengths of the shimmering material draped over one arm; inevitably sooner or later somebody would ask what it was and

The Making Of A Legend

within a few minutes he had another customer.) Madame Krull founded the company to run The Oriental, made up of both Thai and foreign partners, and by 12 June 1947, she was able to advertise in the newly founded *Bangkok Post*:

ORIENTAL HOTEL
OPEN AGAIN
CUISINE FRANÇAISE
BAMBOO BAR
EUROPEAN MANAGER

Getting it to this point had not been an easy task. "After the first weeks of intensive cleaning and getting organized," she later wrote in a memoir, "I was faced with the problem of renovating the hopelessly shabby rooms…" She had to scour the city for sheets, blankets, towels, and mosquito nets, and also for electric wire and paint. "There was no wire whatever and no paint could be found except for some poisonous green or unpleasant pink, and even then, only a few tins…We could not find enough leather of the same colour to re-cover all the in the lobby, so five were covered in red and five in blue…While many things were slowly getting under control, water remained a big problem. It took about a month before we were able to put down on paper just how the water system worked…"

Somehow, though, it was done. Soon afterward the Bamboo Bar opened, and quickly became one of the hotel's most popular features, offering light meals and a cosy place to meet and chat. Due to the large number of Americans passing through, cheeseburgers and club sandwiches were included on the menu. Neither Madame Krull nor the local cooks, however, knew how to prepare such exotic fare, and rescue came in the form of two guests, Al and Frieda Lyman, who offered to serve as instructors.

In a possibly misguided effort to give the Bamboo Bar some elegance, Madame Krull made the gentlemen wear neckties. The management provided ties to those without. "We made hundreds of ties with the cheapest satin and the children of the Chinese boys painted cocks on them. These ties went round the world as they were collected by visitors and local guests."

The Lymans, who were in the process of setting up a law firm in Bangkok that continues to thrive today, were typical of the varied population that called The Oriental home in

Below: The old Chartered Bank building, once next to the hotel
Top left: Four Americans who settled in Thailand after World War II. Left to right: Herman Seiler, who started a bakery; Alexander MacDonald, founder of the Bangkok Post; Jim Thompson, who revived the Thai silk industry; and Jorges Orgibet, a journalist

159

those hectic years. "Our guests were of every type," wrote Madame Krull, "from newly arriving diplomats to fortune hunters, spies, and crooks."

Alexander Macdonald, another former OSS member who stayed on and founded the *Bangkok Post*, paints a vivid picture of the scene in a book he wrote about the period:

"The Oriental was made for mystery and plotting. Its winding, mouldy halls and dim rooms provoked at once an air of suspicion. In its shabby, crowded lobby, every other man – or woman – might have been an international spy. They were not tall, elegant spies such as Lisbon knew, but rather nondescript people. The short, stout Chinese in the crumpled linen suit with a row of fountain pens and pencils studding his front pocket had registered as a leather-and-hide buyer from Hong Kong, but more likely was a Koumintang hatchet man. The buxom Dutch housewife, waiting for months for her husband to join her from the Hague, was probably feeding intelligence daily to the French Legation. The white-jacketed No. 1 boy with the passive smile was probably a graduate of the Sorbonne doing his under-cover bit for Vietnamese freedom."

Everyone met at The Oriental. It was one of the first places of call for the planeloads of tourists and commercial men and the agents among them. Dates were made and kept in its dim-lit lobby. Its register was full of fraudulent names, but most of the agents were easily identifiable. They were the ones who would, at some time or other, saunter over to the desk and take a casual look at the new names on the register. The day's newspapers were sold at the desk, so it was easy to make a quick check while buying a paper.

Another glimpse of the hotel, this time by an outsider, is provided by Ira Morris, wife of the managing director of Louis T. Leonowens and Company, who arrived in 1956 with her husband to celebrate the 50th anniversary of the firm founded by one of The Oriental's early owners. They arrived very early in the morning, around 4 a.m., and pulled up to an unpromising flight of steps that led straight up to the hotel from Oriental Avenue:

"We mounted the steps and walked in between a dingy, shuttered reception desk and a coolie flicking a broom. The hall widened and...

'But this is enchanting!' I exclaimed, giving

*Below: View of The Oriental from the opposite bank of the Chao Phraya River; the River Wing is on the left, the Tower Wing on the right, with the old Authors' Wing in the left front.
Top right: The hotel's original logo*

away to J. at least, what I had thought of the place up to then.

On our right rose a central flight of blue stairs, carpeted in bamboo matting and flanked on either side by tall blue urns of spiky palm. It led up to a small open landing framed in scrolled white archways overlooking an inner garden court. Then two flights led off it left and right, and the white arches mounted along them with trains of flowering creeper encroaching indoors round their slender dividing pillars. Off the hall, on our left, stretched a cool, dark lounge furnished with king-sized red and blue armchairs round small tables; it opened out into a pillared stone terrace dotted with cane *chaises longues* cushioned in white linen; then came a slope of lawn and the river.

Straight ahead of us, past a couple of jewellers' display cases, was a white screen wall fretted into a repeat pattern of bottles, and a white door with a modest blue neon sign above it: 'Bamboo Bar.'"

Ira Morris found to her dismay that her bathing facilities consisted of a large stone jar and a dipper, but this inconvenience made no difference: "I could never fathom then, and I still do not know why this casual layout should have added up to such enchantment. It gave you a feeling of well being just to be there…The Oriental had more charm than any hotel I have ever visited over an extensive map of Europe and America. During our stay it had a good chef, too, which made it almost unfair."

✼

On April 1, 1958, The Oriental opened its Tower Wing, architecturally the most significant addition since Andersen's original structure. It rose ten storeys, making it one of the tallest buildings in Bangkok at the time. The city was experiencing a major tourist boom, and The Oriental was working hard to meet the demand.

Among the most talked-about amenities of the new wing – even more than the novel lifts, the first in Bangkok ever to rise to such dizzying heights – was Le Normandie, the hotel's French restaurant, which had an open grill and a brick chimney, gleaming copper cooking pots, and two rampant lions, emblems of Normandy, which Madame Krull had managed to find in a local antique shop. The *Bangkok Post* reported on its attractions the following year:

"Ranking third, next to good food and good service, a good location would be specified by most diners, something unusual (even bizarre) in the surroundings to add that final rare touch that

Left: General Manager Kurt Wachtveitl (centre) with Interior Designer and Architect, John Rifenberg (second from right), and representatives from Hong Kong Land, discussing plans for the new wing
Above, left: Dr Chaijudh Karnasuta and Giorgio Berlingieri, who bought The Oriental in the 1960s

NORBERT KOSTNER

The Oriental has always been a place to dine for locals as well as travellers, in high times and low. Today, with no fewer than seven in-house outlets, plus a chain of Oriental Shops and meals served aboard a cruiser on the Chao Phraya River, this is more true than ever.

Each restaurant has its own particular chef, but all the hotel's kitchens are under the supervision of Executive Chef Norbert Kostner, a native of South Tyrol who has been with The Oriental since 1974. His duties involve not only a comprehensive knowledge of various cuisines but also a constant effort to find the best ingredients, local as well as imported.

Chef Norbert has been advisor to the Royal Project for the last 12 years. Launched 30 years ago, this groundbreaking initiative set out to convert opium fields in the mountains of northern Thailand into organic farms that cultivate unusual fruit, vegetables, herbs and spices previously unavailable in Bangkok. Some 253 villages and 90,000 people from a dozen hill tribes in the country are now a part of this programme, which also pioneered the rearing of Bresse chickens outside of France.

---

makes for complete gastronomic enjoyment. At Le Normandie, there is nothing bizarre but it has probably the best location for tourists of any restaurant in Bangkok, and combined with good food and service, this roof-top establishment is deservedly the first place that residents usually take their visitors from overseas for a meal."

Two years after completion of the Tower Wing, Germaine Krull left the hotel business – she took up the cause of Tibetan Buddhism and died among exiles of that faith in India – and a series of managers followed. The Oriental's reputation among travellers remained high, but as more and more rivals opened – many of them following the relentless growth of Bangkok far from the river – it became clear that a new infusion of energy was called for, if the hotel was to maintain its position. The pattern was familiar to those who had followed its history. This time rescue came in 1967 with a now legendary telephone conversation between two businessmen, one Italian and the other Thai.

The Italian was Giorgio Berlingieri, an engineer who had formerly worked on ship salvage in Vietnam; the Thai was Dr Chaijudh Karnasuta. Together in the mid-1950s they had formed Italthai, which would eventually comprise more than 60 companies and be involved in almost every aspect of Thailand's economy, from building and road construction to hotel management. Berlingieri was in Italy on a business trip when Dr Chaijudh called him and said, "There's a hotel for sale."

Belingieri's instinctive response, as he recalled it later, was "Forget it."

"It's The Oriental."

"Why didn't you say so? Of course we'll buy it!"

"That's what I thought you'd say."

Italthai immediately set out to raise The Oriental's standing, not just among Bangkok hotels but internationally. One of the first steps was to find a new manager. A likely candidate turned up in the person of Kurt Wachtveitl, who was then managing one of Italthai's hotels in the seaside resort of Pattaya. Young and full of ideas, he accepted the challenge and came to Bangkok. He began by recommending an upgrade of the hotel's restaurants; this led to a complete redecoration of Le Normandie, requiring over a year and resulting in a much more sophisticated dining space, but with the same spectacular views that had been such a part of the room's original

The Making Of A Legend

appeal. A renovation of the Tower Wing followed, after which the new owners and manager turned their attention to even more ambitious improvements.

At this point, The Oriental consisted of what is now called the Authors' Wing, the oldest section, with Andersen's Rising Sun pediment, and a later addition known as the Ambassador's Wing. The latter was a long, low structure, set at an angle so that its rooms offered few views of the river; moreover, its facilities, including the air-conditioning system, were sadly out of date. As Italthai was considering what to do about this in 1972, a dramatic solution presented itself. The Chartered Bank had stood for some 80 years on a large adjacent piece of riverside property. Now, like many Bangkok businesses, the bank was deserting the river for one of the newer commercial districts and the property was available; it was the perfect place to erect an entirely new wing.

To achieve such an expansion, however, which meant transforming The Oriental from a fairly small hotel into a major one with more than 400 rooms, would require finding a new partner with the necessary resources. Several international chains and airlines were considered before the right one was found in the Hong Kong Land group, then eager to expand its chain of prestigious Mandarin Hotels.

As Berlingieri recalled it, after only two telexed messages he met the head of Mandarin International Hotels Ltd and in just 35 minutes they reached an agreement that was later put into legal form without a single change in substance. The Oriental was ready to move.

In the meantime, though, it had suffered a tragedy. The venerable Authors' Wing, only a few months after it had undergone renovations, was severely damaged by fire in August 1973. Within a day, workers were on the scene to begin restoring it to its former status as the true heart of The Oriental.

The 350-room River Wing opened in 1976, which as we have seen was the year the hotel chose to mark its centennial. Five years later, on 1 December 1981, Giorgio Berlingieri died suddenly in his office. But he had seen his dream of a new and grander Oriental come true, and also another one: earlier that year the *Institutional Investor*, a magazine of American bankers, had become the first of a long list to vote The Oriental the best hotel in the world.

Left: The Oriental today as seen from the Chao Phraya River; on the right is the former headquarters of the East Asiatic Company
Below: The Oriental Queen, on which guests can cruise in the historic Chao Phraya River; the Grand Palace can be seen in the background

WRITERS AT THE ORIENTAL

The Oriental has long enjoyed a special relationship with writers. Joseph Conrad, who is honoured today with a suite in the Authors' Wing, but who almost certainly never passed a night under its roof, possibly visited the hotel when he was still an obscure seaman named Jozef Teodor Konrad Korzeniowski.

He arrived in January 1888 to take over the command of a sailing ship whose crew was stricken with illness. The Oriental would have been far beyond his means, and so he chose instead the more modest Universal Hotel favoured by most mariners. He could have visited The Oriental for a concert and after, probably treated to a drink by Andersen, who was always hospitable to impecunious sailors.

In 1922, Somerset Maugham, novelist and playwright, made his first trip to Burma and Siam. As always on his Asian travels, he was looking for material and no doubt, he hoped these countries would yield the sort of gold he had already begun to mine in Malaya, those steamy stories of Europeans going to pieces in the tropics. If so, he was to be disappointed. The difficult journey resulted in a single travel book, *The Gentleman in the Parlour*, and one short fairy tale which he penned on The Oriental's terrace overlooking the river, while recovering from a bout of malaria.

Noel Coward, on one trip, was persuaded to try one of the newer hotels but left after a few nights, declaring it "beastly," and returned to his favourite spot. "There is a terrace overlooking the swift river," he noted in his journal, "where we have drinks every evening watching the liver-coloured water swirling by and the steam tugs hauling rows of barges upriver against the tide. It is a lovely place and I am fonder of it than ever."

James Michener, author of *Tales of the South Pacific*, was an early post-war visitor and returned many times over the years. Alec Waugh, who would write a whole book about Bangkok in 1969, spent ten weeks at The Oriental in 1958: "I was working on a novel, the difficult early stage was past. I breakfasted as soon as it was light, and by seven o'clock as soon as the balcony was clear of mosquitoes I was at my desk." In between trips to Cambodia, where his novel *The Honourable School Boy* is partly set, John Le Carré used the hotel as a base. Graham Greene came, and so did Tennessee Williams, Gore Vidal, Morris West, William Golding, John Steinbeck, Paul Theroux, Barbara Cartland, Iris Murdoch, Han Suyin, and

Right: At the top is the Noel Coward Suite and below is the Somerset Maugham Suite, two of the most luxurious accommodations in the Authors' Wing named after famous writers who stayed there

Ian Fleming, among many others.

With this tradition of literary visitors, it seems only fitting that The Oriental was one of the organisers of the S.E.A. Write Award in 1979. The awards are presented annually to honour writers from the Association of South East Asian Nations (ASEAN), a group that now includes Thailand, Malaysia, Singapore, Indonesia, Brunei, Myanmar, Cambodia and Vietnam.

The winners, each selected by a committee of writers in his or her country, gather at The Oriental for a week-long series of festive events that culminates in a gala dinner.

A member of the Thai royal family, usually His Royal Highness Crown Prince Maha Vajiralongkorn, presides over the final evening, and a guest writer delivers an address. James Michener was the first invited speaker; others have included Nobel Prize winner William Golding, perennial best seller Wilbur Smith, and Thailand's multi-talented M.R. Kukrit Pramoj, author of several novels, journalist, movie actor (*The Ugly American*), and former prime minister.

A STAR-SPANGLED GUEST BOOK

Hospitality is another part of The Oriental's mystique. The countless awards it has won over the years are really based on the friendly smiles and thoughtful attention offered to its guests. Many of the staff have been with the hotel for years – Ankana Kalantananda, in charge of guest relations, has been there since 1947 when Madame Krull was still trying to solve the plumbing problems – and all of them are expert at meeting even the most unusual demands, from Caesar Salad prepared in a certain way to a personal mosquito net despite the air-conditioning. Just arranging and serving a room-service food trolley has been elevated to a fine art and involves 22 different steps (one of them: "Check guests' name and room number and memorise the name.") outlined in a special manual.

The demands may come from visiting royalty (among them the Prince and Princess of Wales, for instance, or the Sultan of Brunei, the Crown Prince of Japan, or the King and Queen of Jordan), heads of state (Lee Kuan Yew of Singapore, Richard Nixon of the United States, and Dr Helmut Kohl of Germany, to mention only a few), or stars of stage and screen (an endless list that includes everybody from Julie Andrews and Lauren Bacall to Elizabeth Taylor and Sir Andrew Lloyd Webber). Or, just as important to the hotel's reputation, they may come from an uncelebrated Mr and Mrs Anybody, making their first round-the-world trip and grateful for that personal touch that makes them feel more at home.

Nor is such attention limited to visitors from abroad. The Oriental remains a centre of Bangkok's social life, and every week its various function rooms are booked for some sort of event. The sumptuous Royal Ballroom, redecorated a few years ago with nostalgic mural paintings of river life in the past, has been the scene of innumerable wedding receptions, birthday parties, national days, product promotions, business gatherings and other affairs; and smaller facilities are also kept busy. Thai royalty, businessmen and society leaders, along with more ordinary residents, continue to think of The Oriental first when planning such events. The fact that Bangkok began to move away from the Chao Phraya at least 50 years ago, and that most such people now live in distant suburbs, has had little effect on the hotel's status as the preferred place to entertain and be seen in.

Above: Author and playwright, Somerset Maugham
Top: Joseph Conrad, the seafaring novelist

Her Majesty Queen Sirikit greets winners of the coveted S.E.A Write Awards

The top writers of ASEAN are honoured annually at the hotel's S.E.A. Write Awards.

Khmer King Norodom Sihanouk

The grand dame of romance, Barbara Cartland

Roger Moore

Charles, the Prince of Wales and the late Lady Diana

Elizabeth Taylor escorted by ex-husband Larry Fortensky

French singer Johnny Hallyday basking in Thai hospitality

A warm welcome for former United States President George Bush

A souvenir from the King of Spain Don Juan Carlos de Borbon and Queen Doña Sofia de Borbon

Sir Richard Attenborough takes centrestage

General Manager Kurt Wachtveitl greets His Majesty the Yang Di Pertuan Agong and Her Majesty the Raja Permaisuri Agong from Malaysia

French President Jacques Chirac pens memories of a great stay

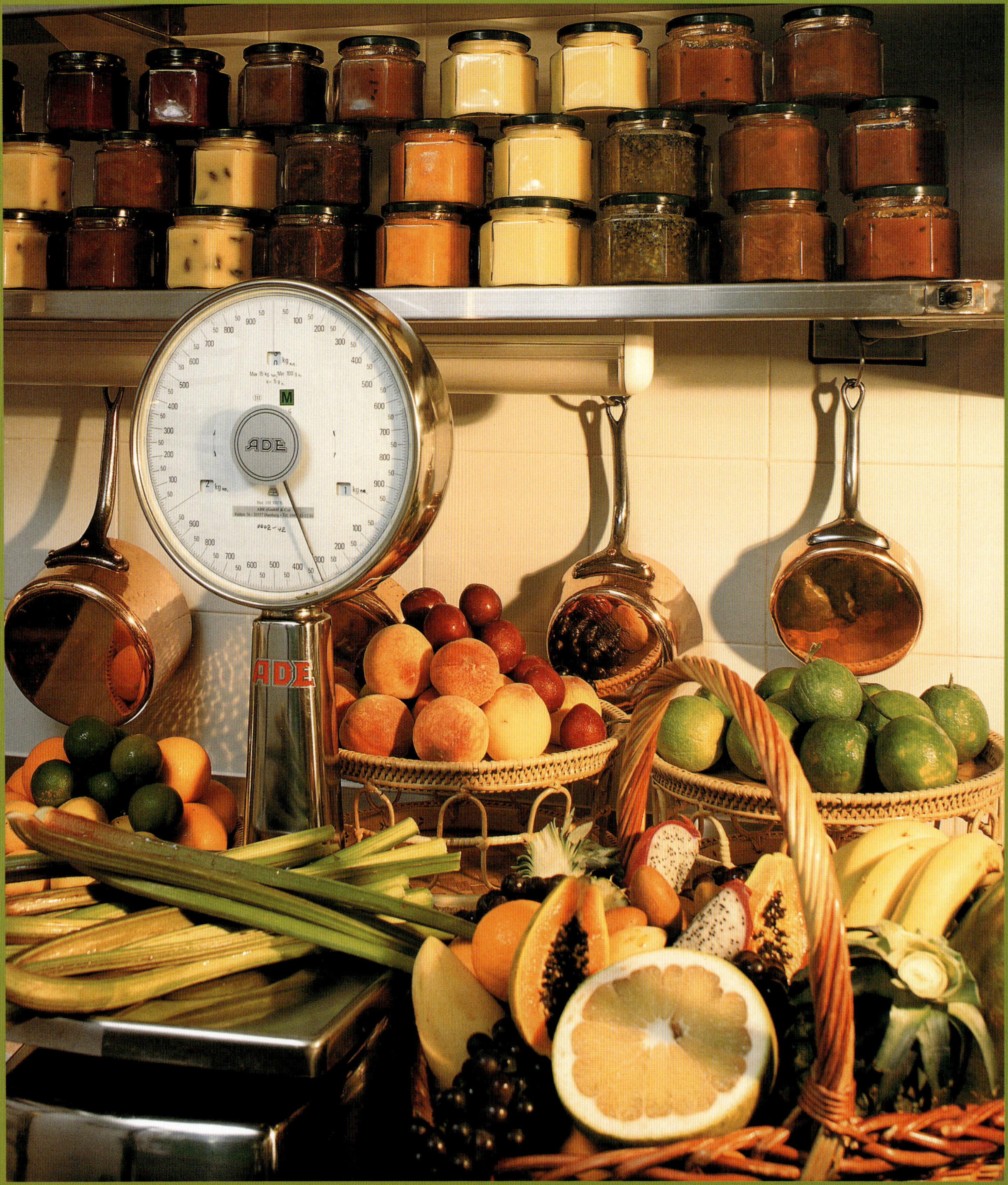
ADE
ADE

[ANNEXES]

CONVERSION TABLES

Weights and measures used in this book are metric. A reliable set of gram/kilogram scales is recommended.

Metric Equivalents

1 metric teaspoon	5 ml
1 metric tablespoon	15 ml
1/4 metric cup	60 ml
1/2 metric cup	125 ml
1 metric cup	250 ml (0.25 litre)
2 metric cups	500 ml (0.5 litre)
4 metric cups	1000 ml (1 litre)

Measures

IMPERIAL	LIQUID MEASURES	METRIC
1 fl oz		30 ml
2 fl oz	1/4 cup	
3 fl oz		90 ml
4 fl oz (1/4 US pint)	1/2 cup	125 ml
5 fl oz		150 ml
6 fl oz	3/4 cup	185 ml
8 fl oz (1/2 US pint)	1 cup	250 ml
10 fl oz	1 1/4 cups	
12 fl oz	1 1/2 cups	
14 fl oz	1 3/4 cups	
16 fl oz	2 cups	500 ml
20 fl oz	1/2 cups	

Weights

IMPERIAL	METRIC
1/2 oz	15 g
1 oz	30 g
2 oz	60 g
3 oz	90 g
4 oz (0.25 lb)	125 g
6 oz	185 g
8 oz (0.5 lb)	250 g
12 oz (0.75 lb)	375 g
16 oz (1 lb)	500 g (0.5 kg)
24 oz (1.5 lb)	750 g
32 oz (2 lb)	1000 g (1 kg)
3 lb	1500 g (1.5 kg)
4 lb	2000 g (2 kg)

Temperature

FAHRENHEIT	GAS REGULO	CELSIUS
225	1	105
250	2	120
275	3	135
300	4	150
325	5	165
350	6	175
375	7	190
400	8	205
425	9	220
450	10	230

(Note: Always pre-heat your oven 15 minutes before use.)
(The Imperial to metric quantities listed are approximate conversions only. North American readers may want to follow American Standard measurements and use a gram/kilogram scale. To measure liquid or dry cup quantities, you will also need a cup graduated in millilitres (ml) and litres.)

Left: Shallots in a traditional 'boat' basket weaved from pandanus leaves
Opposite: Fresh ingredients form the foundation of a winning recipe
Pg 172–173: Home-made preserves, curds, relishes and chutneys from The Oriental's celebrated kitchens

GLOSSARY

Agar-agar Powder – gelatin substitute derived from Asian agar-agar seaweed.

Alkaline Water (red lime water) – made of crushed sea shells, this is like chalk water with a reddish colour and is used to give crunch to batters and cookies.

Arugula – also called rocket, this spicy salad green is similar to dandelion.

Banana Blossom – a deep purplish-crimson coloured, heart-shaped flower used as a vegetable. Also called plantain flower or banana bell.

Bird's Nest – a luxury ingredient made from the dried spittle of cave-dwelling swallows. The gelatinous saliva contains undigested seaweed and adheres the nests to the cave walls.

Black Fungus – also known as cloud ear, wood ear or black jelly mushroom. Usually sold dried, but available fresh.

Blue River Prawn – large variety of river prawns with very long front claws. Found in Thailand, this is an attractive blue colour before it is cooked.

Bok Choy – also called Chinese chard or white cabbage because of its thick, white leaf ribs and dark green leaves.

Bombay Onion – called *bawang Bombay* in Indonesia, this is a small round red variety from the onion family.

Bouquet Garni – a combination of parsley, sage, rosemary, thyme, marjoram and bay leaves, tied in a bundle.

Cake Flour – an American variety best used for making cakes and soft pastries. This is the softest flour of all as it contains only six per cent protein.

Candlenuts – hard oily white nuts, usually ground and used to thicken curries.

Cardamom – a member of the ginger family. Pale green oval pods that contain 15–20 black seeds. These have a sweetly fragrant, almost peppery flavour.

Chat Masala – a dry spice mix sprinkled over crispy snacks, sliced fruit or boiled potatoes. Usually a mixture of roasted fennel and cumin seeds, mango powder, chilli and seasonings.

Chinese Kumquats – also called cumquats, this is a small, citrus-like orange coloured fruit with edible skin.

Chinese Orange – a sweet, loose-skinned orange also called a Mandarin.

Chinese Celery – smaller, greener and stronger in flavour than the Western variety. Used as a flavouring in soups.

Couverture Chocolate – high in cocoa butter, it melts easily and smoothly. Needs tempering before setting.

Dried Yellow Bean – this is also known as yellow lentil or dahl.

Fennel Seeds – seeds of the fennel plant, this looks like a larger, paler version of the cumin seed, with a distinct flavour of aniseed.

Fish Maw – dried stomach lining of large fish used to add texture to a dish.

Fragrant Jasmine Rice – lightly perfumed, long grain variety which is eaten throughout Thailand with all kinds of savoury dishes.

Gelatine Leaves – a type of commercial gelatine made into brittle, transparent sheets. Must be weighed before use as sheets vary in weight between 3–5 g.

Green Peppercorn – the immature berries of the *Piper nigrum* species sold fresh in bunches.

Garam Masala – Indian spice mixture added at the end of cooking. Traditionally includes cardamom, clove, cinnamon, black pepper and nutmeg.

Grappa – a potent Northern Italian brandy distilled from grape skin, stems and seeds left over from winemaking.

Grana Padano – a sharper and less subtle cheese than the Parmigiano-Reggiano and often used as a substitute for it.

Greater Galangal – also known as *lengkuas, kha, laos* or blue ginger; this is an aromatic and fibrous red rhizome from the ginger family. Sold fresh, or dried in slices or as *Laos* powder.

Hot Bean Paste – a chilli bean sauce from China, also known as *min sze jeung*.

Iranian Caviar – top quality caviar from the Caspian Sea and its river systems.

Jicama – the tuber from a plant that also produces beans, hence its other name, yam bean. Similar appearance to the round variety of turnip, its flesh is white and it has a thin, brown skin.

Lesser Galangal – a rhizome, this is in no way similar to the greater variety. Also called *san bai* or Chinese keys, this is a native to Hainan Island where it is only used in Chinese medicine.

Lemon Grass – tall lemon-scented grass used to flavour curries and soups. Use the lower 5–6 cm only.

Lotus Stems – stem from the flowering water plant, available fresh or canned.

Nam Pla (fish sauce) – a pale, amber coloured liquid made by fermenting fish with salt. Gives a distinctive and complex flavour to many Thai dishes.

Oak Sawdust – This is sold as aromatic

chips for smoking foods and flavouring for barbecues.

Pandanus Leaf – also called pandan leaf or screwpine. Green flat leaves used in both sweet and savoury dishes for its perfume and colour.

Palm Sugar – also called jaggery, *gula melaka* or palm honey. A sugar produced from the sap of the palmyra and sugar palms, varying from almost white to dark brown in colour.

Pectin – a setting agent found in the skin, seeds and core of fruit. Commercially available in liquid or powdered form. Used in making preserves.

Mekong – also called Thai rice whisky.

Morning Glory – vegetable with long, pointed, dark-green leaves with paler, hollow stems, also known as water spinach, water convolvulus or *kangkong*.

Risotto Rice – medium-grained Italian rice essential to making risotto.

Roasted Chilli Jam – made by slowly cooking chillies, ginger and sugar into a syrupy jam. Used for flavouring and garnishing. Can be purchased.

Roasted Ground Rice – powder made from rice which has been roasted then ground. Used for thickening sauces.

Sesame Paste – a thick brown paste made from toasted sesame seeds.

Soft-shell Crab – the blue crab or shore-crab caught when shedding its shell. Soft and translucent, it is trimmed of the tail, gills and eyes and eaten whole.

Stracchino Cheese – ripened version of Taleggio. Used on pizza or eaten fresh served at room temperature.

Straw Mushrooms – this is Asia's most important fresh mushroom. It boasts a high protein content and is available fresh, canned or dried.

Sugar Syrup – used in dessert making for sauces and sorbet as well as Thai cuisine. Equal quantities of sugar and water are boiled, then stored for use.

Superior Shark's Fin – the dried dorsal or ventral fin of the shark, regarded as a tonic and appetite stimulant.

Szechuan Pepper – also known as *sansho*, fagara and Chinese pepper, these small reddish-brown berries are sold dried or roasted.

Tamarind – also called Indian date, this is a reddish-brown pod with thin brittle shell. Seeds and fibres are strained from the thick acidic pulp, which is used for flavouring, as well as for tenderising.

Tapioca Grains – this is derived from peeled and grated cassava root that has its juice extracted and pulp soaked in water to release the starch grains. Fibres are removed and the residue heated until it becomes tapioca balls.

Tatsoi Leaves – tiny leaves with pale green stalks, similar to silverbeet in appearance and texture.

Taro Root – also known as dasheen or colocassi. A root vegetable valued for its carbohydrates, it is often boiled, deep-fried or puréed, and has flavour similar to chestnut or potato.

Thai Asparagus – the thin, green, flavourful variety.

Thai Basil – also called *krapow* or Holy basil. Leaves are small and dark green; younger leaves are distinctly reddish purple. Used only in strong-flavoured dishes.

Truffle – this luxury ingredient is a subterranean mushroom that grows mainly on the roots of oak trees, but can also be found on those of the chestnut, hazel and beech trees. The most esteemed is the black truffle of Perigord, France, while the white truffle of Piedmont in Italy is also very popular.

Truffle Oil – good quality extra virgin olive oil infused with truffles to flavour salads and dressings.

Turmeric – a member of the ginger family with brilliant orange-yellow flesh.

White Jelly Mushrooms – white variety of the black fungus.

Winged Beans – also called asparagus bean, frilly bean or *goa* bean. Very decorative with four serrated edges and tiny seeds contained inside a central rib. Very popular in Thailand, this is usually served as a salad, lightly cooked, or dipped into *nam prik* sauce. Usually green but may also be pink or purplish. Can be tough if longer than a finger.

Winter Melon – also known as ash gourd, wax gourd or preserving melon.

Yellow Chives – a flat-leaf chive, covered with a bamboo whilst growing to keep it a pale, yellow colour. Also known as Chinese chives.

Yunnan Ham – Processed during the winter, this ham is selected from the best pork leg, which then has the pork blood completely pressed out of it. The ham is then rubbed with salt and smoked or air dried. It is also called *Xuanwei* ham and is usually sold canned.

Xeres Vinegar – a type of sherry vinegar made in Xeres, France.

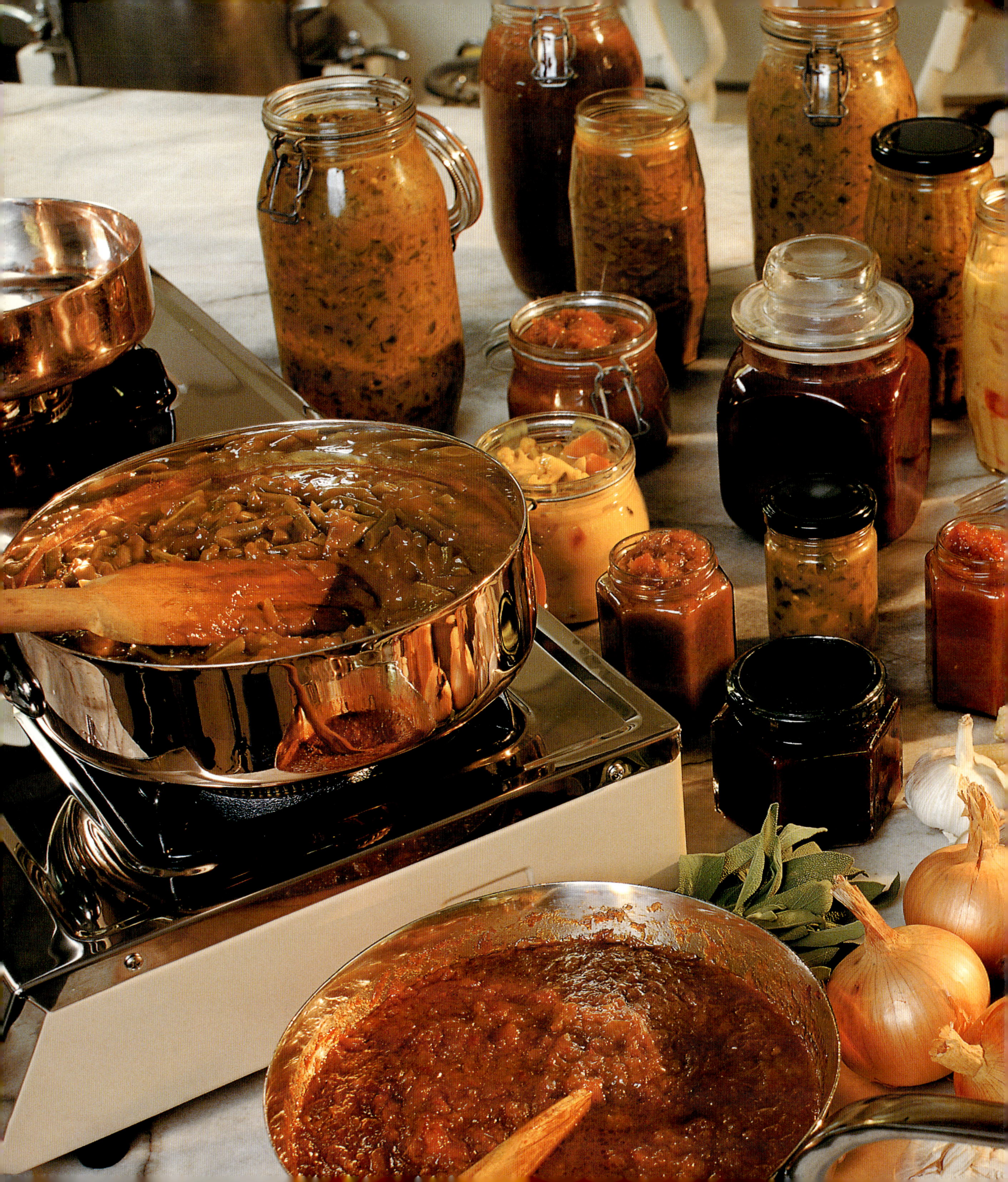

CULINARY INDEX

A
abalone, sliced chilled, with vinegar sauce 88
allspice 24
apple and passionfruit preserve 132
Authors' Lounge 121
Authors' Lounge chocolate cake 122

B
baby pumpkin custard 44
Bakery 121
balsamico dressing 48
Bamboo Bar 121
banana blossom salad 42
bay leaves 24
beurre blanc, mango 48
bigoli with anchovy tuna sauce 66
Bird of Paradise 130
bird's nest soup, Imperial, with winter melon 86
blackcurrant and rum curd 132
blackened beef sandwich 128
black pepper sauce 90
blue river lobsters, giant, pan-braised with sweet Thai basil 41
blue river prawns, herbed, with lotus stems in coconut milk 39
braised shiitake mushroom cups filled with crabmeat and minced pork 32
brown sauce 75

C
cakes
    – Authors' Lounge chocolate cake 122
    – mango cheesecake with pistachio sponge base 126
cappuccino of goose liver with white and black truffles 101
cardamom
    – cardamom pods 24
    – green cardamom pods 24
    – white cardamom pods 24
Caribbean Sunset 131
carpaccio of Coral Reef trout with Mediterranean herbs 69
carrot and jicama juice 119
Casablanca 130
caviar, Iranian, with home-smoked salmon and tomato jelly 99
Chao Phraya Dream 130
char-grilled spiced salmon tournedos with eggplant marmalade 56
char siu garoupa with star anise and Szechuan pepper sauce 53
cheeses
    – mango cheesecake with pistachio sponge base 126
    – penne pasta with Stracchino cheese and spinach leaves 70
    – ricotta and silver beet green gnocchi with gorgonzola and grappa 70
chewy coconut cookies 44
chicken
    – chicken consommé 96
    – chicken stock 101
    – clear chicken soup 118
    – cold-marinated chicken with peanut sauce 84
    – corn-fed chicken and slipper lobster with fennel ragout 60
    – egg noodles with chicken curry 35
    – mung bean noodle salad with shrimps and chicken 115
    – red chicken curry 116
    – river prawn and straw mushroom soup 118
    – Tandoori chicken in pita pocket sandwiches 76
chillies
    – bird's eye chillies 24
    – cucumber-chilli dip 34
    – green chillies 24
    – long dried chillies 24
    – small dried chillies 24
    – yellow chillies 24
chocolate
    – Authors' Lounge chocolate cake 122
    – chocolate and cherry dome with almond crisp 109
    – chocolate and ginger tart with kumquat marmalade ice cream 78
    – chocolate and pistachio nut cookies 125
chutneys
    – savoury Chinese snow pear and onion chutney 134
    – spicy tomato-chilli chutney 133
Ciao 59
Ciao's seafood soup 62
citrus fruit tart 126
clam, bacon and okra chowder 50
claypot fried rice with meat and yam 88
clear chicken soup 118
cloves, white 24
cocktails
    – Bird of Paradise 130
    – Caribbean Sunset 131
    – Casablanca 130
    – Chao Phraya Dream 130
    – Coconut Cooler 131
    – London Calling 131
    – Oriental Sling 131
    – Oriental Sour 131
    – Sunrise 131
    – The Oriental Hotel 131
    – The Oriental's Mai Tai 130
coconut
    – chewy coconut cookies 44
    – Coconut Cooler 131
    – coconut milk/cream 42
    – herbed blue river prawns and lotus stems in coconut milk 39
    – iced banana parfait with coconut crust 122
cold-marinated chicken with peanut sauce 84
cold tofu and jelly mushroom tournedos 60
cookies
    – chewy coconut cookies 44
    – chocolate and pistachio nut cookies 125
coriander seeds 24
corn-fed chicken and slipper lobster with fennel ragout 60
crab
    – braised shiitake mushroom cups filled with crabmeat and minced pork 32
    – crabmeat and green papaya salad 64
    – crabmeat cake with mango beurre blanc 48
    – crabmeat timbal with sweet corn and red capsicum soup 50
    – sautéed fresh scallops with crab roe and potatoes 86
    – soft-shell crab salad with green mango 29
crisp fried seabass on ratatouille Niçoise with basil infusion 102
crispy gnocchi salad with rock lobster in lobster-vanilla essence 54
crispy perch and herb dip 42
crispy Thai pancake 43
cucumber-chilli dip, with fish dumplings 34
cumin seeds 24
curries
    – egg noodles with chicken curry 35
    – pork fillet and water spinach curry 38
    – prawns with cream sauce and curry leaves 84
    – red chicken curry 116
    – red curry paste 41
curds
    – blackcurrant and rum curd 132
    – exotic sparkling lime and ginger curd 132

D
desserts
    – Authors' Lounge chocolate cake 122
    – baby pumpkin custard 44
    – chewy coconut cookies 44
    – chocolate and ginger tart with kumquat marmalade ice cream 78
    – chocolate and pistachio nut cookies 125
    – citrus fruit tart 126
    – crispy Thai pancake 43
    – emerald tapioca sweets 44
    – fresh fruit tart 124
    – gratinated passionfruit parfait with exotic fruits 99
    – iced banana parfait with coconut crust 122
    – miniature yellow bean marzipans 43
    – panna cotta 81
    – tiramisu 81
    – warm upside down spiced pudding with praline ice cream 111
    – white sesame ice cream 125
dips
    – crispy perch and herb dip 42
    – cucumber-chilli dip 34
dressings
    – balsamico dressing 48
    – lemon-oil dressing 128
drinks (The Oriental Spa)
    – carrot and jicama juice 119
    – low-fat yoghurt, cucumber and dill drink 119
    – mango and tangerine juice 119
    – melon and watermelon juice 119
    – papaya-pomelo drink 119
    – tomato, celery and parsley juice 119

E

egg noodle dough 65
egg noodles with chicken curry 35
eggplant
- char-grilled spiced salmon tournedos with eggplant marmalade 56
- eggplant, tomato and capsicum flan 80
- grilled green eggplant salad 26

emerald tapioca sweets 44
exotic sparkling lime and ginger curd 132
extra-bitter lemon marmalade 135

F

fennel ragout, with cornfed chicken and slipper lobster 60
fish
- carpaccio of Coral Reef trout with Mediterranean herbs 69
- char-grilled spiced salmon tournedos with eggplant marmalade 56
- char siu garoupa with star anise and Szechuan pepper sauce 53
- fillet of red mullet and oven-roasted vegetables 72
- fish dumplings with cucumber-chilli dip 34
- fish stock 65
- fried fish maw and cashewnut salad 26
- fried fish rolls with two-mango salad 31
- fried red coral reef garoupa with sweet-salty chilli sauce 36
- home-smoked salmon with tomato jelly and Iranian caviar 99
- lettuce, fresh herb and seabass salad 114
- pan-fried garoupa steak with morning glory and carrot sauce 62
- pan-fried turbot on asparagus-pumpkin ragout with potato-chives broth 108
- spicy crisp fish with sparkling lime rind 28
- spicy tuna and vegetable salad with lemon-oil dressing 128
- steamed fillet of white seabass with lime and lemongrass 118
- steamed garoupa with soy sauce 91
- Thai-style herbed rainbow trout salad 51

fresh fruit tart 124

G

garoupa
- char siu garoupa with star anise and Szechuan pepper sauce 53
- fried red coral reef garoupa with sweet-salty chilli sauce 36
- pan-fried garoupa steak with morning glory and carrot sauce 62

Genovese, pesto 65
ginger, Matore 24
gnocchi
- crispy gnocchi salad with rock lobster in lobster-vanilla essence 54
- ricotta and silver beet green gnocchi with gorgonzola and grappa 70

goose liver
- cappuccino of goose liver with white and black truffles 101
- goose liver dome with Perigord truffles and celeriac 96
- pan-fried escalope of goose liver with grape sauce 100

grappa 70
gratinated passionfruit parfait with exotic fruits 99
green peppercorn 24
grilled green eggplant salad 26
grilled vegetables and guacamole on sunflower bread 129

H

herbed blue river prawns and lotus stems in coconut milk 39
herbed fruit salad 116
herbed soup of vegetables and prawns 31
home-smoked salmon with tomato jelly and Iranian caviar 99

I

ice cream
- kumquat marmalade ice cream 78
- praline ice cream 111
- white sesame seed ice cream 125

iced banana parfait with coconut crust 122
Imperial bird's nest soup with winter melon 86

J

jam, pineapple and ginger 135
jelly mushroom tournedos, and cold tofu 60
jus
- lamb jus 105
- pigeon jus 106

K

kaffir lime 24
kaffir lime leaves 24
king prawns, sautéed with lemon and capsicum 72
kumquat marmalade ice cream 78

L

lamb jus 105
lamb loin, baked in salt crust, with black olive sauce 105
lemongrass 24
Le Normandie 95
lettuce, fresh herb and seabass salad 114
lobsters
- crispy gnocchi salad with rock lobster in lobster-vanilla essence 54
- lobster stock 54
- pan-braised giant blue river lobsters with sweet Thai basil 41

London Calling 131
Lord Jim's 47
lotus stems, with herbed blue river prawns in coconut milk 39
low-fat yoghurt, cucumber and dill drink 119

M

mace 24
mango
- crabmeat cake with mango beurre blanc 48
- fried fish rolls with two-mango salad 31
- mango and tangerine juice 119
- mango cheesecake with pistachio sponge base 126
- soft-shell crab salad with green mango 29

marmalade
- eggplant marmalade 56
- extra-bitter lemon marmalade 135
- kumquat marmalade 78

meatballs, with pumpkin pappardelle 75
melon and watermelon juice 119
miniature yellow bean marzipans 43
morning glory, and pan-fried garoupa steak with carrot sauce 62
mung bean noodle salad with shrimps and chicken 115
mustard pickle, The Oriental 134

N

noodles
- egg noodle dough 65
- egg noodles with chicken curry 35

nutmeg 24

O

Oriental Sling 131
Oriental Sour 131

P

pan-braised giant blue river lobsters with sweet Thai basil 41
pancake, crispy Thai 43
pan-fried escalope of goose liver with grape sauce 100
pan-fried garoupa steak with morning glory and carrot sauce 62
pan-fried turbot on asparagus-pumpkin ragout with potato-chives broth 108
panna cotta 81
papaya-pomelo drink 119
parfait
- gratinated passionfruit parfait with exotic fruits 99
- iced banana parfait with coconut crust 122

Parisienne potatoes 102
pastas
- bigoli with anchovy tuna sauce 66
- penne pasta with Stracchino cheese and spinach leaves 70
- pumpkin pappardelle with meatballs 75

peppercorn
- green peppercorn 24
- Szechuan peppercorn 24
- white peppercorn 24

pesto Genovese 65
pickled lemons 65
pita pocket sandwiches, with Tandoori chicken 76

pigeon
- pigeon jus 106
- roast pigeon in potato coat with mustard sauce 106

pineapple and ginger jam 135

prawns
- herbed blue river prawns and lotus stems in coconut milk 39
- prawns with cream sauce and curry leaves 84
- river prawn and mushroom soup 118
- sautéed king prawns with lemon and capsicum 72
- wing bean salad with prawns 118

preserve, apple and passionfruit 132

pudding, warm upside-down spiced, with praline ice cream 111

pumpkin
- baby pumpkin custard 44
- pan-fried turbot with asparagus-pumpkin ragout and potato-chives broth 108
- pumpkin pappardelle with meatballs 75
- roast pumpkin soup 77

R

rainbow trout salad, Thai-style herbed 51
ratatouille Niçoise 102
red chicken curry 116
red curry paste 41
relish, telegraph cucumber and onion 133

rice
- claypot fried rice with meat and yam 88
- saffron seafood risotto with arugula and mushrooms 66
- vegetable fried rice 116

ricotta and siver beet green gnocchi with gorgonzola and grappa 70
river prawn and straw mushroom soup 118
roast pigeon in potato coat with mustard sauce 106
roast pumpkin soup 77

S

saffron seafood risotto with arugula and mushrooms 66

salads
- banana blossom salad 42
- crabmeat and green papaya salad 64
- crispy gnocchi salad with rock lobster in lobster-vanilla essence 54
- fried fish maw and cashewnut salad 26
- fried fish rolls with two-mango salad 31
- grilled green eggplant salad 26
- herbed fruit salad 116
- lettuce, fresh herb and seabass salad 114
- mung bean noodle salad with shrimps and chicken 115
- sardine salad in lettuce cups 28
- shellfish salad with orange and red onion 69
- soft-shell crab salad with green mango 29
- spicy tuna and vegetable salad with lemon-oil dressing 128
- Thai-style herbed rainbow trout salad 51
- wing bean salad with prawns 118

Sala Rim Naam 23
Salon de l'Oriental 121

sandwiches
- blackened beef sandwich 128
- grilled vegetables and guacamole on sunflower bread 129
- Tandoori chicken in pita pocket sandwiches 76

sardine salad in lettuce cups 28

sauces
- anchovy tuna sauce 66
- black olive sauce 105
- black pepper sauce 90
- brown sauce 75
- carrot sauce 62
- cream sauce 84
- grape sauce 100
- lobster-vanilla essence 54
- mango beurre blanc 48
- mustard sauce 106
- peanut sauce 84
- star anise and Szechuan pepper sauce 53
- sweet-salty chilli sauce 36
- vinegar sauce 88

sautéed beef tenderloin with black pepper sauce 90
sautéed fresh scallops with crab roe and potatoes 86
sautéed king prawns with lemon and capsicum 72
savoury Chinese snow pear and onion chutney 134
seafood tartare 48
shallots 24
shellfish salad with orange and red onion 69
sliced chilled abalone with vinegar sauce 88
soft-shell crab salad with green mango 29

soups
- cappuccino of goose liver with white and black truffles 101
- chicken consommé 96
- Ciao's seafood soup 62
- clam, bacon and okra chowder 50
- clear chicken soup 118
- crabmeat timbal with sweet corn and red capsicum soup 86
- herbed soup of vegetables and prawns 31
- Imperial bird's nest soup with winter melon 86
- river prawn and straw mushroom soup 118
- roast pumpkin soup 77
- superior shark's fins with Yunnan ham flavoured broth 84

spicy tomato-chilli chutney 133
spicy tuna and vegetable salad with lemon-oil dressing 128
sponge base, pistachio 126
star anise 24
steamed fillet of white seabass with lime and lemongrass 118
steamed garoupa with soy sauce 91
stir-fried minced seafood in golden cups 86

stocks
- chicken stock 101
- fish stock 65
- lobster stock 54

sunflower bread, with grilled vegetables and guacamole 129
Sunrise 131
superior shark's fins with Yunnan ham flavoured broth 84

T

Tandoori chicken in pita pocket sandwiches 76

tarts
- chocolate and ginger tart with kumquat marmalade ice cream 78
- citrus fruit tart 126
- fresh fruit tart 124

tartare, seafood 48
telegraph cucumber and onion relish 133
Thai Cooking School 24
Thai ingredients 24
Thai-style herbed rainbow trout salad 51
The China House 83
The Oriental Hotel (cocktail) 131
The Oriental mustard pickle 134
The Oriental's Mai Tai 130
The Oriental Spa 113
The Verandah 59
tiramisu 81
tomato, celery and parsley juice 119

truffles
- cappuccino of goose liver with white and black truffles 101
- goose liver dome with Perigord truffles and celeriac 96

turmeric 24

V

vegetable fried rice 116
vegetable stock 76

W

warm upside-down spiced pudding with praline ice cream 111
white sesame ice cream 125
winged bean salad with prawns 118
winter melon, with Imperial bird's nest soup 86

Y

yoghurt
- home-made unsweetened yoghurt 119
- low-fat yoghurt, cucumber and dill drink 119